Acknowledgement

I want to thank my lovely wife Mary, and our three beautiful children for believing in me - again. I had put my family through a hell they didn't deserve, but over a few years of making things right through lots of apologies, forgiveness, and compassion they embraced a once undeserving man.

I also want to acknowledge and thank Rev. Salvatore Sapienza, my Pastor and friend, who through his powerful messages and life example gave me the courage to be myself and write this book. In doing so I know I am ostracizing myself from family and friends. But God is calling me to love others, not to conform.

Love Beyond Truth

Awakening to the Truth of Love

STEPHEN K NYHOF

ISBN: 9781521125908

CONTENTS

Introduction

As far as childhoods go, I believe I had one of the better ones. I grew up on what I would call a hobby farm, where there were chickens, some goats, a cow and a few horses, and of course more than enough cats and dogs all occupying a large old barn.

I enjoyed shooting guns, fishing by the creek and catching frogs. I'm sure you have seen some good old movies or shows that show families living out on farms and having all sorts of fun and adventure. That is what I remember as I look back on those days.

But there was another part of our lives as with others, and that was going to church three times a week, listening to long sermons that put you to sleep, singing songs and attending Sunday school where we heard all the common Bible stories about Noah and the flood, Jonah and the whale, David and Goliath and of course the stories of Jesus.

As time passed, it was as though the frivolous childlike living was replaced by just day to day life, work, and religion. We spent more and more time unknowingly learning how to judge each other and our neighbors for failing to live up to the lofty standards and expectations of a holy and righteous God we were learning about at church. I didn't know it then, but maintaining a shining example of our righteousness for others to see was paramount and protected by our father who taught us all very well by example how to be shining righteous examples to the people in which we would engage.

This book is about a journey that took place in my middle forties. A journey that opened my eyes to everything I had become over the years that was lost to this once fun loving little farm boy. I want to share this journey with those who know there is more to love than the truth they been told all their life that no longer fits the paradigm of their heart. Again, in case that sentence rolled by, let me ask the question. Are you willing to come face to face with a truly loving and unconditional Creator by following a path that leads you on a personal journey to joy and peace?

Roger Perkins of Higher Ground Foundation, said to me one day when I was really hurting, I had just separated from my wife and children, *"Steve, what would it hurt to trust God?"* I will go into this more in detail as we move ahead. But you may want to tuck those words close by because we are going to use that lens to view this journey.

My story is my story, but you have a story too, and it is important to look within while you read my words. These words are mine, but they may very well be similar to yours. There will be times while you read, that you find me a very angry, judgmental and an unlikeable guy, and that is fine. But if you look at me in judgment, you may become blind and miss the very essence of the message as it pertains to your life. I ask that you reflect deeply on your experiences of life as I share my experiences of life.

You may find fault with some of my words, possibly even find contradictions. But if you allow yourself to step back and view the whole picture I am painting from cover to cover, you will recognize a message of love that I have come to know that you may want to consider.

When I stopped believing for only a moment in what I've been told, I was surprised to hear God calling me from a different path. Psalm 46:10

Throughout the book, I include quotes I have gleaned out of my time in contemplation and meditation that I wrote down throughout the years of this journey. My hope would be that you take the time to be still with a journal and write your thoughts down as they come to you. When we begin to listen carefully, we will hear that small voice inside waiting to lead us on our journey of life.

There was a part of me that did not want to write this book because I have come to a place in my life where much of my past meant nothing to me anymore. I had come to a place of great peace and no longer felt the need to share my story as it was filled with judgment. Love had become the all-important attribute in my life and I just wanted to move forward enjoying my family and friends within this new place of being.

As I tell my story and share my views, judgment will be present and will offend those who hold tightly to their beliefs. However, after facing who I was and who I really am, I recognized that the path I was on was filled with fear and judgment and void of true compassion. I hope as you read through the book that you will gain a glimpse of the unconditional Lover that is waiting patiently to embrace your soul.

When life falls apart

I want to preface this first chapter by sharing more about my marriage and family life prior to everything falling apart because I believe the life we lived for years parallels many marriages and families who grow up in the church and follow a doctrine they unwittingly grow into and make their own and then unwittingly pass onto their children.

I was in my thirties when I stepped out of the job market and started my own business as a home designer. We had just built our first home. My wife and I had two boys by this time, Jordan and Travis who will of course be part of this journey. Life had its ups and downs, but we were committed to our expectations of a life of working hard every day and attending church on the weekend. As the business grew, we built a large home and two story hobby barn where I had my office.

I continued to hire a few people now and then, and within five years I had a manager running the design company, so I began to get things in place to put another company in place to build custom homes. Around this time, we had also adopted our daughter Alicyn from Korea.

From the outside, and for those in our church, we were the epitome of middle class, well-dressed Christians living the American dream - on credit. On the inside, we just went about living as expected within the system. The love that was more romantic at first, that kick starts most marriages was fading and waiting for the real thing to take its place. Only it never did, and we didn't know what to do to fix it.

I was engulfed in code and programming or working on company issues to maintain the over-bloated financial crises we were living in as the years passed. I was good at juggling accounts and using cash flow to survive, robbing Peter to pay Paul.

Mary was busy working full time as well as taking care of the house cleaning, laundry and caring for the kids. We both knew something was wrong and missing in our lives, but I was typically putting all the blame on Mary. From my understanding, she was not living up to the woman found in Proverbs 31, or obedient like we are taught in Ephesians and 1 Peter. If only Mary would learn how to be a good Christian Biblical woman, things would just fall into place, so I thought.

I was taught I was the man of the home and leader of the marriage by the churches example, which also placed me in control as the head as Christ was the head of the church – right? How can the head be in control if the person who is supposed to submit to the head is not submitting? Again, Mary was amazing having put up with me, but my expectations were always a little beyond reach.

While Mary is one of the most loving and kind people you will ever know, she did not take too kindly to my righteous demands as they came from an overbearing Christian doctrinal point of view. I was only trying to follow in my father's footsteps. I read the Bible often and studied scripture using local and Internet dictionaries and concordances. In fact, my father would call me quite often because I could give him answers in seconds to references of scripture he was looking for but could not always find.

By 2008 both my businesses were beginning to feel the slowdown in the economy, and one by one I was letting my employees go. In October of 2008, my mother passed away which hit me hard as I was what people would call a momma's boy. When we were young, my brothers were playing football and other outdoor activities, but I was very happy inside the house building model airplanes and drawing pictures.

And so, two businesses I had built were no longer producing an income, and now my mother also passed away leaving me in a very bewildered state of mind. I was very social with everyone on the evening at the funeral home for visiting. The morning, however, trying to find the cemetery turned into a nightmare for me. It turns out there was a new cemetery I was unaware of, and the ceremony took place without us.

I cannot begin to tell you the feelings that were running through my mind. We drove back home and shortly after I took a phone call from my oldest brother who asked if we still wanted to come to the luncheon. I declined. I then got back into the car and drove out to find the cemetery. On the way, I repeated "Mommy, mommy and sobbed knowing I would never see her again on earth. I drove all over looking for the cemetery and finally found it, not a half mile from the old one but around a few corners. There were several places where the dirt was fresh, so I did not know, but guessed on one spot and fell on my knees and cried while grasping the dirt in my hands. I know, a little cliché, but it is what I did. While I was there, I felt a peacefulness come over me as I realized that God had given me my space and time completely alone with my mother to grieve.

In November of 2008, we filed for personal bankruptcy as we could no longer afford to pay for our home and vehicles. Over the next few weeks, I made sure we kept the cars in the garages so the repossessor could not get them. I remember my oldest son left my car outside one evening and I came home to the car being taken away. I hollered at my son for failing to do as I asked. I was a very angry person and did not even know it then.

By January 2009, we found a rental home and moved our belongings out of our home and into the place we would call home for the next few years. Mary's parents graciously purchased a used van for us as we needed a vehicle to get around. Not a week later, I took a phone call from a lawyer telling me that he represented a company that was going to sue my business for copyright infringement unless I did a few things related to my website. So, I did, but they sued me anyway, and the case lasted over two years and settled out of court causing me so much stress I did not care much about anything.

I was still doing some drawing to make a few bucks, trying to figure out what to do next to provide for my family. The pressures of all this was too much, and Mary and I grew further apart. We still didn't know how we had come to this place in life, or what to do to fix our marriage.

I remember a well-known preacher doing week long seminars came into the area, and so I went because I believed it would be God that would save our family. Mary did not want to go, which only made me angry as I was too stupid to see I was only pounding my version of this "Christian" righteousness thing down her throat. I remember coming home after the seminar and sitting on the bed, looking Mary in the eyes and saying, "I don't like you, but I love you because God tells me too." I believed in God and his "truth," but I had no clue what love was.

Mary started to hang out with other people related to a different church associated with AA. When I asked if I could come to church with her, she just said no, which made me feel completely out of control and very angry. Honestly, I do not even like to write about this now (so much has changed in our lives) and while I never lifted a finger against Mary physically, I used very cunning verbal or well-written attacks, not even with a raised voice, but just mean Biblically judged verse filled verbiage that could cut down a redwood tree. Somehow, she was stronger and held on to life. I grew up in a family that communicated this way, what I call verse punching - the regurgitation of programming trying to make itself right or solve a problem. I just was too stupid to see how judgmental and destructive it was.

Believe me, I am completely humbled to know she loves me today. As I think of what Mary went through and endured under my self-righteous Biblical manipulation, I am amazed by her stamina to remain steadfast. Based on some of the things I have learned recently, I believe Mary is my soulmate, and came to the earth at this time to challenge my belief system and shake me to my core, only neither of us knew at the time what that would look like.

Mary was working at a local Christian bookstore, and a man walked in by the name of Roger Perkins. He was in his late sixties with white windblown hair. Mary helped him at the counter, and he asked if she would be interested in joining a group of women at his foundation called Higher Ground Foundation. She agreed.

After a few weeks, Mary invited me to call Roger as he was also leading several men's groups. I told Mary that if Roger wants me to join he can call and invite me. I believed I was perfectly sound in my doctrines and knew all I needed to know to live a God fearing Christian life. After all, I held the "absolute truth." Because of the turmoil we were in, I studied even more and wrote often documenting things to prove my beliefs and why I was right in what I believed, all Biblically backed.

If you want to create a solid Biblical argument you can. The key is knowing enough verses to prove your points and a crafty mind to form the words in just the right way. The better you become at it, the better you feel about yourself. My father loved to tell us how he debated people and stumped them at their beliefs. Why would I be any different? I just wanted to do it better them him.

I do not recall why I finally went to see Roger a few weeks later, but he and his partner, the former chief of police, was also there. I only learned from Mary a few months ago that he was there specifically because of how afraid Mary was of me and believed I was capable of really hurting someone. It made me sad to learn that, and while I don't think I could hurt anyone, I do know that I gave that impression at times, and it sickens me to know I frightened my wife and children to that degree.

Roger let me know of some rules they had, like "we do not give advice to anyone," "we do not confess another person's sin," "we do not correct another person's point of view," and of course things shared were kept in strict confidentiality. In all cases, there was an understanding of no judgment or talking about others. This was new for me, for the church for that matter!

Without even knowing just how wonderful those rules were then, I recognized the freedom and safety those rules created in this place. I didn't skip a beat and went on rambling and raved about my beliefs and how I was right, and after ten minutes of further vomiting my doctrines all over the place, I found I was very pleased with myself. I remember Roger distinctly asking me about my relationship with my father. I assured him that my father was a great man and never did anything wrong, he loved his family, God and preached the gospel all over the world. A pillar in my mind.

I joined a group that met once a week. I did it only because my wife was in a group and I thought I better also be in a group if I am to set an example and be a leader. Weeks turned into months, and I fought much of what was being taught as it seemed to focus on our childhood and recalling things that happened in our past that may have caused behaviors ingrained in our actions today. This seemed more like psychology, and I knew my father was dead against it, and therefore so was I. You just forgive and move on. That's what I was taught. (Of course, it doesn't really work quite that way.)

When we are in judgment of someone's message, we become blind to the essence of what we should learn from it.

In my very cunning way, I shared my Biblical views of forgiveness and sin, guilt, and shame and our depravity without a savior. I'm sure all the guys wanted to vomit having to listen to me preach each week and then by the rules remain quiet. I was too arrogant to know they apply to me also. I hated being there but stayed because Mary also stayed in her group. I also hated it because Mary and I could not share the discussions with each other, so I was feeling further out of control. I tried several times to get Roger to counsel us together, but he refused as he was more interested in our personal relationship with God than in Mary and my relationship or marriage, which seemed at the time to counter what I believed. I believed that Mary needed to comply with my authority and then work on following the Bible and it's every word "as I was doing," and all would be ok.

I know many women live under this mentality today but do not even know the fear that exists in them that keeps them in bondage to their religion of submission, and call it love. I'm just thankful today that Mary would not stand for my religious abuse any longer. Somehow, she found the strength within great fear to challenge me and cause me to face whatever this great darkness was that was destroying our marriage and family.

Week after week in the group we dug into aspects of our lives I would have rather left untouched. I mean, I just never spent any time at all thinking about why I behave the way I do. I still had no idea of how angry a person I was because I was so blinded by my self-righteousness. When I left in the evening I would mull over what I was learning, and it wasn't that Roger was telling me of anything about what he believed, but through the sharing from all the men, I was beginning to realize how little I knew about myself and about compassion. Coupled with questions Roger would ask that I just never thought of before gave me cause to begin to question a number of things I believed. Back and forth for several months, I questioned what I was now thinking. It was a most frightening time as I found myself now and then really wondering about all that I held as true. What did I really believe? But I was determined to put my marriage back together, so that as the driving force kept me facing my internal fears and beliefs week after week.

Regardless of what I thought was progress my wife and my lives continually unraveled and anything I was trying to control only convinced me more of how out of control things were, which only caused me to try and control things more, which only made me wonder more about what I was trying to control. It was not really in the teaching as much as it was about getting real about myself and realizing how hidden I was to others of who I really am. How afraid I was all the time and reacting out of that fear and calling it godliness, hiding behind the Christian facade I wore.

What I am trying to convey is that I found myself in a place for months, where I did not know what was true or what I believed anymore. But without knowing it then, this was and is the only path a person must take to find out who they really are in Christ. Everything before this place of unknowing is made up of belief systems and false realities we call truth because it is all we were taught and knew. It is nothing more than a comfort zone we know nothing about and yet claim a stake in it as our own.

This is what I call an investment because we live out and proselytize our investment to our children and others so they too can develop their own lifelong investment. Investments are hard to let go of as they define us and our egos!

As more months passed within meditation in the morning in the presence of God as we were taught, and God revealing hidden things within me, I was beginning to learn things that started to make some sense to who I was and why I did the things I did. I started to see myself in a new light. In fact, you might say I was beginning to stop fighting to prove myself right, and resting in what Roger was always trying to get us all to do, and that was to spend time in the presence of God which was our number one goal and still is today. On March 23, 2010, I wrote the following letter to myself as God was revealing to me things that were coming to the surface through the men's group and within meditation as God's loving grace shed light on the things in my life I needed to expose.

Never good enough

It begins with love, the perfect love story, connected over the miles through letters and phone calls. Then face to face, I beheld my beautiful wife, and I was her man, strong and proud. A man who by his words proclaim a love for Jesus she has never seen in another man.

Later, while standing next to Jesus, my arms around His shoulder I look to my wife with loving eyes and tell her this is my buddy Jesus, and ask her to take His hand. She moves forward happy to do it, only I step in the way, still with the look of love in my eyes, I tell her she is not doing it right.

Oh, she says, loving me back, how should I do it? I explain how, so she moves in again. Again, I step forward and stop her. No, I say, you're not doing it right. I tell her that Jesus is the King of Kings and Lord of Lords. He is mighty and demands our best.

Again, I ask her to take Jesus' hand. She trusts and loves me, so she does as I say. Again, I step in the way and tell her she is not doing it right. Mary looks at me, confused and hurt. Now questioning what I want her to do to do it right, a little raise of her voice.

I can see that I hurt her, so I say I'm sorry, please here, take the hand of Jesus. She moves forward and reaches out, and I slap her hand away, disappointed with her for how she did it.

Angry now and desperate to hold Jesus' hand she sidesteps me and grabs for Him, My anger strikes back at her and push her away, how can you approach Him like this, thinking that you can come to Jesus without my approval? I know what is best and you don't.

Mary's heart is breaking, pleading with me to let her come to Jesus. She screams, I just want to hold His hand! Again, I'm sorry for the way I acted, feeling bad, I am so sorry. Please come and hold His hand. She reaches for Him, tears running down her face, afraid, her trembling hand reaching slowly to her savior. Again, I slap her hand away telling her that she's not doing it right.

Resentment begins to settle in, she stops trying and just hopes that sometime she will learn how to approach Jesus where it will be ok with Steve. Maybe she can do it when Steve isn't around, then she can hold tight to her loving savior. Only I find out that she's thinking this way, and am very upset that she would question me and my authority as the man of the house under Christ, and what I know is the best way to approach Jesus.

Bitterness and hatred begin to take root, desperate and longing to be loved by Jesus, just to feel loved, if not this man she once believed she loved. Yet, I would not let her. Now I begin to question her salvation, telling her that she cannot approach Jesus when she holds so much bitterness and hatred for me. Don't you know that Jesus said if you hate your brother the love of Christ is not in you?

Completely confused, desperate now for life itself, she begins to question the love of Jesus, she begins to lose the faith she once knew. Why is Jesus not reaching for me? Why does He allow Steve to step in the way? Steve, she pleads over and over, please let me touch the hand of Jesus.

Of course, you can I reply, Jesus loves you and wants you to come to him. We both want the same thing, why don't we do this together I ask? Why are you fighting me?

A little ray of hope left, she wants to believe that I will let her this time. She reaches out slowly, she can only see darkness now but believes Jesus may still be there, but I shove her away, and she falls to the ground. Jesus, she cries looking past me, please save me from Steve! Please reach out and touch my hand! I tell her she doesn't understand. If you just learn to forgive me I say, to let this all go, then Jesus will be available to you. It's so simple.

Finally, that day came when Mary told me that she thinks it would be best if we got a divorce. Strange how I used those words in the past on her to shock her into some controlled reality I had. But now when I heard it, I may have for the first time felt the pain of those words as she felt it coming from me. Mary needed to do something to save herself, her life - from me. I didn't understand how it came to this. All I ever wanted was to be a man of God. Wasn't truth and righteousness the goal?

In the pages ahead you will learn how I being a once very dogmatic, Bible believing, fundamentalists Christian came to find a love that dug me out of a pit of darkness. The message of Jesus was for those who lost sight of who they really are. Today, Jesus' message is specifically pointing at those who are self-appointed righteous Bible believers who stand on a throne of "godliness" looking down on all the "sinners" that desperately need salvation.

---

*Jesus taught, But I tell you, love your enemies and pray for those who persecute you, that you may be children of "**your**" Father in heaven.*

*Followers preach, But I tell you, convert your enemies to believe as we do so they become friends, that they may be children of "**our**" Father in heaven.*

What would it hurt to trust God?

We maintain denial because we are bent on proving the voices of the past wrong. But freedom comes in the face of reality whether the voices scream "I told you so." We win when we listen closely to our heart and follow our soul to the place where peace resides.

I don't remember how long after Mary told me she wanted a divorce, but it was in November that I talked with Roger who suggested I find a place to go for a few days just to allow some space between Mary and I. This horrified me, but I agreed. I had no friends so found a cheap hotel I could stay at for a few days. Further talks with Roger suggested that I find a place to live for a few months. And so I found a place to rent about a mile away from the home Mary and the kids were staying at.

I distinctly remember the last night that I would stay with the family. It was Monday, Nov. 8, 2010 – 9:00 PM when I wrote down these words...

I just finished watching Toy Story 3 with Alicyn (our adopted daughter). For about 45 seconds I felt something I never felt before overtake my mind. I slipped from my reality which included everything I had ever known to what seemed like a more real reality. I was startled and needed to use the bathroom. The moment had gone, and now I was sitting there wondering what was going on.

I was questioning many things of what was happening, I knew I was not in my right mind or was I? I took a bike ride to the park across the street to shake it off. It was dark, and I found a bench where there was some light from the lamps. My mind went to a movie I seen several months ago where the whole story made you believe that the main character was right in his thinking, meeting and talking to people that were crazy and telling lies. Only as it turned out, in the end, he was again playing over all the lies he had made himself believe, and he was really in an insane asylum replaying something that happened years before. While it seemed everyone else was crazy, it turned out that he alone was the crazy guy.

I was talking through this whole ordeal out loud while it played out in front of my mind. I remember being panicky and desperate and telling myself to remain calm. I really was questioning if what I knew of my life was real at all. I was wondering if I was somehow connected to a bunch of wires somewhere while lying on a bed all my life.

It seemed darker now as though the lamps were not emitting any light and I had a type of vision of a multitude of dark figures dancing around in front of me. I prayed and asked God to remove this from my presence, to stop this. Then over the next few seconds I seemed to calm and what I knew as reality came back, and the area I was sitting became visibly lighter making my visually small area of view broaden as many areas of the park came into view.

I felt at peace now and realized that I was placing my life, my wife's life and my children's lives into the hands of Roger who I believed by this time truly loved God first above all, and also loved us. I am sitting in my office chair here writing this as soon as I returned, and Aliy's voice "daddy, look" is music to my ears. I hope this is the real life I am leaving to save.

The next morning, I got up as normal, packed some things and headed out the door to go and live in my own home. It all seemed so surreal. I know this was a time to separate and heal if possible, but to me, I was walking away from the only life I had known for twenty-two years. I had failed.

That night I remember the thoughts that crammed for space in my mind. I couldn't shut them out, and it was driving me crazy. The night came, and I was all alone. Standing in my door looking out into the night sky wondering what this is all about. I didn't know if I should scream or cry or cut my wrists. When the thought of ending my life came to mind now and then over the next few days, I would think of the kids, and so the thought would pass into utter despair and loneliness. I cried a lot the first few weeks, especially as evening fell and one more day ended in silent nothingness.

I went to our men's group that Wednesday and Roger talked to me before the other guys showed up and asked if he could specifically call me out on the event that just took place. I agreed even in my pain. Roger asked me several questions which tore into my very essence, and through tears and sobs, I shared from a new broken place in my life. It did not take long before I came to understand that things like scripture verses about truth and sin, that I made a big deal over meant nothing at the moment. All I wanted was to sit and hear Mary's voice. And not that I could not call her, or talk to the kids, but I agreed with Roger to stay away for several weeks at first and to have as little of contact as possible with Mary.

One thing to note is that the street I moved in on had rental homes all with names of the Wizard of Oz. My house happened to be called the "Tin Man." When I saw that the first thought that ran through my head was that I truly was a tin man, who if you recall did not have a heart. At the end of this journey, an event will take place that I personally found as a small and yet amazing synchronicity of encouragement. It was also November and therefore too cold to sit on the front porch. That will make sense later.

A few days after moving in I headed to Las Vegas for the company I was working with. I arrived there and found my hotel room. I felt very alone so I called Roger and told him I couldn't do this, I cannot take the pain of being away from my family or thinking that our marriage could end. I just cannot fathom how things could change and how in time other people and families would come into the picture of our lives. Roger said to me, **"Steve, *what would it hurt to trust God?"***

We hung up, and those words would become the platform for which my journey would rest. What would it hurt to trust God? Well, I was a Christian, I certainly trusted in God with all my life, didn't I? What does it mean to trust God? Did I really trust in God?

Anyone reading those words as a Christian understands them very well and know that belief in the word of God is the fundamental foundation of the Christian faith. I believed in the Bible, and therefore I believed in God… Right? Well, that is not what went through my head when Roger shared those words with me. What I heard was,

'Steve, what would it hurt to trust in God alone?' Meaning to me, that anything and everything was set aside and I stand before God, naked, the same way I came into this world. All I am is what I am, and at the moment I had no idea what that was.

Well, I know now after talking with many people, that those words mean trusting in the Bible as that is their source of information *about* God. However, that is not how I took it upon myself to face the days, weeks and months ahead.

The days after coming home to my rental house continued to remain impossible. I couldn't shake the noise in my mind pulling my attention to things that caused me to point blame and offer excuses to my current situation. But I would fight it over and over and tell myself that only I am to blame for my situation, but it was difficult to believe. *If only the rest of the world would conform to my desires!* That is kind of a funny statement, and yet it is a statement from the arrogant self-righteous among us of whom I was still a strong believer of.

I remember one night I felt an incredible darkness, a black nothingness come over me. I realized at that moment that there was nothing I could hold on to that would provide any security. There was not even a rope I could grab hold of hanging in the blackness, and if there were, what was the source of the strength of the rope? In this very dark place, I remember thinking that the only thing I know is true, is that I will die one day and that I am alive now. That's it! If we are honest with ourselves down to the core, that is the only thing we truly know for sure, outside of faith.

As I looked at anything I have ever clung to as a source of safety or salvation, I could find nothing. I became increasingly desperate to find an answer, and yet nothing came to me. The only thought that ran through my mind was if there is a God I have no idea at this point if it is good or bad, and what does that even mean? If my life rests in the hope of life and after death, then whatever happens when I die is placed into the hands of this thing we call God.

At that same moment, I felt called to put everything down of external information and put my trust in this God I thought I knew, but realized now I knew nothing outside of what was told or taught to me. My trust was in other people's trust in God. I got all my information from the Bible and my father, my siblings, and church, and of course school, books and the Internet. The world was filled with information up to its eyeballs, and the diversity of religions and denominations all claiming theirs is the one true way made anyone on the outside wonder which one is right, or laugh yourself crazy at the very idea of such a conundrum.

Intellectual wordiness is a clanging cymbal, but God is found in the experience of silence.

Filling a heart sized hole

Happy Father's Day Dad! It is hard to see you so tired and sick. You were once so strong, a mighty man among men. I know you look forward to a better place, but somehow through a skewed belief I fear many hold to, miss the fullness of life God has given to us while on earth.

My father will not read this, but I will visit him today to share some time. What about you? Are you a father who is just getting along in life, hoping for an eternal destination to begin to live? Do you really think God made such a beautiful world as a place just to pass through and then destroy?

I talked with my father now and then, and several of my brothers either stopped by or called me at least once or twice, and that was very special to me. My father was telling me one day that once you move out of the house divorce is the next step and it is very hard to bring the marriage back together again. Those were words I didn't want to hear because that was on my mind more than other things. But he went on with telling me about a book he would like to send me some money for so I could go out and buy it for myself to read. A book about divorce and how bad it is for the children. I was thinking, do you need a book to educate someone on that? Surely there is more than enough advice already doing very little in the world, we need an intervention with a loving God in a much more honest and authentic way. I was only just beginning to learn what that meant.

At the time, I was working on a number of things in the group about childhood situations that may have caused some of my current life's behaviors. One thing I recalled was when we had to learn Bible verses. In our family, we didn't just have to learn a few verses, we had to memorize complete chapters and books of the new testament. I began to put a tune to the verses I was learning and making it into a type of song to help me memorize. Then my father came into the room and told me that we do not put music to learning our verses.

I was about twelve years old and so not only did I feel ashamed for doing so, I believe a part of me as I grew older made more sense to the resistance my family had toward music that had any rock or beat in it. Something in me enjoyed the music, and yet I felt it was wrong, and of course my father did not approve. As we grew older and with Christian music becoming more "secular," we all told people it was of the devil. Some people might find that a bit of a silly connection, but what I knew at the time was that my father loved me and was my only source of protection and truth, so if putting music to Bible words is bad, who am I at twelve years old going to know if he was wrong?

In my twenties, I stayed with my parents for six months in Africa. During that time, I was reading through the Bible but also a number of books dad had sitting around. I remember one day going to my father excited to share what

I was learning. In response, he told me I was not doing it right and offered me some advice. I remember getting angry with him and telling him that I would find God in my own way.

This he misunderstood as me saying that I will not listen to how my father would have me seek God, and therefore wrong, but what I meant was that he needed to give me time to study and allow God to work in my life. It was bringing some of these things up in the group that allowed me to see why I was acting the way I was with my sons and with Mary, and why they could never do it right as I always had higher expectations for them to reach for.

Back at the rental house, I remember talking to my father on the phone when he told me to go back home and kick Mary out! Said in his voice that meant you better follow or else which of course made me feel like I was twelve again. Another favorite of his sayings when sharing something he disagreed with was "Baloney!" said with a very strong voice that was meant to be condescending and shut you down completely. I think it made him feel very proud of himself in doing so. It made me feel like a stupid little boy, which of course is what it was meant to do.

Well, when he told me to go home and kick Mary out, it really hurt, because while we had our differences, I still respected my father and believed in him as an honest and good man. He was my father! I still trusted him. I was just shocked to hear him suggest that I break up our marriage further, and with force. Now I was beginning to understand the control freak in me. I was working hard every day on myself with a great hope to save my marriage and family. I hung up with him and got in the car and just drove around until I began to cry from what I felt was abandonment to the little piece of hope I still had left in my father. My mother was gone, and now I felt completely alone. The next day when I got up, I wrote the following story to a new understanding.

The little boy inside

Stevie boy didn't know what to do with this new information he was being told by his father. It seemed to contradict, and it hurt more than anything he can remember.

Stevie boy didn't dare to cry because dads are always right, and dad's love their children. But Stevie boy was afraid of being alone. Somehow this had left a sharp pain, a seemingly large hole in his heart. But being only a young boy, who trusted his father, didn't know what to do about it. It just hurt.

But something new happened today. Stevie boy found a new friend, big Steve! Turning and looking up to me when I called his name, I smiled at him, and he smiled back, knowing instantly that he was no longer alone.

I said, I know you are hurting, and it's ok to cry. So, I lifted him up into my strong arms and held him tight, and we both cried together. Both of us feeling the very same pain.

I could still see in his eyes that he was still afraid. Afraid of not knowing what to do or what to think. He counted on his father to be his hero, his savior. Without dad, I could hear him thinking - I would die! I held him tighter, assuring him he was going to be alright.

In a short time, I felt his small muscles relax, and the grip he had on my neck loosen. I set him down on a chair opposite from me and looked into his eyes. Stevie boy I said, I need to tell you something. This pain you feel will fade, but it will never be forgotten. It will be a constant reminder of the love that only God can fill.

You see, you can only see a giant hole left from words that left you in fear, but I know now that it is actually a blessing. With that, he wiped away the tears still left on his cheeks, and his eyes grew a little bigger, dancing back and forth as he studied my face, anticipating with the hope he already knew I was going to share with him.

I said you have been relying on your father all your life, and I have too. I said that I loved God with all my heart, but I recently found out that I really didn't. Our faith and trust had been with our earthly father. The hole that has just been made is so large that only God can fill it. What a blessing it is to know that your heavenly Father can now fill the hole, the void you feel, with a perfect Love.

Shifting in his chair a little, knowing I was not done, he breathed deeply and said, tell me more. I smiled back at him watching his eyes as he was being made aware that the night was over, birds were singing outside, and the smell of Spring flowers filled the air. I could sense that he was being set free, that the world he once knew was small compared to this new reality.

I said, there is no reason to be angry with your father. Do you know he was also hurt when he was a boy just like you? He was nodding his head, letting this information settle into his young mind. I watched as tears again began to well up in his eyes, and mine did too. Sadness came over his face, and he reached for my hands which were folded on the table that separated us.

We held each other's hands and cried again, only this time for the pain of our father's childhood. After a minute, Stevie boy spoke again and said, Steve, I am so glad that you took the time to learn about this. If you hadn't, I would have lived my whole life in fear, pain, and bitterness. I had become very angry over the years and felt ashamed of myself for thinking poorly of others. I judged them because of their sin, but now I feel sorry for them, for their pain.

I nodded my head in agreement, respecting this little guy for who he is. We both got up and took each other's hands. I said I think you have grown a little since the last time I remember seeing you, messing up his hair. We both laughed, knowing he is me, and I am he. I said I want you to meet a Friend of mine who is just like us. He has a little boy who is also Himself. And so, we walked out into the warm sunlight, telling ourselves what a great day this is going to be.

He walks with me and talks with me

A few years ago, while walking down the road, I was thinking that if Jesus were walking with me, how would I position myself.

At first, I thought he would lead so I could follow him. No, I thought, he would not want me to feel he was above me.

Then I thought he would follow so he would have my back. No, I thought, I would not want him to feel I was above him.

Then he said to me with a smile, I do not lead or follow my friends, but walk side by side and hand in hand.

The thing that is worshiped cannot be loved or of love, for love is a companion to you, as you are a companion to love.
~Steve Nyhof

The one thing we learned at Higher Ground, was that we did not study the Bible to find or learn about what Jesus or David or Paul was conveying, but that in what they said, how did it speak to our life where we are today. This concept was foreign to me as I grew up being a part of Bible studies where the focus was to learn what the Bible was teaching us from that history, which always creates division because we all have different perspectives depending on where we are in life, the family we grew up in and the culture we move around in.

This approach assumes the perspective of what the Bible is saying is understood in a specific way, or that the purpose of the study is to agree on a doctrine that everyone agrees on as true of what is being said about the authors or characters message. Now I was being asked while reading the verse(s), to pay close attention to that still small voice inside talking to me. It may be sharing something completely off topic, that is fine. The goal was to listen and write down what was coming to mind related to me in this moment and then address that in truth.

It took me literally months to deprogram out of coming to the group and telling others what I thought the meaning of the verses were instead of how the verses spoke to me personally in my life this week. Roger was not interested in our disconnected from personal life doctrinal opinions and perspectives of what scripture was saying two to six thousand years ago because he knew this had no solution or would not serve anyone, myself or the others. He was interested in how the scripture was bringing thoughts to mind in our personal lives and what in the verses brought attention to us about our current situation.

Because I grew up in the Baptist church and know how the fundamentalist and literalist mind works, if this is your background or similar, the previous paragraphs I just wrote have been thoroughly judged because what I just wrote seems to be contrary to "like-minded" words, or words used in specific ways that are allowed or not allowed by the doctrine of your teaching. In other words, they do not fit the Biblical definition of how the Bible should be studied, and therefore wrong.

But that is the purpose of this book, and especially this chapter. I was asked the question about trusting God, and now I am asking you, "what would it hurt to trust in God alone?" Can you put your Bible down for a while and step away from all you've been taught and told, good or bad, and step into the presence of God for a time to hear his voice speaking specifically to your heart? And do you even know what that means?

I had someone tell me they would die if they could not have their Bible while ignorant that billions of people died before the compilation of the Bible ever existed or lived and died without knowing a thing about it. The Mayan civilization, one of many existing before Jesus, lived and died without a Bible or knowing who Jesus was. The Jewish people prior to knowing of Jesus walking the earth and had scriptures in the form of scrolls that told them about God, but nothing yet of a new testament, nor desire it today.

My point is that the Bible has become the new God of contemporary Christians. If God were to speak to the common Biblical follower, they would test what they heard by the Bible. Well, you say, then the message was not from God because the Bible is God's word. I am saying, if God spoke to you would you listen to Him, or dismiss His voice because of Biblical doctrines you hold more dear as truth? If yes, then the Bible holds more power to you than God and makes God as small as your understanding.

There are over 30,000, and some say over 40,000 different Christian denominations practiced today. When I learned of this, I needed to give some thought to what that meant and meant to me. If you talked to each of these groups, you would get the same answer from each one when asking if they believe that their denomination holds the correct translation and perspective of scripture. I have not found a single person yet who said they follow their doctrine knowing what they believe is wrong.

Beliefs are the result of truths held as correct based on the personal understanding of the information available over time and at the time. We do not believe in something until we first are convinced of the truth of it. The truth at times is based on facts, but also on faith. When truth is based on faith, the belief is now only something held onto in hope by the individual or group who holds the same hope as truth. Meaning, when we step into faith, (and I am a strong advocate of faith) we step into a place of hearsay based on one's own experience or desire to hope in what another trusted person may believe in based on their experience and knowledge.

These were some of the things now running through my mind as the weeks slowly turned into the first month away from my family. In a way, I felt for the first time a freedom from the guilt of desiring to step into a world filled with wonder I was told never to adventure into for fear of being led astray.

As I spent time each day in meditation for 10 to 20 minutes, mainly calming and training my mind to be quiet, but also in contemplation, allowing thoughts to arise, whether good or bad and let them go, I would consider a thought and expand on it. I would spend time with the thought for as long as necessary. Sometimes, and in many cases, I wrote in my journal or got up and went to my computer and began to write as the thoughts flowed through my mind. Other times I completed my quiet time and would just get started on my work day.

I have hundreds of documents of my time resting in the presence of God as I understood it then. In this place, I felt no condemnation or any inclination that some dark force wanted to take control of my mind or body. Of course, I wondered about it because I was told from my family to be afraid of doing such a thing as "demons" are waiting in sheep's clothing. I was learning so much from this space and so excited about the place I seem to be in that I could only describe the next months ahead as pure bliss. I was alone, running out of money to live on, even considering going to the city mission to live just to experience that, and yet I held a profound peace and joy in my heart that was nothing short of an amazing and compassionate presence.

I began walking every day with Jesus as he seemed to be a large part of my journey at this time. We would walk down the sidewalk, and I would stay to one side, and we talked for extended periods of time. This became so real to me that one day while in a deep conversation we walked around a corner that had a high bush, and a fellow came around the other side and would have walked right into Jesus except that Jesus quickly sidestepped to avoid the collision! And then we both laughed as we walked on.

At that very moment, I realized that I was laughing alone and to anyone watching I must've looked like a crazy guy with some serious problems. But that is how real it was to me, and I shared my stories with the men in my group. One story of when I was meditating, I saw myself resting my head on Jesus' lap, and when I stood up in front of him, I was wearing white shorts and a white button up shirt outside my shorts. Jesus was telling me that God sees me filled with light, perfect and blameless just as I am. It was at this moment that I was beginning to realize that salvation was not something we receive as though we are lost sinners as my doctrines would determine, but that we are innately perfect and filled with light and love from eternity past. We are somehow always as God is always.

Roger had me read the book Codependent No More by Melody Beattie. I filled up a complete wire bound notebook with notes as I was learning how I was codependent on Mary and especially my father. Liberation was a word that was being used more often in my vocabulary as I shared my experiences with the men. I read the book Emotional Intelligence 2.0 by Travis Bradberry. I had picked it up at an airport and was the book that helped me to begin to understand the difference between those that use intelligence and those who use compassion to communicate. A business leadership book, but it's implication to marriage and relationship is all there in the pages. Highly recommended, as it offers very insightful and practical information for anyone that find themselves at odds with their partner. And remember, the path to God is never about changing others, that is impossible and futile. This is about learning and changing ourselves.

The Power of Now by Eckhart Tolle was the book that really began to challenge me with new insights and change my outlook on living in the present, basically letting the past go because it does not exist except in the mind. Eckhart Tolle shares his disparaging evening and the unexpected morning and months ahead of a present bliss he enjoyed that changed his life. The Road Home: The

Journey Beyond the Spiritual Quick Fix by William Frank Diedrich was a book that took me further outside my box of fear I was told never to step out of. I read many other books and information as I felt for the first time in my life I was learning more about the greatness of God by learning more about the diversity of the world cultures and all of God's unique children. I was beginning to see everyone as beings of light, knowing that we only lost sight of who we truly are – children of God.

The main thing I was learning was that Mary and I were very different people. I was an analytical thinking person, and Mary was more of a feeling person. The book The Personality Code by Travis Bradberry was a great eye opener for me because it helped me understand that I was much more analytical in how I communicated, whereas Mary was more feeling based in how she communicated. Wow! Mary was looking for compassion from a stone-cold machine. No wonder we had no clue to who we were or what we wanted for our relationship. I realized that I grew up in a family where emotions and feeling were purposely suppressed as they could be untrustworthy. It was as though our doctrine crushed the very essence of who God is at the core and replaced it with a robotic informational manual of knowledge and instructions.

The more our group got into the Bible, the more I saw that the whole thing is one story of experience after another and filled with feelings. In fact, all of life is experience and only experience. Experience has everything to do with gut feelings, intuition and the senses of the body talking to us. Recognizing I had feelings was a new thing for me and another step of liberation that I felt missing from my life. I had been so afraid of my feelings and therefore hid them beneath my facade of knowledge and self-righteousness.

We comment that women have intuition, said in some way of answering how she just happened to know something before it happened. Yes! Because women are typically more emotional so they use their intuition unknowingly to guide them. Men have a lesson to learn from women. It is the analytical, truth-demanding, knowledge-driven intellectual that is the farthest away from his or her heart, and therefore, out of touch with the Great Lover, who is trying to get their attention.

I do understand that there are facts and truths of things that we grab ahold of to guide our way, but much of these also originate from spiritual teachers of love, such as Siddhartha Gautama, Jesus, Krishna, and Mohammed. These were the ones sharing their spiritual experiences with their culture so they might see the light and unity of God within them. It is the followers who did not experience the same thing but instead shared what they think they believe is the truth about what was told to them by the teacher. Their faith becomes their truth as they trust the teacher with what was shared without experiencing the same thing for themselves.

It is impossible to experience someone else's experience. If anything was supposed to be transferred to another person from the teacher, it was the message of love and unity, the feelings, and emotions that were present within that experience. Followers turn the words shared about the experience into a new religion because the words shared drives the followers to want to hold on to it like a treasure. Then spend their entire lives trying to live out and experience this treasure from another, missing their own opportunities to experience God on the path designed for them.

To expand on this a bit, I started to look at someone like David, in how he wrote down his songs and the messages they conveyed. If David were here and learned that we wrote hundreds of books about him, he would be perplexed at the very least in the wonder of our stupidity. David would say, *"I wrote down the things I did because I experienced a relationship with God that was so real and exciting that I wanted others to seek after God like I did. You cannot know God by studying my experiences, you know God by experiencing God for yourself."* David might say, *"Go and write your own experiences down about your relationship with God so others might be intrigued to go and seek after God to find their own experience."* He may further say, *"I wrote this down to intrigue you to seek God, not to study my experiences and then create doctrines around them."* I can see him standing there with that "are you kidding me" look on his face.

You go to Disney on vacation and enjoy all the parks and rides and then came back and tell a friend all about your experiences with all of your emotion. You do your best to share your experiences, every moment, every sight, every sound, smell, and taste. Your friend in the meantime is not looking at you because she is busy writing everything down as fast as she can. About a minute into sharing with great excitement, you stop and ask what she is doing. "Oh," she looks up and says, "I'm recording the whole thing because it sounds amazing! Please continue!" You tell her that it is amazing and she should go for herself. "Oh no." she says, "this is good enough for me! I will just read this whenever I want to know what it is like to spend time at Disney. I will also share it with my friends so they too can know all about Disney and how great it is, please continue!"

This is exactly how we treat our relationship and experience with God, by going to a written record of other people's relationship and experiences *about* God. Yes, I know there is much more to gain from reading the Bible, but today, the Bible has taken the place of having our own experience with the Father. Jesus said that he came to show us the Father, not words about the Father.

What I was also learning is that within meditation I was coming to know things, what I began to call a "knowing," something from the heart and not of the mind. I began to see the opposite take place in what was coming into my mind and heart. In the past I would not ever allow myself to think there is truth outside the Bible or the words presented to me from within the doctrines I held as true, or what I believed my father would agree is true or false, what I called my father filter.

Now the things coming to me in meditation were being answered within hours, days and weeks within the Bible and other books, or listening to music or talking with someone about anything. I was becoming more aware and recognizing that the truth was within me as it was with David or Abraham or Jesus and others in scripture, or outside of it who shared their stories of their relationship with God. The truth and love to be discovered is alive within me and within you. It was always there and is always there.

But you may be afraid already because I used those eastern names in this book. If you haven't done your history study on these people, then you live in fear as a result of ignorance and call it being spiritually discerning. Trust me, the Christian uses these words to justify their fears. In fact, once I started to pay closer attention to my thoughts, my mind could produce the longest string of lies through the justification and rationalization of scripture. You just don't know you are doing this while engulfed within the very belief system. Right now, you may not believe me because you are afraid to stand with me on the outside of your faith. You may not even know what I'm talking about.

Again, I would ask Roger about our marriage because he was also leading the women's group my wife was in. He would typically say that he was not really interested in our marriage but mainly interested in our relationship with God. As the months passed Rogers reply to my question would be that Mary and I were talking less about each other or blaming each other and focused more on our relationship with God.

For the seven months I was away, Roger never gave me any inclination of whether our marriage would get back together, and so while I did live in fear of losing my marriage and family, my relationship with God was growing stronger every day. One day I was asked in my heart, will you love Me even if you lose your family? Yes, was my answer without hesitation. My relationship had become so amazing and filled with joy by this time, I could not imagine ever giving up on my relationship with God for anything or anyone. But more importantly, I also knew that this was the only way back home. I just didn't know how but trusted God would open the doors to our lives when the time was ready, and I was no longer in a hurry.

It is in the place of the know that people connect. This place is void of words and reason because it is of the heart. It is also in this place where we are present with God.

The death of the father filter

I once relied on my father to show me the Lord.
Now I rely on the Lord to show me, my father.

As I continued to attend the group and share, and others sharing their stories, I slowly began to recognize that much of what was still popping up in my mind as I faced day to day life situations was my father. In fact, prior to facing some of these things in my life, my reactions or actions to anything in life was filtered through my father's approval or disapproval without my knowing it. Prior to joining Higher Ground, I had no clue to the thoughts that ran through my mind, and therefore my behaviors were just reactions to their control.

I remember pacing the sidewalk in front of my home for several weeks chain smoking one cigarette after the next, mulling over all the things where dad was interacting with me in actions and thoughts. I thought of things I said to Mary and the children based on this father filter that existed subconsciously in my mind. I recalled so many other conversations or situations where I debated some doctrinal beliefs and realized that while I had my own take on things, all I was really doing is regurgitating words and verses my father would say, or reacting one way or another as if I had to answer to him at some time. I was afraid of upsetting or disappointing my father should he ever find out I made a wrong choice or choices that would gain his approval even if he would never know. Trust me I made poor choices all the time myself, but I am referring to those choices where I knew my doctrines were being challenged.

I paced the sidewalk for months while contemplating much of the things that were coming into my mind, and often darted into the house to type these thoughts down as fast as I could as they flowed so I would not forget them. One topic that I have documented was the time I was testing all of God's attributes against my father. I know it is strange to think I did this, but I share this because I know I am no different than many other people who live their whole lives regurgitating the thoughts and behaviors of their fathers and mothers unaware. This was an exercise to help me see more clearly who I was placing my trust in.

I thought of a bar chart and placed my father under one bar and God under the other. Then I began to think of the things we know about God, like power, where did dad stand up against God in power? Well, I thought, if God is infinite, then dad's bar would remain at zero. If dad's bar did raise a little in my mind, it was only because I lost sight of God. Dad's bar was quickly brought back to zero time and time again when I raised God's bar to a greater infinity.

I did the same things with love, grace, kindness, longsuffering, etc., exhausting each one and thinking about situations where dad displayed love or patients, etc., and how God would display himself within these situations. As much as I tried to find something, dad's bar remained at zero in comparison to the attributes of God. Then the words ran through my head, "why on earth am I following dad"? In comparison to God, my father was a big zero! It was another very strong message to me that I needed to trust in God alone.

When we grow up and leave home, our fathers should make it clear that he is passing us from his hand into the care of God, and therefore making the once cared for child grow into a man or woman and put away childish things. But like my father, I took on the role of treating my wife as a child when I took on the role of head of the home. The Bible talks of this, but no adult should feel like they need to answer to anyone except God, and then what does that mean? Some may say, well Steve, this was your fault for not letting go, you are the one to cling to your father.

Yes, I had come to realize that I was still holding on to my end of the rope, but my father also in his very presence made it very clear that his children better pay close attention to a righteousness that existed within the family (what I call a facade today) to adhere too or else. My older adopted sister could attest to what happens when you crossed dad, the same thing the Amish parents and culture do, shun their children and send them away and out of the only existence they ever knew or loved because of a truth demanded above tolerance and compassion. And this was still going on after she was married and had children! My sister was abandoned twice by the only thing a child knows as safe, her parents.

The world has never been more lost of its love because of clinging on to a hope of truths some will die for, misunderstanding they are completely giving into the desires of righteousness over compassion, therefore stepping into the same darkness they claim to resist.

As long as truth is demanded over truth, an intolerant fear remains in control, and love as part of its nature steps aside allowing our free will to control the illusion we created when we lost sight of love long ago where we once remembered Its benevolent power.

So how does love prevail? By loving the enemy. It is only our fears that manifested separation from love in the first place. Dying for truth never worked and always separates. Love is always there waiting to show Its unexpected outcome through compassion.

This journey has taught me a great deal about how my wife and I should let our children go with the understanding that they are responsible for their personal relationship with God, and that I would love them no matter what through childhood and adulthood as the love I have come to experience in the past few months was completely different and opposing to the love I grew up with that could judge, punish, accuse, and even cast out for all eternity.

"God is love," "Love has no fear," "Love remembers no wrongs." These are words found in scripture that I believe to be true. But you can also find words that contradict these, as in "but the wicked and him that loveth violence his soul hateth" or "And whosoever was not found written in the book of life was cast into the lake of fire" (love apparently does remember wrongs and is capable of hating if you believe all of the scriptures). These were the things I was wrestling with in my mind, but I was also by this time trusting in God more than the Bible to guide my heart to truth knowing there existed no authority greater outside the truth he put within my heart, a truth I have always been a part of but somehow forgot because of all the things in this world that distracted me from who I am.

What about the Bible Steve? That is the Word of GOD!

Well, if you think about it, how big is God if (He/She/It) is confined to a small book that has only in recent centuries had its followers claiming it as the word of God? And what does that mean? We say that God is infinite and all powerful, all knowing "Behold, God is great, and we know him not" and yet we are so sure about what scripture says according to our very tiny historical blink of an eye existence of understanding, and therefore make God tiny and finite if not completely something else we CAN imagine. That the Holy Spirit guides us, and yet we don't listen to Him because He is confined by our very literal definition of scripture based on where we grew up, what church we attended and a thousand other things that would confine God to the small box we find ourselves in because we can't stop ourselves from defining God by our very literal Sunday school childlike minds.

But before you get all uptight with me, at this time of my journey, this was not easy for me either as the doubts of my upbringing and indoctrination (programming) were telling me I better be careful. If hell is real and God is in charge, then wouldn't it be safest to take no chances with eternity? Well, I would have to ask myself, how is this of love? When does love draw a line in the sand? And if it does, then how safe am I anyway?

While holding to beliefs where I "knew" I was right, I was completely blinded to the underlying control that guided my life. Within this spirit I would also claim I understood love, that it was of compassion, but also judgment, placing me in a perpetual conflict with how I wanted to engage with my family and with how God engaged with humanity throughout history.

While I stood on the "solid rock" pointing a finger outward in judgment, my heart wanted to be more tender and kind "as a hen her chicks" with my wife and children. Surrendering to a greater truth placed within me was the Great Lover Itself, who is slowly shifting my awareness from what I believed and was taught to an understanding of a love unbound by doctrines.

I am learning that I know so little of love because behavior understood per doctrines and belief systems were mainly the subjects of life. Today I am trying to live on the side of grace, and any conflict to my desired compassion for others is still often thwarted by old judgmental doctrines fighting within me pointing the finger at the faults in the very person I claim to love.

Love's compassion and belief systems of judgment will always be in conflict with one another. For two thousand years, we have tried to fit this puzzle together by creating more doctrines of judgment and further separating itself from God. Love was never meant to stand in the same line and behind doctrines or belief systems. Love's grace is greater than truth.

The next morning after concluding that I would do all I can to be mindful and aware of when I was using my father, I stepped from my front porch onto the only step down to the sidewalk and in the flash of a moment, the following is a recount from my journal of the vision I had.

Steve, you are a man made in the image of God. You don't "need" anyone or anything to fulfill your life. You don't need to filter your beliefs through your father anymore. The reason you don't trust Me is because you never had to rely on Me, you always relied on your father, and he is only a finite man. I am God the Holy Spirit, my knowledge and wisdom are infinite. I have never hurt you, and I never will. You have a lot to learn and unlearn, and as you focus on Me alone for your "needs," I will hold your hand and never let you go.

I then saw a vision in my mind play out instantly... The life I was living was in a tunnel, where I made my own ideas of what the sky was like, and grass and the world as I knew it. There was light on each end of the tunnel showing me that there was hope. And then my spirit was lifted up to God's viewpoint as I seen the tunnel lifted and myself left standing there in an endless sea of flowers. The sky over me was forever, and I was able to see for the first time the finite existence I made for myself and believed was real.

And then it left me as I was standing on the sidewalk where I stopped to wonder what I had just witnessed.

I shared my stories with the guys, and by this time, whether they believed a word I ever shared, there was no question from any of them by my excitement that I believed in what I experienced over these months on my own. This is why I often refer to it as my journey because it was nothing less than a most wondrous adventure in the presence of a most loving God.

With each step I took like this, I felt more and more liberated from what was becoming clearer to me as bondage, but not of sin, no, of indoctrination to things I was told was true only because those before them were told were true. And fear was the driving force behind all of this insanity and belief systems we bow our knee to in worship and call it love. How can love ask you to worship it?

I had followed a god that demands my best and then shames me for failing impossible expectations. I was following a god that would damn my son to hell while holding my hand, smiling and leading me into "the promised land." I would still be doing the same to my wife and children the rest of my life if it were not for Roger challenging me to trust my heart to God. Two years ago, my words did not come across like this as my fears and doubts would not so easily give up to the wonders of the love and light that guide me today.

There is a river that flows within like gravity grounding each step we take. From the beginning man was aware of this downward force long before he knew its name. You might say, he believes in it, he lives by it. The same for him who becomes aware and lives by the flow of God within is saved into this knowing and presence. God is calling everyone into these rivers, the "always is" gift within that no language can express except that which is shared between you and God. John 7:38

You have my full attention!

I traveled a raging sea in a ship of beliefs where hope held tight to the rudder guiding me to a shore where Love resides. Standing on this shore of unspeakable joy and peace, I wave goodbye to the ship that once carried gentle truths within the storm that would bring me into the arms of Love.

I was busy with building a website platform for a company I was partnered with. We were selling systems to our clients, and I was holding webinars, or what you might think of as seminars, only held over the Internet where hundreds of people joined me in training about things related to the Internet and how to gain a presence to help grow their companies.

I remember I was getting behind and needed to get some things done for another partner who was also busy with other aspects and different relationships but all connected to the development of the content management system I had built for people wanting to get onto the Internet. So, there was this pressure that existed as you can imagine at any job, and so I did my best to remain focused on my work.

However, after months into this journey, there came a time where only a few minutes would pass, and I would find myself writing and researching spiritual things that were running through my mind and back to writing again. Then I would notice that several hours had passed so I would tell myself to put this down and that I needed to get some work done. So again, I would focus on what I needed to do and get into the code and other things, and before I knew what was happening, I was documenting more of my inner thoughts down. Back and forth this went on for a week. Then it dawned on me what was happening.

God had something else in mind for me now, and it wasn't building website systems. I stopped the fight when I realized what was happening and told God that he has my undivided attention. Lead me wherever you want me to go. I went to sit on the front porch because by this time it was Spring and everything was beginning to turn green and beautiful in our neighborhood. I was reading the Bible and always several books at the same time. I could tell my insights would slow down when I stopped reading for only a few days. I continued to meditate for longer periods of time and just basking in the light of this Great Lover of my soul.

I wrote a lot by hand in my journal but also on the computer that my writings could fill a dozen books. As I look back and read some of the things I wrote, I am not always sure where I was at on this journey, or what I was specifically thinking about at the time to have had these thoughts. Here are a few statements I wrote down during times of reading and meditating.

Life in the body on earth and today's circumstances become our playing field. Our unique personalities along with God's ever-present Light create the relationship of his foreseen final and perfect design.

I am only now seeing God as a true friend, just like the guys, where He wants to talk about the day and my feelings. He's not interested in solving anything with me, He just wants to talk.

There is a place I am finding that I know exists. The closer I come to it, or whenever I enter it, I feel my earthly existence is only a shadow compared to it. I am finding that my earthly physical mind is not a part of it.

There is something I am beginning to know in my heart that is not of the earth or of the physical body. Awareness is also a part of this spiritual thing or presence. Awareness is not of the mind or of understanding, it is a part of the knowing of the heart.

When I enter my past, I do so in my mind only. I am missing the beauty of the moment, the warm sun, the sounds of birds singing, the fragrance of flowers in the air, the very presence of love.

In this state of being, God opens up the eyes of our heart to see others as God sees us. In this place, there is a knowing that words cannot express. This is the place where joy lives.

God's design for oneness is through the unique, seemingly opposing characteristics operating in a constant cycle of growth of giving and letting go to lift all involved to a higher level of knowing each other and God.

Joy is not of this world, it cannot be found in the mind. The best of circumstances will only offer happiness, but never joy. Joy is found in the presence of God which can only be known in the heart.

While sitting on my porch over the next few weeks, I had several strange experiences. One morning while sitting on my porch looking out at the neighborhood I had a funny feeling like something was different, and yet everything was as it always had been. It was like everything I was looking at, whether a house, a car or the lawns, it was somehow more real. It was vibrant and filled with life. I really felt like I was in another reality that was in some unknowing way different and more real, more alive. To this day, I cannot make anything else out about it, other than I felt like life was fuller and more real that morning. When I read Eckhart Tolle explain his experience the morning that started his journey, his recounting of his experience was very similar to mine, only he was able to articulate it more clearly.

Another experience I had was in the evening. Again, I was on the front porch reading by the ceiling light because the sun was just going down. I stopped reading because I noticed that the light in the room was fading quickly into darkness. The ceiling light was still on, but the room felt dark and a bit intimidating. I then saw a type of vision is all I know it by, of a doorway that opened into a dark black room where I found myself alone and a little frightened. Then the door closed behind me, and any light showing around the door jamb, faded away until the door itself no longer existed.

The thought came to me that I had stepped over a threshold in my beliefs where I could no longer go back. I had for the first time just realized what it was like to look back on a once held belief system with new unblinded eyes and see it for what it was. The person who grows up and builds on their childhood belief system has no idea of what I am sharing by this statement, because until right at this moment, I didn't know this could exist. The darkness in the room faded away after about 5 minutes, and I sat there just pondering on this new revelation.

About a month later I traveled to a conference in Texas for a few days and stayed at a beautiful place where there were lots of parties and great times just socializing with hundreds of other people there, and I was on such a high cloud that more and more people were gathering around me just to hear what I was learning and had to share. I know that I was radiating light and love within my countenance. The joy and peace I held was very inviting to them.

On the morning of the day I would be heading back, I was sitting on a small balcony off the bedroom of the hotel. I had a chair there and was just sitting looking out at the grounds. Then a vision came to me where I was sitting at a small square table with God, The Holy Spirit, and Jesus. They pointed my attention over to a white car in the parking lot.

I was being told that I am not my body, that like a driver is the life of the car, without the driver, the car is nothing. I cannot explain in words the next moments I had of feeling as though I was outside my body while this insight was happening to me, but it gave me tremendous strength to think of my body as the form of which my essence resides for a time on this earth. My temple. I felt like I always had been, and always will be like there never was a time that love or God could separate itself from itself, and I was somehow a part of that everlasting presence. The intense realization of this faded, but the thought of the feeling stuck with me for several months.

God certainly had my full attention, and my faith and trust in his love and guidance have never been greater in my life. I was beyond excited to see what God had in store for me next. I was still sitting out on that balcony when my mind was now going back to the movie, Ratatouille, where there was an inspiring rat that wanted to become a chef, but there was this extremely egotistic and judgmental food critic that over the course of the movie had a change of heart about a rat running a kitchen and cooking food. In the end, the waiter came out to the critic who stopped by for dinner and was asked what he wanted for dessert. The critic turned and glanced over to the kitchen where the rat was looking back through the door window in anticipation.

The critic smiled and said, "surprise me!"

That is where I was at. I was feeling completely outside of my once held desires, and yet learning that the closer I got to God, the more his desires were my desires. And it was not as though I was giving up to something different than what I wanted, it was that God was merging into my will overjoyed to help me experience the joys of my heart.

Over the next month or so I was completely at peace living on my own, broke, and was going to be ok if the marriage did not come back together. I was in a place where God was truly at the helm, and I was more excited to see where the next adventure would take me. I had such a strong trust in God, and a deepening love I had never known or been taught about that whatever the next steps would be I was confident and completely at peace it would be for the best of all of us. Somehow, I knew that the amazing love and unbelievable joy that was very present each day in my life would find a way, sooner or later, into the reconciliation of my wife and children's lives.

It was in my extolling of great effort to preserve what I made out of my imputed belief system which proved it was not true. It was in following my heart that my efforts began to lessen because I was beginning to find peace and rest in already having and being.

There was also an effort at first against my indoctrination (that truth was somehow something I lacked), and slowly became aware of the distortions as they compared to my already being. Liberation also continued to step in to give me affirmation that my efforts were slowly becoming unnecessary as the truth of being is truth itself.

Therefore, the truth may be less of something we seek, which takes effort, but more of letting go of that which we have attached to it, hiding a most brilliant essence within. It's not in the "newing" of the mind, as though from outside, but in the "renewing" because it is already within.

The time for reconciliation

The amazing pain of getting real is of no consequence to the peace and liberation I have come to know in your presence.

Higher Ground for me was the place where I felt safe to share whatever I wanted or needed to without worry of someone judging me for not saying something doctrinally correct, offered advice to why I was wrong, or for saying something stupid that others would laugh at. I shed many tears in that place as I confessed to so many things the Spirit was bringing to mind in meditation and when I went for my walks. I started to write a few emails to my family telling them of what I was learning, but I don't think I quite fit into the mold they envisioned for my life or how repentance should look. I was stepping away from my faith into a new light of seeing the world. But it came with facing the wrongs I had made that hurt my family.

The Higher Ground slogan verse was *"And be not conformed to this world: but be ye transformed by the renewing of your mind, that ye may prove what is that good, and acceptable, and perfect, will of God." Romans 12:2.* Change takes time, and it is more than just learning a knowledge of scripture others can be in awe of. That is how I felt at most Bible studies in my younger years. It was those that really studied and memorized and could share their findings that rose to the top as leaders, completely missing the essence of how scripture should change our lives to be more unified. Instead, we dig in harder with innovative ways to prove and solve the contradictions, forming new and more dogmatic doctrines of separation, mainly because the god of the Bible and the God of Love are truly two separate realities, and we try to fuse them together to make sense of the insanity.

I began to send Mary an email now and then telling her I was sorry for things I had done to hurt her through the years. Nothing I wrote to her now had any indication any longer of a man being clever with his wording or trying to manipulate. God was shedding light on the things in my life where I had missed the mark at times, and others where I was downright insensitive and mean spirited to maintain my dominant male ego. Every week the men would come together to share stories of their week and where they may have made a wrong choice, saying something hurtful or not saying something when they should, and then confessing these things one to another along with the steps we would take to correct the wrongs or possible choices to prevent the wrongs from happening again. Renewing the mind.

The devil is in the music!

I was completely sucked in by the teaching of our family beliefs as well as beliefs of the church and preachers that would come to tell us that rock music was of the devil. Back in that day, there was more than enough talk about how satan was destroying our children through this music. So, what is a self-righteous parent to do to protect his holy facade but do his part in keeping his children safe? Mind you, most country music was ok to listen to in our family, go figure! When I was younger, I had several friends that burned all their records after certain preachers shared their stories of fear and damnation in the church, the prime tactic of the church to bring about conversion and control of its sheep. It worked then and is still working today.

One day I told my oldest son Jordan that he needed to burn his CDs. (Funny how it needs to be burning. Seems to be something there about killing and sacrifice and burning, and calling it love that makes the church feel approved unto God. Or it is that god vs God thing we can't seem to get right.) I do not remember him resisting much but certainly upset. But I would guess that he was too afraid of me being the self-righteous control freak that I was. In fact, today I believe this behavior crosses the line into psychotic.

I remember standing on the deck in the back of our house as Jordan took a box with him to the rear of the back yard. He was on his knees and trying to light them on fire with a lighter, and when that didn't work, he began to bend them in half. I was about 40 feet away, and it was getting dark out, so our house light was on, and even at this distance, I could see the tears flowing down his fifteen-year-old face as I watched on, a dictator in God's army. A righteous father protecting his child from destruction.

Honestly, I hate recounting this story because it breaks my heart that I really did this to my son.

I was conflicted about what I was having him do as it broke my heart then and yet my father, most siblings, friends, and preachers were my reason to be strong and unwavering in doing "the right thing." Truth must prevail at all costs – right? We needed to "purge the devil" from our home. Back then I didn't realize just how deep the superstition ran in my family, in me and within the church, and is still there today driving its sheep into a darkness of fear.

Now back to the time my wife and I were separated, I stopped by the home where my wife and children were staying and went upstairs to Jordan's room. This would be the first of many times I began to face Jordan with confessing of the things I did that hurt him. He was laying on a bed on the floor, and so I sat on a chair at the foot of the bed and began to recount the time I had asked him to burn his CDs. With a stone-cold face, he listened to me tell him that I was sorry for disrespecting him and his property. That what I had asked him to do was completely uncalled for and an attack on his person as a child of God.

Jordan had come to hate God and me for numerous reasons related to family, church, and school, but on this day, there remained some hidden place of hope still in him that came forward as he could not fight the tear that slipped out of one eye and down toward his ear. I told him I loved him, got up and walked out. A few days later when I stopped at the home, I met Jordan outside in the driveway and told him that I would like to replace all of his CDs and/or buy him any music he wanted, which he was very happy to hear.

Have you ever tried to apologize to your children for something you said or did that was hurtful? There is no child alive that doesn't long for the reconciliation of the love of their parents. I don't care if you are eighty years old and your child is sixty. He or she will melt in the presence of the love that is presented.

I remember Roger asking the men who were often my age and older, maybe a few that were younger, if their father ever told them he was sorry. I was surprised how often this question was asked over the months to newer men joining, that very few men recall ever hearing those words. I never did. I never expected to. Why would I say them to my family? But I found that those are the most powerful words of change a person can share with those he or she loves.

When my younger son Travis who was nineteen began to join me at Higher Ground, the men witnessed firsthand how a father apologizes to his son. One day Travis and I were working on a construction job, and I wanted the nail gun, but Travis insisted that he could do it and I became very angry and swore at him. In the group, this came up as Travis shared how he felt about this attack on him which broke my heart right there to hear this first hand of how I hurt him and how he felt caring this pain of my words with him for several years. I began to weep in front of the guys and in tears I told Travis I was very sorry and that I was wrong for how I acted. Over the months ahead I confessed other things God would bring to my mind of wrongs I had done to hurt Travis, and our relationship grew stronger and stronger.

I was not only blessed by how confession restored the relationships with my wife and sons but also how being real about our living each day includes failures and victories. Why are we bent on making sure the facade we create out of our doctrinal investment be perfect all the time? I think we got the message about being holy all wrong. It is not about how we appear righteous to others that attract them, it is about how we present ourselves as broken and normal people that make mistakes like everyone else that draw others to Love.

I found it very profound how when I shared the hurtful or unkind things I had done and just being real about life, how quickly people opened up to me. It took seconds for me to be engulfed deeply into a conversation with someone who then completely opened up about their life revealing things they kept secret all their lives. There was something about how I shared within my brokenness that made them feel completely safe with me. And they were.

People are sick and tired of the holy-than-thouers, the I-never-sinners, the I-hold-the-answers and the we-do-not-huggers. These are the same people that point at the Pharisees in the Bible with disgust and then live exactly like them in every way. This is what I grew up into and how I behaved. I stood with Paul pointing my finger at all the evil people and their corrupt ways, completely blinded by my own self-righteousness.

It was when I finally really listened to Paul preach that I turned and looked at him. He was angry and did not see these people as his brothers and sisters. I was no different than these and so stepped away from the pulpit and sat in the seats next to the people Paul was addressing. That is when I recognized that I was the very same in one way or another as those I claimed to be opposite of. Jesus said to pray in secret, and yet before every meal at a restaurant when I bowed my head I was telling everyone else there, "see this is what godliness and holiness look like, I am so glad I am not like you heathens who are not thankful for your food." So, I stopped offending these people I didn't know with my self-righteousness. They didn't ask for it nor do they want to be shamed by me just because I was raised to feel guilty or told I was ungrateful for not praying before a meal in public. And just for those who are hoping to reach the "lost," praying in public is not an act of witnessing.

I needed to also come to Alicyn, our adopted daughter, now ten years old at this time. I remember when she drew pictures that I was always happy to see her draw, but being artistic myself I never knew how to leave things alone without suggesting what she might do to correct some things in how she drew. You know there is a place for training your children, and then there is a time to really think about the situation and take a breath and leave some things go for the sake of allowing the joy of a little girl's masterpiece to be praised by her daddy for what it is - a time for a daughter to reach out to her father for adoration and acceptance by way of drawing a picture.

I have learned a great deal about when being loving in the face of wrong is a whole lot better than being critical and justifying it as love because you know you are right. Maybe this is what Jesus meant when he asks us to love our enemies. I came to Alicyn several times to tell her I was sorry for being critical of her drawings and that I treasure all of her pictures with all my heart.

Aliy and I often connected in the evening on the phone while I was away, to read stories and then I would also pray with her. In prayer, I needed to be careful and through that learned how to compromise my thoughts and words mainly asking God to heal our lives, to help us love one another more and other things that would not be indicators of manipulation of what I wanted or even hoped for. I did not know what would happen and was trusting that God would guide us to what end was right.

Sometime after I came back home and was in the process of moving to another home we could buy on land contract, I was cleaning the rooms of the home we were moving out of and picked up a little booklet off the floor in Aliy's room. She had written the following only weeks before I came home but never shared it with us. I had since had the pages put into a picture and frame and given to Roger for being such an amazing mentor and friend over the months, for showing us the real God of love that changed our lives and brought our family back together again.

WILL

Aliy titled what she wrote WILL and underlined all the words 'will' in her message.

> *My parents will get reunited. They will love each other, again. They will know how to treat each other with respect. They will be a better husband and wife plus parents. And soon we will be a better family and love God more, including Jordan. I know God will help us with it, that's why he gave an angle like* Roger.
>
> *Dear Lord,*
> *Thank you for people like Roger who can help issues, like, you know. And thank you for the progress that my parents have made on learning to love again! Amen. Love Aliy.*

Well with a broom in my hand the tears began to flow knowing that the faith of a child's intentions is about as powerful as anything can be. I was never prouder of Aliy and never happier to be back home as a completely new person. But I am getting ahead of myself.

I had also written long emails to my father who lived in Texas, and he would write back. At first, I was blaming him for things I was learning as we went back into our childhoods at Higher Ground, and while we should take the time to recognize these issues that happened in our childhood as reasons why we act, say and do the things we do, I lashed out against my father in anger. I even hated him for a time. But as time moved on and I learned more about these things that happen in our lives and similar things happen in our parent's lives, and in their parent's lives, the more I learned to feel sorry for how things just seem to happen. The last few emails were lighter and in a deeper discussion of things, and the last email I wrote was just telling dad that I was sorry for the choices I made in my life that hurt him and mom and our family. Nothing in that email had blame left in it as I had come to a place of forgiveness for my father, I had let the blaming go.

One day when dad was not doing as well and had moved back to our town from Texas and put in a home for the elderly, I came to visit him, and I brought up my adopted Korean sister Sai Lee. I was telling him more about the group I was involved with called Higher Ground Foundation where we practiced James 5:16 with our family and those we hurt - *"Confess your faults one to another, and pray one for another, that ye may be healed."*

Sai Lee was "shunned" is all I can name it by my father for making choices to believe differently than the way we grew up and were taught. I'm sure there was more I don't know, but all stupid I'm sure compared to one's own love for a child. I said, dad, give her a call and just tell her you made some dumb choices in life that now seem so ridiculous. Tell her that you're sorry that you hurt her. His eyes no longer looking into mine, he just said, "there are some things you do or say in your life that cannot be undone." I said that was not what you taught us, nor do I believe that based on how I saw God restore my marriage and relationships with my children to a place few fathers will ever experience. Again, I prodded him to call my sister, even send a letter as it will set her free of the anger and abandonment I'm sure she carries. He just said no, and then changed the subject. So, I let it go.

A few weeks later I came to see dad in another home because he was not doing well and needed blood transfusions to restore his energy. He was tired but alert, and while putting my hand on his arm, I told him again I was sorry for how things happened in life and that I loved him. He didn't respond to that, but I didn't expect him too, and that was just fine.

Honestly, I believe those two statements were just too much for him to handle. Saying I'm sorry and I love you were words I never heard from him vocally all my life. He did sometimes sign his emails to me with "With love Dad." Dad was a very devoted Christian and Bible reader, but I believe his childhood was very traumatizing at times, and he never heard those words either. Recognizing and displaying a broken spirit is not something you will find in a family whose ego drives their religion.

A few weeks later I was taking Aliy to see her grandpa who was not doing well. When I entered the room my next older brother was sitting with dad reading the Bible to him when dad breathed his last. I did not let Aliy in the room, but just looked at my brother and put my palm on my father's chest to feel any movement. He was gone. I turned in silence, and Aliy and I walked back to the car.

On the way home we said nothing, but tears streamed down my face and sounds of my whimpers were heard by Aliy as she learned that her grandpa had just passed away. I was heartbroken, I wanted more time with my father. There is not enough time in a lifetime to work through the issues that divide us at times. My father was a man who sought the truth. Based on his upbringing and the hard life he faced, he did not live long enough to come to know of what I was learning about the power of love and forgiveness that covers truths and rightness as a hen covers her chicks with her wing. Yes, dad had a head knowledge, but any feelings associated with love or apology were off the table.

Jesus taught a great deal about a love that was unconditional. The Bible as a whole, when believed as the inerrant word of God and smashed all together creates devoted followers to view love as dualistic and conditional, the very opposite of the very essence of what love is. I am only just now learning that we as a church know so little about love because of how distorted it has been taught by those that never give up on their investment of proclaiming a contradictory truth. We know in our hearts, but we tell ourselves we must be wrong because the Bible says so.

I thought I had lost this entry in another journal dated July 2011, shortly after I came home I took a phone call from my father. This is what I journaled.

A Father's Confession

As soon as I got off the phone with my father, I ran into the house and recorded statements of what he said because they were so profound to me and my journey. It was in response to a letter I mailed to my whole family, about the pain I had caused them and other things I was learning about living daily in the presence of God.

Dad said, "I was reading over the last letter you sent to the family, and reread it several times to get the 'feel' of it."

He said, "I always seen you as a nice little boy. I have many children and grandchildren, and thought about all the pain I caused them all."

He said, "I can see that I caused more harm in my inaction than in my action." He quoted Ecclesiastes 6:9 "Better is the sight of the eyes than the wandering of the desire: this is also vanity and vexation of spirit."

He said, "I realized that while all the wonderful things, like a beautiful wife as a gift from God, my mind was wandering to other desires. I wished I had paid closer attention to the first 5 verses in Proverbs in my 20's, 30's and 40's."

He said, "I was walking in a park in Arkansas and noticed the flowers, and Ecclesiastes 6:9 came to mind. My problem is that I miss and have missed living in the present."

I didn't realize it then, but as I read this to Roger, Roger smiled and said, "it sounds like a very wonderful apology from your father." I was amazed to the thought and agreed. But I was moved even more and the reason I wrote it down at the time was because, for the first time in a long time that I can remember in talking about the deeper things of life, dad seemed very real to me. For the first time in my adult life I was no longer his little boy being taught by the regurgitation of scripture, but a fellow man and friend sharing life together for what it is.

And I will always remember something else dad said to me in one of our conversations about creation...

"At the center of the universe is love and laughter."

I remember that statement fitting more closely with things I was reading in the Power of Now by Eckhart Tolle. I remember when I was younger when dad told me that he believed we would become creators ourselves once we got to heaven. He did not think we would create human life, but that we each would possibly get our own planet and create the animals and trees and the creatures in the seas. These were the few words based on dad's knowing and dreaming of his heart that I remember.

He also talked about 4th dimensional stuff with me now and then, something outside our current 3rd dimensional understanding of linear life. From the things I'm studying and learning, I think dad was onto something that is being discussed and studied a lot more today with quantum physics and other sciences revealing so much more about life and our planet and the universe. There was a time I believed in only one life, but with overwhelming evidence today to the contrary, dad and mom will be back and enjoy a most wonderful time in the history of which has never been witnessed before in our planet's history.

The multi-faces of righteousness

While a person may agree he does not know the full truth, he will often still stake his life and beliefs on the truth he holds at this moment as infallible and unabridged. This only tells me that the seeking for truth is never over and that some truth or parts of truth in time is fallible.

As soon as I claim it is over, that I know all the truth, it only means I have settled for truth as it is known to me now. Therefore, our life is lived within a falsehood or darkness of truth and a reaching for new truth, but in time proven unattainable.

Is truth than worth pursuing? Of course, it is the pathway to and through experiences. But never fully knowing the full truth should encourage us to keep striving, but it should also tell us that Love is gently waiting to cover the sins that truth creates when demanded.

It was still winter and plenty of snow to deal with when Jordan came to live with me. Travis and Aliy were still living with Mary. The home had only a one bedroom, but the kitchen and dining where its own room so we set up another bed for Jordan in the corner of the dining space which worked fine as we spent most of our time in the living room.

Stepping back to just months before Mary and I separated, Jordan brought home some beer and put it in the refrigerator. Alcohol was just not allowed in the house to drink, although we did use it for cooking. I grew up in a home where it was, of course, evil, and I even remember having discussions about what the wine was that was talked about in the Bible. You know, like when Jesus turned water into "grape juice," or Jesus saved the best "grape juice" for last. Yep, in our home, it was grape juice and not fermented. Somehow in Biblical days, they could prevent fermentation because Mr. Welch was on the scene to save the day.

This is one of those things again where in the old testament it says do not be drunk with wine, of course, it was wine in that verse. No one ever brought up the verse that says, "Give strong drink unto him that is ready to perish, and wine unto those that be of heavy hearts." Here we read two opposing views but allowed because of situations in life. Righteousness moves into our situation in life where we are at. Knowledge is often like mathematics, we as humans like it when we can add things up, so there is no room for error. Absolute truth is what we call it. But love is different in that it finds us where we are in our own personal life with God and allows different outcomes.

I walked over to the refrigerator for something, opened the door and seen two brown bottles of beer on the shelf. I was immediately angry because I was being defied. So, I picked them up to go and dump them into the trash outside. Now I was already attending Higher Ground and learning some things about respect, personal space, and boundaries. And Jordan was already old enough to drink and by law an adult. I remember fighting in my mind, closing the cover of the trash can and looking around to where I could put them outside. So, I set them on the grill tray and started to head inside, but stopped and thought I am still invading his space, but he was invading mine, but how can I show him love? But this is my home, and he needs to respect me! Nothing I thought of made me feel any better, so I picked them up and brought them back into the refrigerator. As I look back on this, what is really in the forefront is my father filter telling me my dad is not going to be happy I gave in to this. Fear is crippling, demanding and controlling and leaves no room for compassion to step in and help address the issue. However, on this day, Love won the battle!

So fast forward again to when Jordan is living with me. By this time in my life, I am learning so much and feeling a love of God I just never experienced before that these things in me that once needed to remain in control no longer meant anything anymore. Jordan came home every day with a few beers or sometimes with some special whiskey or who knows what. I stayed busy with my work during the day and in the evening when Jordan was around, and at first, we stuck to our own things. He often watched some show on the Internet, and I was typically reading and writing.

Over time we were watching shows together, and Jordan loved comedians, and I did too when I was his age. There was still that edge in me that was trying to make sense of righteousness as I felt some of the things Jordan was watching was not good, but then I would question myself, good based on whose demands. Well, you would say, on God's standards, the Bible! I slowly gave into Jordan's requests as I was more interested in what was driving him or offering him some happiness in life while he I am sure wondered every day if his mom and dad would ever get back together again. The bigger picture is often lost to our petty nit picking of our shallow focused singular righteousness.

One day I noticed he was not coming home with alcohol anymore. So, I asked him, why are you not bringing home any alcohol? He said, "you don't care anymore. It was kind of fun when I could bug you." That statement to me was an affirmation to me specifically testing the workings of compassion over righteousness. You see, love allows, it does not demand from a place of fear. I was learning that the whole of the Christian life is based on fear, inventing places of torment and punishment which did not exist in the Jewish scriptures. I bring up the Jewish scriptures because if hell was a thing, then wouldn't God address this rather significant issue when sin entered the world? No, God sent his Son in as a lover and forgiver, and introduced hell at the same time. Just think about it. Let's move on.

"Love remembers no wrongs" 1 Corinthians 13:5. From the onset, the Christian scriptures (the new testament) were a manipulation of some writings while many other gospels that existed at that time were destroyed and burned to make sure the history was lost of the true teachings of Jesus. Many of these have been found in recent years and are very interesting and help answer a lot of questions. One such change was capitalizing the S in satan making a Jewish symbolic idea of an adversary within a dualistic world existence into a literal being created by God who is god-like. How superstitious and childish have we become having lost sight of the depths that mythology offered from a personal spiritual perspective?

By trying to literally convey the experiences of other people's spiritual experiences we demand a spiritual truth through limited human language while completely devoid of the fact that our understanding through our own life and experiences will determine our understanding and interpretation of that truth.

Therefore, maybe instead of being dogmatic and therefore egotistic about maintaining an interpretive truth as "the truth," it would be a better intent to convey spiritual experiences metaphorically for the purpose of the edifying of the lives and experiences of others to whatever end God leads them, thereby expanding on the truth.

It seems to me that we are more interested in proving a truth full and complete based on some original source, thereby making it stagnant and small vs. allowing truth to be a living thing that grows and matures with the uniqueness God created into every soul.

Perhaps the solid rock on which I stand is not a rock at all, but an ever moving and growing mountain that encompasses all of humanity where God is speaking truth into each of our experiences throughout our lives, thereby offering an endless flowering of experience to and from our neighbors.

I might ask, how does one literalize the experiences of another being?

> *"There is no fear in love; but perfect love casteth out fear: because fear hath torment. He that feareth is not made perfect in love." 1 John 4:18*

How is it that we ignore verses like this? God is love. Love has no fear, Love remembers no wrongs. Yes, I am repeating these verses, because it takes only a single sidestep of another verse or thought to capture our minds away from what is being said for something we want to make work for us because of the grand investment we have into our belief systems. Stop here and put the book down and give some thought about a God of love, where love has no fear and remembers no wrongs.

Yes, you will fight if you face these questions and face your fears of being wrong. What if all you put your trust into is wrong? Could you put your Bible down and walk away for some months to spend time with God alone? You have no idea if you have not traveled this road of facing your fears and doubts into new truths when putting your Bible down and coming to God empty. The Bible has always been a part of your knowledge and that it was the power by which you live and breathe. Put it down long enough to know you can still breathe and that God is so much bigger and wants to speak to you every day if you are willing to be still and listen and trust in Him alone.

I have learned that Jordan has an incredibly deep understanding of the art of scripting in movies. He loves things in movies I completely miss. He asked me to watch a movie with him and warned me that there were some things in it that I will not be comfortable with. I agreed because I was more interested in growing the relationship between us than on being righteous about it. We watched several movies that had sex and strong language in them, but what I was witnessing was a bond of trust Jordan was placing in me as I respected him for who he was and what he loved. I also found myself seeing things within Jordan I would not notice before if I was in a constant protection mode and spewing out righteous truths.

We become fathers or mothers and think we know what is best for our children. They grow up, and we think we know them. Think of your own childhood and the secrets you keep that run through your mind you wish you could be free of, or at least talk about with the ones you should trust the most. Does your father or mother know of these things? Do they really know you?

I am proud to say that I have come to a place because of my being real and honest and setting aside a standard righteousness and judgment based on my doctrine, that I now have conversations with both of my sons that few fathers will ever have. I used to be in judgment of what is right and wrong, or what is appropriate or not all based on my family's interpretation of a biblical righteousness, some absolute truth we invent out of thin air to build walls and strongholds with mortar made out of fear. I'm not saying that everything is appropriate, I am saying that there are times depending on the situation that may not only be appropriate but expected when love has something more important to address than interpretive truth.

There is no one ultimate righteousness. Not only does that not exist, but when it is believed and pushed it becomes the driving force behind the dualistic mindset that creates new doctrines. The fundamentalist Christian spends his or her life steeped into trying to make it all make sense, as though solving the questions and having answers to everything is paramount in saying they in some way have arrived at "the truth." There is nothing to arrive to. There is nothing to solve. Love is calling us to engage with others no matter who they are or what they believe. Love does not wish to convert a soul to some doctrine based on someone's perspective of truth according to a scripture interpreted thousands of diverse ways. Love only seeks to open the eyes of those who are blinded by their own belief systems of duality.

Jordan as a young man and within his rebellion helped me step out of the very small religious box I didn't even know I was in by asking me very profound questions from what I believe now is a truth he knew within that resisted what he was being told by the church and me. I fought so hard to convince others that I was in the right place and held the right truth, not just because I really believed it, but more so because my blind investment at this point was almost fifty years old. I better be right! I have an ego to protect! Although we dare not believe it is our pride behind this.

You might say that the process of a childhood belief taught by parents and culture is reinforced when the relationship between the parent and child is good, and there is no reason to believe the parent is wrong because you wouldn't know anything else. Then the child grows into adulthood and carries on in the same belief system, especially because by this time there are many within the same group all believing pretty much the same thing and gaining an unaware affirmation every young person longs for, to be approved and loved. This all proves it is right in our minds or makes us feel right.

I asked myself if I grew up in Pakistan, would I really think that my Islamic belief was wrong and recognize the Christian religion if it happened to cross my doorway? We hear the stories of those that convert, and we praise God that another lost sheep entered the fold. We will go on and tell that one story for years not knowing if the person converted back or just no longer follows anything. We love stories of salvation because it gives us validity and affirmation to our doctrines and invested beliefs. Converting an Islamic person to Christianity only moves him from one small box into another small box. Both boxes believe that their god rewards good and punishes sin for eternity.

How many people have you converted to what you believe is the right truth in the last thirty or forty years? How many do you ignore every day that you believe will "die in their sins" and go to a Christ-less eternity? What justifications have you rationalized for this? This is a good question to know if you believe that people should be punished beyond life. Do you hope Hitler is in hell? Surely, he is a man who should still be suffering for his choices, right?

When people get older, we think it is time to help them find Jesus before they die. Maybe someone should begin the process of acting like their friend so they trust them, then proselytize to them and bring them to church. We now call "intent to convert", friendship! I call it deceit as that is the only thing it can be. Fear drives these ignorant ideas and calls them love when it is the very opposite. No wonder we have no clue of what love is because all of what I just wrote is engulfed in fear.

> *"There is no fear in love; but perfect love casteth out fear: because fear hath torment. He that feareth is not made perfect in love." 1 John 4:18*

Steve, why do you keep sharing this verse, I thought you no longer trusted the Bible? There are many statements and messages in the Bible that my truth meter finds as true. When a person is willing to look deep into their heart and pay attention to what it is saying, they too will see the fear that exists in most of the doctrines.

When someone steps in the way of all we know to be true of a different belief, we fight to hold on to our investment using the teachings that best fit our belief system to further convince ourselves we are on the right path, typically listening only to what we want so that we don't have to face something we don't know. In fact, we feel like martyrs when others "persecute" us for standing up for our beliefs. This again offers further affirmation to our perseverance, and little by little we become more dogmatic about our doctrines and love becomes a word we use in passing replaced by a truth that must be followed at all costs.

By the time we are in our forties, we have built a fortress that is impenetrable, coated with many layers of self-righteousness we call truth, and try our best to convince others through our fake smiles. And before we even know how we got sucked into this thing, we don't even know we are, and look out from our very little box of perfectionism we call "loving God" like a single soldier, armor on and ready to fight anyone that dares to move a single brick from the wall we built out of needing to be right. This is mine, and I stand alone if I must guard against tens of thousands of others who all got their doctrines wrong and are heading to a Christ-less eternity.

The sins of the fathers is not talking about some crazy killer who teaches his sons the same skills. No. The sins of the fathers are those who remained asleep to the lies they were sold because they were too filled with fear to step outside their box of lies they called truth because their holy book told them they better not or else. Teaching that to your children is the sin.

The teaching of hell bothered me greatly and was on my mind often now as I was trying to make sense of how a loving God would send his creation, not only to eternal separation but to torment them for all eternity. Jesus (who is "God") paid for the entire world of sin and went to hell for three days, but we go for all eternity for our own personal sins. How does that make any sense, and how does a god demanding punishment justify it?

The further I step away from my childhood indoctrinations, the clearer I see the very childlike clinging of egocentric behaviors grasping to truths that completely drown out love in its wake.

A love that demands worship and sacrifice, offers grace while judging and punishes is not love at all no matter how much we smile while claiming these false ideas as truth and righteousness.

The person sure about their beliefs is also a person blind to the truths known by their enemy. It is not about proving one truth over another, it is about surrendering truth to the compassion of love.

I was five years old when one evening my older brother told me that if I did not accept Jesus into my heart, I was going to hell. You know, the good news of the gospel message! The one filled with fear and control to get what it wants. I remember praying and telling Jesus I needed him in my heart because I did not want to go to hell. When I shared my testimony, I enjoyed saying that my brother scared the hell out of me. In reality, that is all it was because that is what it is.

For the next fifteen years at least once a week after doing something wrong or bad or unkind, I would beg God to save me, that I didn't feel saved and I didn't want to go to hell. I had several dreams of getting up in the morning and coming downstairs and seeing mom by the stove with her back to me. I could see she was crying, so I asked her why she was crying, and she told me that the rapture had come, the family is gone, and we were left behind.

"There is no fear in love; but perfect love casteth out fear: because fear hath torment. He that feareth is not made perfect in love." 1 John 4:18

One day when I was about thirteen years old, I wanted to stay home from church one evening. What thirteen-year-old wants to go to church anyway? I said I was not feeling well and that I would sleep. Well, we had a television on and off over the years, and so I stayed up and watched TV. As the time came for the family to be home, minutes turned into more minutes, and it began to frighten me that something happened. I went to my oldest brother's room and looked out to the road across our large yard. There were no cars driving, and I could not hear a single sound in the air which was completely calm. I began to think that the rapture had come and I was left behind. Why you ask, does that thought come to a thirteen-year-old mind? Because my father was a prophecy freak and talked about the rapture and revelations and all the other creepy things related to that.

It seemed to me that at least thirty minutes had passed and the same stillness crept into my mind as I began to think I would soon find myself in the presence of demons and evil spirits for all eternity. Finally, I saw the car coming from way down the road and I was elated to know I was not doomed. So, I ran over to my sister's room just so my family would see me in the window when they drove up. However, they, of course, did not know what I had just experienced, so they jumped straight into what a family of judgmental freaks do, accuse and yell at me for lying to them as I should have been in bed. One brother would put his hand on the TV to see if it was still warm just to accuse me of watching it thus making me even more of the bad and wicked person that I believed I was.

Fast forward. One day while I was still separated from Mary, I wrote a story of myself as God and my son Jordan as Jordan. Mainly because most of my extended family believed he was not "saved." (Which you can even tell by Aliy's prayer of WILL… "even Jordan." Is it any wonder why Jordan resented anyone and anything to do with Christianity?) Again, that is just another avoiding way of saying, he's on his way to hell. Which is just another way of saying that the God we worship will send our child to hell. But we make lots of excuses for that statement by saying it is our choice, which means that God is incapable of finding another way.

Here is the story I wrote mainly to get this idea further in my mind. I still believed in original sin, and that Jesus somehow saves us from hell by dying and rising from the dead.

Note: The Hebrew text states "born into sin," other newer translations changed that to say, "born a sinner." Psalm 51:5 - It is funny how we create entire doctrines around a few verses found here and there that are often misinterpreted. But a little study into church history will explain how it happened. It was not love that consolidated the canon, but leaders with an agenda that wanted to remain in control.

I was only just learning some new things and working them through in my mind, writing things down to help me make sense of a new understanding I was being faced with. I still believed at the time of this writing that Jesus was the son of God and therefore I can see the justification of my writing as I work to fit things together. But hell was starting to change for me into something else, different from what I was taught because love was becoming something more to me. Below is some of my thoughts I wrote down.

Dec - 2011

Love and Heaven and God is. Hell Isn't and is a place that exists only in my mind, in the absence of the Presence of God.

Grace, therefore, is the conduit that comes from the Love of God, that which is, and enters into my mind created hell, which isn't to God, but is to me. Jesus is that Grace who came to earth to save me from myself, to save me from hell.

Righteousness is my recognition of knowing Grace and seeking to do His will so that I might enjoy a heavenly relationship with God.

Faith is my knowing that God is, my heart sees Him as is, where my human eyes only deceive my mind which is absence of the invisible - which is.

I stand alone with others standing with me, there in the presence of God. I can do nothing to earn salvation - heaven, but by God's free gift of grace, He wills me to enter into this relationship. However, as I stand here, I am already in the relationship.

To walk away from God and this relationship is to walk into the void of God, or sin, a type of hell. Therefore, I create with my mind my own hell within me. God does not cast me into hell, I cast myself into hell by stepping away from His grace and love - again, only in my mind.

Jesus, therefore, came to earth to enter my hell and walk with me in it. Loving me by His example of what true and unconditional love is. This is the good news of the Gospel message.

Sin cannot enter the presence of God because sin is the void of what God isn't. When I walk toward God, I enter into His love

- heaven - which is real, an essence. However, when I walk away from God, I enter into Love's void - hell - a creation of my mind.

Grace, however, enters into hell on my behalf. Grace can enter the void and bring me back to God by way of love and truth known in my heart. God is love, and God desires a relationship with me, who is a real created being by God with my own will to walk toward the light, or away from it into the darkness of my mind.

God has not, nor does not create hell - I do. God created me with a will to choose. To be one with God is to be, to walk away is my choice to enter the void which is absent of love and only exists in my mind. This is only an act of my will to create this place, but Grace and Love transcend it.

Entering into my mind created hell, thinking it is better than heaven, God is still there always loving me back into a relationship with Himself - and He always will.

Hell, therefore, cannot stand against itself. God will at times give us over to a depraved mind so that we might enter hell for a time of pruning. Luke 13:6-9 - Mark 4:26-29 - Mark 4:31-32 - Hebrews 11 - Romans 1:28 - Romans 6:18

You have been set free from sin (the hell of our minds) and have become slaves (no choice - by grace alone) to righteousness (relationship with God). Romans 6:18

The LORD will strike Egypt with a plague; he will strike them and heal them. They will turn to the LORD, and he will respond to their pleas and heal them. Isaiah 19:21-24

So, Jesus called them and spoke to them in parables: "How can satan drive out satan? If a kingdom is divided against itself, that kingdom cannot stand. Mark 3:22-30

Does God Love us unconditionally? Can we say that Hell is a place that exists on its own power and energy outside of God? Love at its very core is the power that gives life. How then can life exist outside of God? And if life does exist outside of God, is Love then compromised and made conditional? And then is there more than one god? Do I love then because I am scared to death? Love casts out fear, yet with this mindset, now it is love that embraces fear.

Jordan goes to hell

~~~ I wrote this down just so I could see in writing the truth of the full gospel message as I understood it. The story places me as a father but also God.

Jordan, whether you know it or not, I love you and want to build a relationship with you. I am always standing here with my arms open wide, ready to welcome you into a deeper relationship between you and myself, your father, your flesh, and blood.

Dad, by my understanding, you say you love me, but I know what you will do to me if I do not love you back. I have never seen it done, but if it is true, what you call love, I call the most heinous and monstrous act of hate I cannot even imagine.

Jordan, I'm just asking you by your own will to choose love, I love you!

Dad, please! Or what? Hmm, or what?! Do that thing you and others like you do to their own children?
~~~

Jordan, please listen. Jesus died in place of your sin so that you might believe in Him and have everlasting life! Whether you know it or not, if you die today and in your sin, I will be forced to destroy you in a super created body that never dies but is tortured for all eternity! Please don't make me do that. I love you!

Dad, you listen to me. If Jesus took on my sin - past, present, and future, and you call that grace, then what you are asking me to do by believing is to work for my salvation. What kind of grace is that? What kind of love does that?

On the one hand, you tell me that no one seeks after God, and therefore why should I even seek after you and your "love." On the other hand, you tell me that I must seek after you or be tortured forever.

Jordan, you are just confusing things here. Please listen to me -

WATCH OUT, SON!!!...

Jordan! Jordan can you hear me? Noooo!!!! Not my Jordan! This can't be happening! Why didn't he believe? Why didn't he accept my love?

Oh well. Jordan, even though you are dead, I am now going to recreate your spirit and soul into a new super body that cannot ever die. This body will exist with energy outside of my power - some other god will take over now, but I am going to help set things up so that the torturing may begin.

Jordan, can you hear me?

Dad? What is going on? Am I dead?

Yes, son, you died before accepting my forgiveness, and therefore I have reconstructed you with a super body that will be super conscious of the pain I will inflict on it and you because sin must be punished.

Dad!! I thought you said you loved me? That you are forgiving? I heard of such a thing of this torture, but didn't believe someone like you who showed love to me, could now after I died from an accident in my youth, before I could even understand what you were talking about, now show such hatred!?

Jordan, don't you see, this is love. I love you so much that if you don't believe in me, and you die, even at such a young age and not understanding, that now I must torture you forever and ever. Don't you see the love in that?

Dad, what are you doing?! Please don't do this. What is that? What does it do?!

Jordan, this is a machine that runs on its own power, it does not need me to power it - for reasons I do not know even though I am God, I am love, and through me, all that is and has it's being is from me. But somehow this hell exists, this outer darkness and its power to torture without my presence. Don't ask me how I don't know, I'm only God.

AHHHHH! (screaming!) Please stop! Dad! Please make it stop!!

Jordan, you did not accept my love, so this is what you deserve for your punishment of sin that Adam and Eve did. I am a God of grace, but people still think they need to do something to receive this grace, and so they have conceived the idea that hell and this place you are now living in death is the result of a god that they need to sacrifice to. I said that I desire mercy, not sacrifice - but when no mercy is given, there must be a sacrifice. Oh, how I love sacrifice!

Dad, I thought Jesus was that sacrifice, paid once for all.

Jordan that is what we preach, but we hide in our hearts the fact that if you die outside the works of receiving His grace, then we send you here to be tortured forever.

Dad, please make it stop, it feels like it is ripping my skin off my body with pain I have never before known. It also feels like this new body you gave me repairs itself faster and also with pain. Dad, the machine just ripped my eyes out, but in pain, I feel them being created again.

Dad!!! Dad where are you?!! Ahhhhhh!!! (screaming!)

Hi, Aliy sweety! How are you doing today? Did I tell you about the good news of my love for you and My free gift of salvation?

~~~

At the time I penned these words, tears flowed the whole way through. Even what I used to consider the greatest preachers I have ever heard, preach on hell, none of them ever just said it like it is. Oh, you can go to YouTube and find more than enough Psychopaths trying their best to scare their listeners to convert.

> *"There is no fear in love; but perfect love casteth out fear: because fear hath torment. He that feareth is not made perfect in love." 1 John 4:18*
~~~

"He that loveth not, knoweth not God; for God is love." 1 John 4:8

"But Jesus said, Suffer little children, and forbid them not, to come unto me: for of such is the kingdom of heaven." Matthew 19:14

The idea of hell, the doctrine of original sin, the trinity, the virgin birth, the resurrection of Jesus, and a belief in Jesus as the Son of God are all devised systems and doctrines created by the early Roman and Catholic church leaders who were part of the ruling class and government. And then later with Martin Luther leading the way, similar forms of these same doctrines remained and adopted by the Protestants. The Protestant church only formed a new way to control their sheep. A different box but the same ideas present. Do your research. It was something in my heart that set me on my quests to learn the history of these things. That something is in everyone, longing to wake us up.

The truth was being revealed to me and driving me within synchronicity day by day, and through study leading me to confirm my heartfelt truths. The Spirit was driving me specifically on this journey to show me that the truth resides within me, and proof of this is shown by numerous examples of historical evidence creating a picture of truth used to confirm it. I let myself go into a flow of this leading. This was, in fact, much of the reason I feel God is a Flow of Love vs. some guy standing in condemnation of his creation. It truly was a gentle flow, loving me along the way.

Even the hardest rock in the stream is polished by the Flow.

Spend some time thinking about the verses above and the next time you go to church begin to listen to the fear that exists behind the messages and songs. I used to question myself knowing there are what I used to consider great preachers who were elderly, who preach a message of reward and punishment and call it the love of God. I began to wonder; how can these people not hear themselves talk? Can they not hear the complete lunacy of a message claimed as loving where the same God will punish people for not believing in His son? With a smile on their face they preach a message of forgiveness and grace by way of a doctrine unknown by Jesus, about Jesus being the Son of God, as God, who is sacrificed for the sins of the world and all that is required is a belief that Jesus was, in fact, the Son of God.

I am still waiting to hear this same message being preached to the thousands of children dying of starvation in third world countries. Put them all in a building and tell them that they are sinners, and that their evil and wickedness on this earth has been found wanting by a loving and forgiving God, and that because they were "born sinners", they deserve a punishment far worse than starvation and therefore must repent of their wickedness and believe in Jesus (who they have no clue of). You know, while half of them are curled up in a fetal position with their eyes glazed over, while the other half of them are crying because their stomachs are in pain for lack of food and nourishment, and a few falling over dead throughout the hour you share your message of reward and punishment in the name of love.

I asked this of my father, and he found one verse in the old testament where it says that God turned an eye. Really!? The greatest thing to befall man's condition by default has a remedy if you happen to know the one verse that is most likely completely taken out of context, while not knowing you need even to be looking for it because you never heard the name of Jesus before?

Well we say, we do not understand the mysteries of God or understand his ways, but it is what the Bible says, so it is too bad. Again, I say, really!? That is the best we can come up with? A form of justification to make God appear not so psychotic like he needs help or something? We who are in the church know deep down of these questions but live with them by diverting our attention to other more comfortable verses about how God is good and loving. Or, if it is about bad people, our minds go to Hitler, Jeffrey Dahmer, wicked men that rape young girls and others, once again to justify the God of love we worship.

In fact, most preaching on hell comes from the viewpoint of pointing out toward wicked men and women who have cursed God and therefore satisfy our God-given consciousnesses that fight against such an idea that is trying to wake us up from such controlling thoughts. You know, the thought that we give our lives to a monster out of pure terror, that the same will destroy us if we do not comply. Why do you think words like worship, grace, mercy, and forgiveness exist? True love does not desire this or need any of these things? These attributes make God very needy and little – like how small we made ourselves through fear and then imputed these invented ideas onto the Source of all there is.

Here is a story I wrote while I continued to wrestle with the idea that God could punish, and then in such a twisted and psychotic way. The story is a paraphrase of the Gospel message we share to convert others to embrace what we believe in. Written on September 02, 2015

Once upon a time, there was a father who lived several hundred years and had a son named Sunny. Over the years, the father had many more children and loved each one with such exceeding compassion that everyone who knew the man, loved him too. However, Sunny died one day a young man, and he was a very skilled musician.

The Father wrote a book about Sunny and his love and how to live in peace with one another so that the children would grow up loving and caring for one another, and to follow his son's example. His love came with endless grace and mercy because as children go, they can get themselves into all sorts of trouble and cause pain to the others.

Their father taught them how to be grateful, and to forgive those that cause pain. To allow themselves to hurt in the place of others and to give grace and mercy as we have but one life to live he said, and we should always offer love even when justice is deserved.

Over time some of the children were wondering where some of their other siblings were as months went by without word of them. One day several of the young children heard terrible noises coming from the backfield and ventured to where their father's barn was at. When they looked inside, they saw that their father created an apparatus that was at that moment tearing apart what looked like some bloody fleshly human creature.

Just then their father showed up and pulled them out of the barn and told them that his children who do not believe that Sunny was his child or that he was a skilled musician were to be put into the apparatus for punishment until they almost die. Then the apparatus lets them heal and does it all over again and again for the rest of their life.

The little children said, ok daddy, with glee (you know because that is normal behavior) and skipped merrily back toward the house with their loving father who smiled back at them with great love and compassion. Then one of the little children said that she heard that Sunny was the father's son, but said she did not believe that because she never met him.

The father turned and bent down to his knees to cuddle her face and said that if she did not believe in Sunny that he will need to bring her to the barn. But because the father had so great of love, he said he would show compassion and give her a few more days to decide. She said, ok daddy, and skipped into the house knowing that her father would keep her safe and protect her as he has always told all his children every night before bedtime. She sure loved her daddy!

A few days passed, and the father asked his little girl if she had decided if she believes that Sunny was his child. The little girl said she thought so but was not real sure yet. With a big smile on her father's face and with those wonderful smiling eyes, he said that she must believe 100 percent, as even 99 percent is doubt and a lack of faith. The little girl asked, how can I know that I believe 100 percent, I'm not really sure where I left my dolly this morning? Daddy do you know where I left my dolly? And what does belief mean?

Truly the father thought, this precious little girl is not focused enough to believe 100 percent that Sunny was my son, and so she is a backslider, a wicked and evil person and the worst of all devils! At that, with a very big smile on his face because he loves them so much, he took the little girl's hand and brought her to the barn where she would join the other heathen sinners in the torture apparatus for the rest of her life.

When the father returned to the home and closed the door so the little girl's screams could no longer be heard, he rounded up all the others and began to tell them all about his unending love, mercy, and protection he had for them. You know, because he loves them soo much! But he noticed that many of them did not look so happy, and asked them why. They quickly responded with large happy fake smiles and with pressing happy voices told their father that they were very happy indeed!! The father's face warmed again and said that he thought so.

If you grew up in a family where you were given a book where it's very message was to teach you only that which is in the book, and that part of its teaching called you a fool, and you would be punished for looking outside the book, or that you would die if you should not accept everything in the book, add to the book or take anything away from the book, you would raise a child into an increadiably unintelligent and unloving adult that knew only what was in that book. And yet I ask, is not the controlling doctrines we invented come from a book called the Bible?

They understand that through the book they have a way of escape by remaining true to the book only because the book teaches them that the book offers the way of escape or you will be punished or killed if you fail to do it right. They know nothing or little outside that knowledge and therefore resist anything else other than what they know.

But that is not enough. We go to a church where like-minded non-outside book readers come together actually to worship the god who is in the book. We go and "worship" a god that offers love to us or else the punishment is forever. The same god we worship offers "grace." Why would a god of love need to offer grace unless love wasn't enough? As some would say, with a friend like this, who needs enemies? A truer statement could not be said! Oh, but there are those who will say, *God does not send us to hell, we send ourselves to hell because we choose!* Really!? That is what having free will has brought our deprived minds to? Have we control over hell?

But that is not enough. We sing songs about these same things, lifting up a God given gift of music which holds its own resonance of beauty and apply the same words of the book to reinforce what we know and read in the book, that we are lost sinners and wretched, and God demands sacrifice and blood and worship and grace to save us - from Himself. *Jesus loves me this I know for the "book" tells me so, little ones to him "belong"?* (children do not belong within the original sin doctrines invented in the past number of centuries) Or… *Yes, Jesus loves me, yes, Jesus loves me….* or the missing part of the song that is unsung *…or his father will cast you out if you don't love him back or know his name.*

We maintain denial because we are bent on proving the voices of the past wrong. But freedom comes in the face of reality whether the voices scream "I told you so." We win when we listen closely to our heart and follow our soul to the place where peace resides.

There are those who will read my words and want to reply to me with their theological reasons to show where I am wrong. Find countless verses to regurgitate from their programmed mind and prove that their personal church doctrines are right and mine wrong, believing that is the goal.

I will ask one thing of you if you find what I say is offensive and blasphemous... Be very honest with yourself as I ask this question as to the first thought into your mind. *I know I will die tomorrow... what if I say that I believe that Jesus is NOT the Son of God?*

Let me guess what you are thinking right now. The first thing in your mind, the same thing that is probably on everyone's mind who believe in hell reading this, *"then you Steve, will go to hell."* I have tested this first hand with a number of fundamentalists and it works every time. Sometimes you need to push people past their good side to get there, but you can get there. What does this mean? It means that the whole of the Christian faith is summed up in fear of hell. Meaning, we did not love God because he is wonderful, but because we are told that God will send us away from his presence and into eternal torment. I'm not saying we do not love God, I am saying that when pushed to being honest about the gospel message, hell is there at the core controlling the whole thing.

> *"There is no fear in love; but perfect love casteth out fear: because fear hath torment. He that feareth is not made perfect in love." 1 John 4:18*

I also studied atheism and learned that these people were far more real and safe to talk with than Christians. One show I watched had a number of Christians call in because they felt this was a place they could share their thoughts without being condemned as they were by their family. Several people called in saying they grew up in the church but don't know how to leave it for fear of how they will be treated or kicked out of their family if they told their parents how they felt and what they believe. Ask yourself, do you feel safe asking your parents or siblings about some of the questions I raise? Maybe you're dogmatic and sure of your faith! What about your children? Do they really dare to ask some of these problematic questions, or have you already so stifled them through fear of questioning their faith that they would never dare to ask anyone their deeper questions about what they been indoctrinated into?

If you are a seeker, you maybe still live in fear of even thinking about questioning and know you will be shut down by your peers for even thinking of such things, or you feel ashamed to have ever questioned some of these things, and yet we all do and are silent, hiding behind a fear that has been suppressed so long that we don't even know it exists, much less how to address it. What we know very well is how to use all the pretty words to express our faith, and yet that too has become a cunning skill we don't even know we use to keep us in a comfort zone of lies made to make us feel right. I will get into more of my journey as an atheist, but in the end, they too even in their more honest way, live in their own small box, a making mainly of resistance to religion.

While I do not know this as fact, I believe much of atheism rose out of the extremely controlling and dogmatic churches of the west that claim love but have no idea of what it is. Most of the atheists I have come to know came out of the church. The church's view of God being both rewarder and punisher is what remains in their perspective today, or the lens in which they can view the world from, and therefore, remain blind to a greater truth and an even greater unknown love that we have yet to uncover in the pages ahead. If you think I have just been tough about my views on hell and the doctrines of the church, spend some time listening to an Atheist.

It still took me several more years after this point in my journey to let hell completely go as something that exists. My doctrines hung on strong to me and kept the doubts knocking on my brain, bringing years of memorized verses to mind over and over. Once that day came that I was free of the fear of hell, mainly through a new and much deeper understanding of love, a completely new understanding of all of the scriptures, of eastern scriptures and teachings and even the same songs began to shed new light and meaning. I began to understand things more metaphorically and symbolically and therefore more spiritually personal. The reason the truth resides within is because we are all unique within the Source of all that is (we call God) and within this space offer our own unique truth to the world. If we think there must be only one truth, we fight to maintain this one truth through fear of other truths diluting and corrupting this great truth we found.

Understanding is not in the word spoken, but in the revelation the word is drawing from innate within the listener. The word may fail because the listener's journey in now ready to reveal the revelation as it relates to them. Revelations are truths and/or probabilities of truths that are revealed to each person's knowing from within their experience when the time is appropriate.

If we speak with the intent of conforming our own knowing onto the listener's knowing, we not only fool ourselves but may limit the spirit's movement in the listener's understanding of their personal knowing, and the word becomes smaller and defined. Therefore, share freely, accepting that your word spoken may not be understood as intended and that sharing our word may have much more to offer another than we presently comprehend.

Again, this was another step to a greater liberation that I experienced. If someone asks me today if I believe that Jesus is the son of God, my answer is yes. The road to understanding this more took me through quantum physics and water memory and dark matter and other subjects of science. I grew up believing that science was the enemy of religion, but over time found that not only are they compatible, but religion exists as an attempt to make sense of who God is and to point us to God, where science is at the foundation of what God is. The fight today seems to be creation vs. evolution. But I believe they are both right and both wrong.

Taking a literal, historical interpretation of scripture only leads to a form of superstition that does little more than demand more details to further define and enforce countless doctrinal belief systems, over the infinite mythical depths of spiritual meaning and divine relationship found in the same words.

Falling in love again for the first time

It is in the place of the know that people connect. This place is void of words and reason because it is of the heart. It is also in this place where we are present with God.

The first ray of hope that I thought Mary was interested in making some move toward connecting again was in March. Mary invited me to a birthday party at Johnny Carino's restaurant for one of her girlfriends and a few of her children. Aliy was also there, and I sat next to Mary, which I must confess was strange and wonderful at the same time. Five months had already passed, and I had little to no social connection with Mary, so this was delightful. I remember driving home afterward lying on the bed and crying for hoping to see the family come together again.

I learned later that Mary always felt we were separating for the purpose of healing and coming back together, and while I knew that to be the case, nothing in me told me that this was going to end with us coming back together again. Mary was surprised to learn that I thought that, but in a way, I was thankful I did because it kept me focused on myself and my relationship with God.

As May rolled around Mary and I began to talk a little more on the phone and share more about ourselves and then later as we went for drives around town. It was at a point in my journey that while I wanted to go home, I had come to a place in my life of great peace and joy. I was beginning to share bits and pieces of my journey with Mary as I knew Mary was still scared knowing so little about what took place in my life the last six months. Our time together was allowing her to witness the characteristics of a completely new man inside the same old body. I made up my mind I would not ask to come home, that it would need to be Mary who crosses that bridge when she was ready.

In time, I invited Mary to come and sit on the front porch of my place to watch some movies on the computer or talk about whatever into the evenings. I was doing more of the talking and some of what I was learning at Higher Ground, not a lot, but enough to know that within the conversations between us that my path had taken me down a road completely different than Mary's. In fact, different from anyone else's at Higher Ground. This was a bit concerning to me as I was then a little afraid to come back into the relationship without things being further addressed. But what would that look like I wondered? I knew things would change when I went home.

It was a bit strange and fun as it was truly like getting to know each other all over again for the first time, a little awkward at times like on first dates. To ponder on the dynamic of it, I must admit it is truly the most wonderful thing to experience because there is everything right about falling in love with the same person you fell in love with and married years earlier!

I remember one night we watched Avatar, which for me was like the third time. Avatar was for me a visual representation of things I was learning and coming to believe. The idea of entering an avatar (body) was like the soul entering a human body for the purpose of experiencing the earth we live on. The community of the tribal connection with one another and spiritual connection with other animals and even to the planet itself is deeply felt and appreciated as a more realistic, perhaps even a romantic way of living that I could see myself enjoying.

Stepping back a few months. I was learning a great deal about relationships and how people interact with each other in healthy ways. As I read through the book, Codependent No More by Melody Beattie I was learning about myself and Mary. I was being honest with myself and recognizing where even in my anger and having to control things that I was co-dependent with my wife, and she was co-dependent on me.

Being single again and celibate for seven months did a lot in itself to teach me about the sexual side of our relationship. The more I studied and meditated about these things, the more I began to see the deeper relationships as more of a companionship. Spending time with the guys taught me that great depths to life and conversation could take place without the sexual side of my life. In fact, the thought that came to me is that a healthy companionship would look like a ball, whole and complete all by itself. And that sex, if to be a part of that relationship, would be an additional blip on the ball. I say blip because my understanding at that time was that sex seemed to be a very small part of my thoughts or the thoughts of what I would much rather be a part of. Meaning, sex is not necessary for a perfectly loving couple to deeply share their lives together. Everything else in our lives should be in this higher place of companionship for sex to be an amazing aspect of our lives within the relationship. If sex ever becomes a part of the whole and not the extra, then we may have lost sight of the deeper essence of our partner.

The whole of this journey I was on was for a hope that our marriage would come back together again. But as time passed, I found myself thinking less and less of our marriage and more on my personal relationship with God. I was also falling in love again with God, who for me was slowly looking more like some mysterious benevolent energy touching every aspect of all there is in the cosmos, than some limited deity separate onto Himself and overlooking humanity on earth alone. Like Love itself was a flow that was always gently coming into our lives, but because of our free will, could fight and resist if we like. And love like smoke in the air moves and sways within the wind of our flailing arms of resistance. But when we stop for a time to be still, again the love gently moves toward the center of our being. God to me was no longer an entity, a "Him" or judge looking down from on high. God was now always present, within and without moving throughout life and within my being, making up a part of my very essence.

From a Christian point of view, you might say that I accepted Christ for my salvation and that the Holy Spirit came into my life. This is said in a more literal way, but also assumes I was lost to God in a literally separated way bringing focus to the flesh. Where I expand on this, is that I was never lost as though God can separate Itself, but that I had a veil whereby I was hidden from my true self, my essence, my soul that exists in a truer reality. C.S. Lewis said in his book, The Great Divorce, that the closer the bus took the characters toward heaven the more transparent they became. This was his way of explaining in metaphor that the "kingdom of God" or "the reign of the heavens" is what the true reality is and the earth was then recognized as the illusion we were only experiencing in the flesh for a moment in time. I think he was onto something.

Shame and guilt left me because God was no longer in the business of pointing a finger at my sin. Somehow sin was part of how man communicates with man, a blemish on the vessel I occupied and under the rules and laws of the land I found myself in. The Bible speaks of different people feeling like foreigners on the earth, but the meaning of that was no longer because I was not a part of the earth as though God made a mistake in Its creation, but that I was beginning to understand that I was greater and part of the whole of everything, and the earth was a place where I was born to experience something but forgot or was hidden for a time from my true identity - which I was at this time still seeking.

Well, you can imagine me sharing some of these things with Mary, that what she witnessed before her today was a man who seemed to care very little about doctrines, less about belief systems and was filled with a joy that elevated his life in ways she never saw before. She could sense the guy before her was radiating with a renewed inner peace and wellbeing.

One day while sitting on the porch in the evening with Mary, she said she thought it was time for me to come home. I remember feeling like I would burst inside, but remained calm and cool until she left. Then I went inside and wept as I realized that Love had its way through the months and that the heart of God was bursting with light within my soul. (If you haven't figured out by now, I cried a lot over these months for pain but much more for joy, and to this day my emotions are very attuned to other people's pain and joy.) A few days later when Mary was over, and she got up to leave, she gave me a hug and told me she loved me. I have a note in my journal saying, "she said I love you first." I told her that I loved her too, and maybe for the first time in our marriage, those words really meant something far more to me than ever before. I loved this woman more than anything in the world and was very excited about where we were going from here.

A few days later while sitting on my front porch in the morning, I looked over to my left where a large tree was on the property line between my house and the next. The tree had a large limb cut off at the base of the limb years ago, and someone had painted red paint on the area that was cut. The tree by this time was overgrowing the area where the red paint was left and formed a perfect heart shape only from where I was sitting on the porch. Because I was more in tune with synchronicities at this point, I just sat in amazement that God would let me know after the long winter and journey, and before I left to go home in the Spring, that the tin man with no heart that I came into this house with seven months before now was being reminded that I had a heart and understood so much more of what love was all about. But I would soon find out there was still much more to learn.

Time to come back home

It was June 1st when I packed my bags and headed for home. Aliy greeted me in the doorway and took my picture. I just thought of this now while typing, but what must the feelings be like for a little ten-year-old girl to see her daddy come home again knowing something deep within her knew that things were very different from seven months ago? Her hopes and prayers were answered, and her family was not only back together again, but more in love with each other and with life than ever before.

But it would not quite end in the fairytale Mary and I may have hoped for because there were things we still had to work through. The good part of all of this was that we both were in a much healthier place to speak our minds and talk things out where before not only were we quiet or quick to anger but often had no idea how to move forward to break the darkness that existed just months ago. The darkness I speak of is not demonic, or some other superstition of the churches created imagination, but of fear, a running from love, created in the minds of humans, who are more than capable of creating a darkness that crowds out what light is longing to guide our way.

I remember one topic that changed my outlook on relationships was concerning the differences between wanting and needing. I had spent a great deal of time on this because of how I was taught in the church about only needing food, clothes, and shelter, which is true, but more importantly is that to want was in some way lustful and/or greedy. As I thought about these two attributes, I saw love as codependent if we say we need it. Well, I had come to a place in my life where I knew I did not need Mary nor her love. But I did now want Mary and wanted to love her. Whether Mary wanted me or felt she needed me was something she was still struggling with partly because of how I was approaching her on this. I would tell her when the topic came up that I only need God, but that I wanted to love Mary. Well, Steve, you are just splitting hairs and making a big deal out of nothing. The words we use mold the programming of our minds. The words we use and the meaning behind them play a role in how others perceive our intentions. I was still being kind and caring and allowing whatever time was needed for the dynamics of these two words to work themselves out.

There is something in us from childhood that needs love from our parents. This is true and appropriate. But as we grow into adulthood, we should seek God and come to a place of complete rest in knowing that God is love and all that we need. Nothing else of form can offer hope because nothing other than love exists. It isn't that I was not showing Mary love, it was that I was for the first time showing Mary love by wanting her. In this way is the idea that one can get up and walk away. There is freedom to be. If you don't need me, then what am I good for? Need is clingy, weak and desperate by nature. Want is intention and power by nature. I could leave in all reality, but I want to stay because I love you. If you give some thought to it, you will find that need is not loving at all. Need tells the other you can't leave me or I'll suffer. There is no love in that! Out of all the places on earth I can be right now, I want to be here with you. That is a love that the other can enjoy and be at peace with. We heard it say, if you love something, set it free. Yes, want is also freeing for the other. And that is what happened next.

One day we drove home in the evening from somewhere and stopped in the driveway. Mary wanted to talk, and so we stayed there for some time just talking, well, Mary talked while I listened. I really do not remember what she said specifically, but it was to help me understand where she was at in her journey. The one thing I remember her saying was that she only needs God and that she does not need me. When she said those words, most couples would think the next words were to end the marriage. But the biggest smile came on my face as I realized what she was coming to realize. I also knew that her needing me to need her was fading into want and that this was the beginning of our love growing deeper for each other. Any clinging was done between God and ourselves, but the love we shared was for the other without strings attached. Where there are strings, there is need just around the corner. In other words, we were free to love the other regardless if the other loved back or not. If you think about it, it is the only way love can be love. Love can only give and never take. To need is to take. To need is to stifle. To need is to encourage more needing.

Well, there was more to learn and discover about each other, and we sure did! But there was another step I had to take of letting go of control that still existed within my position as head of the home. I was wanting Mary to break free of her position as a submissive woman as understood by the church, to becoming a more assertive and active person of God living within a relationship of givers. She still felt more comfortable being *"safe"* under the control of her life investment as the woman and her place as recognized and affirmed by those within the group that believed this way. And to tell you the truth, as I was pushing Mary to be herself and do whatever she pleases (which meant at first, my stepping away as head as she understood it), the little freedom steps she was taking were beginning to freak me out.

I remember just spending time telling myself that she still loves me. I realized I was still codependent which forced me again toward God and to trust that love would have its way in my life. I was becoming afraid she was able to truly be and live on her own and maybe would want to, and yet I knew this was appropriate. These were the emotions I was feeling, and the fears we create in our minds that create codependency and then destroy relationships. Well, I held my tongue and just kept loving Mary as I felt God pushing me through this very uncomfortable place. I also remember telling Mary of the feelings I was having and that it was good and that I was proud of her for stepping out into life and with friends as she has not in a healthy way before. As a woman who was complete and perfect within her relationship with God, she was free to be herself. It was good to openly express myself, not to manipulate as I could have done, and of course, that would not be of love. What I was learning about love is that it allows.

There was another dynamic at work which I also began to notice, and that was being afraid to show love back to love so freely given. I remember sharing my feelings with the men in my group as I worked through this for several weeks. I believe that in most relationships there exists an openness that desires vulnerability, and yet at the same time, a resistance is maintained to protect ourself. What I see is nothing other than our egos desire to survive under such pressures of the presence of love that is there at the doorway, knocking to come in.

As Mary willingly gave herself more and more to me emotionally and physically, I felt very awkward and resistant although I did my best to comply with her desires, whatever that may be. And just to help you get your mind around more than just sex, things like just saying good morning with a pleasant joy and glee in her voice that comes from no other place than deep within her heart. Watching her move around the house with a bounce in her step and a permanent bright smile on her face made me desire her more, but at the same time unsure I should as I felt I was undeserving of this great love that was so clearly present and felt radiating around her.

If there was ever a greater example of forgiveness, grace and wanting to give so unconditionally all wrapped up into one amazing and beautiful embodied form, it was Mary. I literally lived within this presence every day. Forgiveness of a long past of emotional controlling religious abuse, to then of grace so abundant that made the past seem as though it never existed, followed by a wanting that made me feel deeply desired and loved. The needy, clingy and controlling past of blame and shame seemed all but a distant thought.

Today, even though I am far more emotional and kinder than I ever was, Mary continues to surprise me with her beautiful and compassionate heart for all people. The thing that drew me to Mary in the first place was her deep love for others and desire to please others with her best. In the past, that existed more out of a desire to fit in and be appreciated and affirmed as a person, and one that I took advantage of to my own benefit. But today those same attributes come from and through a woman who finds great pleasure in giving to others from a much deeper and healthier place of love and compassion within a presence of God that lives within her heart.

Ask, and the door will be opened, was taught to me from a place of need as though I was lost. Now I realize it is a place of want and to receive. The only problem is that the teaching of need has not yet learned how to step off its pedestal and stand humbly with open and accepting hands.

When the real gift of love is so freely shared with me, I find myself resistant. Not that I do not want to receive for we all long for love's compassion, but that I do not know how to be fully vulnerable and fearless to love's amazing fullness when it appears at the door of my heart.

Meditating in the garden

In the beginning, there was only you and me, and we walked in the garden with God. Everywhere we turned there was only the hand of God in all that was. It was beautiful!

Where were the libraries and prophets I asked? Sensing God stepping beside us looking into the distance, stretching out his arms and saying, "be fruitful and multiply," purposely ignoring my question, but instead telling us to enjoy the earth and all within it.

But how will I get to know God I wondered… but my thought was cut short as I felt God loving me with a smile and a hand on my shoulder as if telling me to stop trying to figure things out, that life is not about solving the questions of our mind, but connecting with and experiencing all there is in life with our hearts.

But my mind would not be still, I knew I was intelligent, surely there were many things to solve. Surely there were things that were not right or complete. Perhaps other people who were misguided that needed my advice.

Being very young and still open and aware, God said in a kind voice spoken to my heart, "be still and know that I am God." Pointing to a far mountain I was encouraged to climb, God said,

with your mind solve the steps of your way, but
with your heart enjoy the experience of the journey.
This is how you will know Me.

Finding time to meditate like I did before was not the same back home with so many things going on. Work was still slow, and we were falling behind on bills, and hardly getting by. Both Mary and I had a much stronger understanding and appreciation for life because we were willing to travel down this road of facing our fears and childhood pasts. I realize today that while there are those whose lives have been affected by the months and years within our men's groups, few people stayed long enough to really dig in, or left when the real work began to expose things in their lives they would rather leave buried. Because of the religion I came through, I believed with all my heart that there was nothing buried, and if hidden, it was under control and placed at the feet of the cross, forgiven and let go. Nothing could be further from the truth! Those are pleasant words we use to make us feel we are in the faith as others would expect of us. It's all ego!

Mary and I continued to go to our groups for several more years, and now helping with others that would join who faced similar trials in their lives. I found it very effective to share a condensed version of my story, or parts of my story to guys who were at their ends, either just divorced or within weeks of seeing their entire world fall apart. Several of the men in our groups were recently released from prison for a number of reasons, and part of their coming back into society was to be a part of rehabilitating group like Higher Ground.

I built strong relationships with these men because Higher Ground was a place where we were safe, never under any condemnation to share incredibly deep and painful personal things that were done to these fellows as children or adults, or things that required some help and encouragement to face things that were done to others that needed self-forgiveness and closure. Each one of us were guided by Roger through what we studied as the 4 great outcomes and the 4 habits of a healthy heart, found in a booklet produced by Higher Ground to offer guidance to our journeys. You can also visit their website at www.highergroundfoundation.org.

As I mentioned before, meditation within the presence of God was encouraged before the evening started, but also at home so we could return the following week with what we heard God share with us as we listen within our quiet time. There are a lot of Christians who do not like the word meditation, and I did not either at first because it is related to Buddhism, Hinduism and other eastern religions and practices. I understood prayer, but even prayer is very broad covering an endless scope of meaning and understanding.

While there are differences that I believe are evident between these two words, the commonality that exists is that we are talking about some form or way in which we are connecting with the Christ, the Divine, the Spiritual Source, the Lord, the Holy Spirit, God, etc. But here also we get bent out of shape because of the doctrines and cultures we grew up in and the beliefs we set in stone as truth for our life all depends on the group we may find ourselves in and the language we use to describe our beliefs. If it does not fit our lingo, it's bad! What is wrong with our heads?!

Meditation however for me was further explained as a time to be still and know the "I AM" within. While I grew up and was told that we should be guided by the Holy Spirit, I think that just meant that when I did good things I was guided, and when I did bad things I was not guided. I say this because I know we were all taught never to do anything remotely close to meditating or channeling of any kind because you could end up calling in evil spirits into our brain or body.

It seemed that while the Bible was a book that was supposed to teach its followers how to have a relationship with the Father (human with Spirit – 'the Christ'), that ended up looking more like reading and memorizing Bible verses, going to church to agree or disagree with the message preached and discussing or fighting over verses and their meanings. To be encouraged to go and sit for a time in silence and listen to God speak would never happen, especially in our family as when we heard about people that meditated and then mentioned the clearing of the mind, one of my siblings especially freaked out and said that is when demons come in. So, make sure our minds are always preoccupied with something?

At Higher Ground, I was listening carefully to what Roger would be sharing, and while I did not always comprehend what he was sharing, I knew that he had a close relationship with God and knew things I knew I didn't but wanted to. Roger never really explained how exactly he meditated, perhaps because he assumed we knew, or expected us to find that path on our own as that would be more of his style (not to control or make a rule as that would define and cause judgment). Roger never wanted to be a person seeking to offer answers because he was always more interested in hearing how God was working in each of our lives through our time in meditation and writing. If I were to ask Roger something I wanted to know, he would say, "hmm, that is a great question, you go home and ask God and tell us what He said to you, next week." Roger was all too aware of the programming that was already in place through human advice.

I began to sit with a candle on the table. I kept my eyes closed most of the time, but when my mind would wonder, I would open and focus on the flame to bring my mind back into focus. Most of my meditation was more of what you might call contemplative prayer. But I was slowly training myself to clear my mind of its chatter. What the easterners call the "monkey brain." As long as your mind is thinking of things to do, like, what happened last week at this time, what am I supposed to get done today, that was a strange dream I had a few days ago, etc., you are not doing anything to help yourself come into the presence of Source and hear from It speak to your heart. From a very early age, I practiced clearing my mind or controlling what I wanted to think about when I would have a bad dream. Over the years without knowing what I was doing, I was putting my mind into a still mode or quiet space so I could fall asleep.

As I talk about meditation and hearing from God, this makes most Christians very uncomfortable because like I said, they (and I speak for myself here also at this time of my journey) believe they do speak to God, but that God speaks to us through what is revealed in scripture. *"God does not speak today to people like he did back in the Bible days."* Have you heard this? I have many times throughout my life. Why would I ever hear from God when this is programmed into my mind?

For years now I have done an extensive study on human and animal consciousness and many spiritual topics to have come to a certain understanding, and I am encouraging you to step through your own door of fears and face your belief systems that may be keeping you from hearing from God.

I think it was back in 2012 when I felt that inner voice tell me to go back in time into my mind because I was questioning how David wrote his songs. How did Jesus know and do the things he did? Was what Roger was teaching the same thing? Does God still speak today? And if so, maybe he never stopped and always has been speaking to those willing to listen. We just forgot how and then created doctrines to support beliefs of fear to never engage with the Spirit. Later I would find that many people of the early church were Gnostics and meditated in dark caves for extended periods of time to reach various stages of euphoria or have experiences of wondrous things outside of this world and even experiences outside of their body. Were they able to connect with that higher power from where we are fully known?

Jesus was still a large part of my connection to Spirit, so I believed it was Jesus telling me to go back before the new testament existed. That was in itself a liberating thought I would ponder on, as at the time of Jesus, his gang and fellow religious people were Jews. This had its own understandings and implications, as we often think Jesus was a Christian or that he even created the Christian religion. Far from it!

Days later, Jesus said to me again in my heart, go back further. So, I thought of David and his songs, his motivation to face Goliath without fear. What was that all about? He had a strong trust in God and spent much of his younger life out in the fields, I would guess staring up at the sky, the clouds, the night, moon, and stars. How did he hear from God? At one point he wrote down, "to be still and know that I am God." Where did this and other thoughts come from that David would write down? "…Fearing no evil for thou art with me." These are the Psalms many people rest in.

Jesus said, go back further, so I thought of Abraham and God speaking to him about Isaac. What was that all about? Was it really God as we think of him today asking Abraham to kill his only son? (Talk about listening to the wrong spirit!) I still believed in this story, but study into ancient history of Egypt and even earlier, Samaria began to open the door to other ideas about taller and stronger beings that may have walked the earth, such as the Nephilim, but even others that the church deems as the "fallen angels".

To the common man they would seem like gods. I grew up assuming people were just bent on worshiping something so made these things up in their heads and the battle of whose god was greater began. But there is too much archaeological evidence pointing to these so-called gods that may have lived and ruled over the people of earth. Could these Beings also speak to and through us I wondered?

Greece, of course, had its many gods, and it would be the Jews who would bring the idea of a monotheistic God who ruled over all. The King of kings! The Lord or lords. The idea of rule and worship taken from the past understanding of one in charge, but still with a very literal and linear viewpoint from a very unconscious and blind mind. I grew up believing that God was testing Abraham for his devotion and desire to obey. But that was just another thing we do as Christians to help the god of the Bible out of doing unimaginable things in the name of loyalty.

This makes more sense to me today having learned more about just "what god" may have been speaking to Abraham through some form of conscious communication. The gods of that time or the stories gleaned from earlier history that was brought into the Torah fits closer to the power-hungry beings not dissimilar than mankind with a craving for power and supremacy. These are not the attributes of love, but of greed and great fear of loss of control, steeped in darkness.

Jesus said, go back further, so I went back to the beginning of what I knew at the time was the beginning, the garden of Eden. Depending on where you grew up on earth and in what culture, depends on what you would define as your genesis story, for there are many, and some that date back further than the old testament scriptures. The metaphor of the garden is amazing and filled with meaning, although I still did not see it. We have literalized it to the point where groups will actually fight over what the fruit was that Eve ate, or wonder what that tree of knowledge of good and evil must have looked like to be so pleasing to the eyes.

So here I was, and I realized that God wanted me to spend time here in meditation, to relax and allow all the thoughts, all the programming of all I knew as history and all I had been taught come to the surface to be let go. Then spend time looking at all there is here in this place from a new uncluttered understanding as though I was just born into the world for the first time.

The first days took me through so much of what I was taught, the snake, the trees, how sin entered the world, and countless thoughts that flooded my mind, mostly of things that would be impossible to know if I were alone in a world untouched by man. As these thoughts entered my mind, I let them come and go as they had no meaning in this place. I began to imagine my surroundings and all I was looking at. The deer over there, was it warm, did I even know what warm was? It's fur, and again, I found I had names and labels for everything, and then allowed myself to let these things go as they defined everything.

> *Thought: I remember when I was probably eight or nine when I was learning about mammals, reptiles, and birds and that these things were categorized into groups. For only a moment the thought came to me as to why we group them. It was if the grouping defined them to help us understand things better. I understood that from an analytical standpoint, but there was something else in my thought that said just to let each creature be great within itself. I felt like we were losing something by defining them vs. just enjoying them.*

Back in the garden: I asked myself if I was afraid, joyful, did I even know I was alive, and if I didn't know that name, would I know how to express my feelings about it? I felt I was curious. From where I stood, I realized that I just found myself here, that I have not even walked anywhere yet. I questioned if what I saw around me was good or bad, and then wondered if I would know. I then saw a lion and something in me told me I needed to crouch down behind a nearby rock, although I didn't know to call it that. It was hard and cool to the touch. I knew of fear only when I saw the lion chase after the deer into a wall of tall things with shimmering green things fluttering in the wind.

I knew I would know nothing here of names, but I was just fine to move about within the space, touching things, smelling things, tasting things. I got hungry and thirsty, but I wondered if I would intuitively know to find what I needed to satisfy these desires.

The one thing I learned here was that I was the result of history and culture and family with more than enough to say to point and guide me. I wondered if there was anything of my personality or opinions or thoughts that were me at all. There were no prophets here. There were no libraries or the Internet to offer advice and information about the world. I didn't even know this was a world, but I found it beautiful even if I didn't know how to express myself by that word. Every moment here was an ever-expanding experience.

For several weeks, I spent time in meditation and contemplation in this space to cleanse my mind of all I was told, to deprogram my mind. While I did not know if I would know there is a God in this place, I felt I needed to call out to someone, something that had made this. But even that I believe is bias as I really do not know if I could know unless that it might be instilled in me. But who was me? When it got dark out, I felt I should find a place away from the open space I was in. When it rained, I wanted to get out from under it as it made me cold. The bright yellow disk in the sky was warm, I could feel that. I liked to close my eyes and just stand and feel it's warmth on my face.

Then I began to explore and move around more. There was always plenty to eat from so many different fruit trees and other foods that grew near the ground. After some time, I began to wonder what I was doing here, like something bugging me about what this is all about. I was beginning to hope there was someone else like me around, so I headed into the woods. It's amazing how the woods seem to bring a little fear into my mind, I felt unsure and unsafe, but I think that is mainly because that is what I grew up believing, so it became my reality. But at the same time, I did take myself into dangerous situations for the purpose to question how I would feel and react.

I did finally meet another man and took my mind down the road of being a companion and how that played out, and then what happened when he wanted something of mine, or I wanted something of his. I realized how quickly I could lose sight of what was enough and when I wanted something because I placed myself into a position of significance above the other. I then spent time contemplating about just that to try and figure out why we do the things we do. I realized that this was the forbidden fruit, this dualistic mindset I was facing at this juncture in my mind.

Why was I okay on my own, but now that I had someone to compare against that the dynamics changed. When he took the tool, I made to break open some food, it made me angry. Why anger? What is this anger I feel? I don't like it, and now I feel something between us had broken. I didn't like what I was feeling and felt I wanted and maybe even needed to fix it. Would I allow it to happen and learn to live without my tool? I could just make another one. Yes, so my mind was creative and could expand. Or I could tell him to give it back to me, it was mine! Was it really mine? Should I take it back? My gut was turning with some of these thoughts.

Things continued to get messier the more people I ran into. Yes, I went through meeting a woman, and everything that relationship would bring with it. Where does intrigue turn into passion? What are these feelings I have that have no name and no way to articulate, not even to myself? This was something I wanted even though its desire is not planned out or even thought through like when I built my thatch home. Then from passion to daily living where food was important and whose turn is it to clean up the leftovers, to, I cleaned up last time, and now it is your turn. You would be surprised as to how quickly our giving turns into taking.

Within meditation, you will be far more aware of when and how these dynamics change over time and often by confrontation where my understanding and perspective of truth is more important than your understanding and perspective of truth. This is the place where love is used as a stepping stool to allow whatever it was, to cover and give way to other people's truths that were different than mine. Was there one truth here to provide control, or was love the tool that allowed uniqueness to exist in people even if out of step with others?

I began to realize that the tree of the knowledge of good and evil was a metaphor of life itself. The garden lives within each one of us, it lives within me. The fruit I should not partake in was all around me as I interacted with more people and life and the desires that exist in this world. To want to take my fruit tool back from my companion even though it was "mine" was to partake in eating the forbidden fruit. Being right about something should not overrule an opportunity to offer compassion for another in its place.

I realized that my father planted himself at the base of the tree of knowledge of good and evil and never left it all of his life. And then by example, he taught each of his children how to do the same thing. To spend a lifetime pointing fingers at what is holy and righteous, and what is evil and wicked, thereby existing in this perpetual dualistic mindset of righteousness that desires control, instead of letting it go for the sake of compassion.

So then does truth have a place? Of course, we seek truth in everything to help ourselves grow, but never use it for our gain or to manipulate another person over offering love. To claim for example that belief in Jesus as the only way to heaven is a proclaimed truth with the elephant in the room as hell and torment being the motivator of the truth presented, causing love to be suppressed because of the fear that exists in the offer being sold. How can love exist in an offer of eternal bliss where the underlying fine print tells the buyer they better buy it or be punished for all eternity?

> *"There is no fear in love; but perfect love casteth out fear: because fear hath torment. He that feareth is not made perfect in love."*
> *1 John 4:18*

I began to see more and more of how the Bible was a book written by the very same types of Beings bent on solving a problem that was never meant to be solved. To try and solve sin out of existence by calling it out is to put our focus on the very thing that does not exist and off the only thing that does exist, love.

Jesus was upset with the Pharisees because they lived within a judgmental truth-at-all-costs reality created out of self-righteousness that superseded compassion. There is no difference between those leaders and followers of that day than in our day except we now use a new testament to demand our righteousness over others. God is love and Love allows and so the illusion of our creative minds needing to control continues to take center stage. The ego lives by telling us we must control the form we exist in within the reality we created. And when others take control, we dive in to take it back without even thinking about how that dualistic mindset destroys others.

Jesus asks us to love our enemies, but we don't even know what that looks like. We would much rather convert them first into something lovable and agreeable with our view on life. So, we preach a message of love and fear, of heaven and hell to control those we claim to love. Yet God is love and Love has no opposite. There is nothing to control. There is only giving of ourselves at all costs because Love allows.

I strongly recommend that you take some time each day for a few weeks and spend time in the garden where no one else exists except you, and then begin to bring in the dynamics of others and of life from this very primitive place of emptiness. Take it step by step, as you learn so much about the clatter and chatter of all you been taught and told that controls your thoughts and ultimately rules over your subconscious and conscious life literally keeping you from hearing the Spirit. "Be still and know that I am God." Listen carefully to the Spirit speak to you and begin to let go of all the past things you fight over or run from.

Right now, is the only time where love resides. Love does not exist in the past or the future. It is impossible to love or know and feel love when your mind is mulling over the past or worrying about the future. When we begin to learn to step away from our minds and into our hearts, a whole new world of love becomes present, showing things to you from completely unknown perspectives.

> *But without faith it is impossible to please him: for he that cometh to God must believe that he is, and that he is a rewarder of them that diligently seek him. Hebrews 11:6*

> *He that loveth not, knoweth not God; for God is love. 1 John 4:8*

> *But without faith (that which is only active in the present) it is impossible to please Love: for he that cometh to Love (resides within) must believe that Love is, and that Love is an enlightener of them that diligently seek Love.*

Christianity

I did not come to bring peace but division…
Luke 12:51

Jesus came to share a message of division at a time when people followed a scripture that preached a message of judgment and anger born out of their fears and written down in what was called the "holy" scriptures.

Jesus' message was about a Father of love, grace, forgiveness, and peace, which was a very divisive message to how people believed life operated. Especially divisive to those who were considered the established leaders of his day.

He did not come as the savior of the world as though we were lost to some judgmental deity, but to bring awareness and understanding, to save humanity from the fears they invented about God and themselves. Yes, a very divisive message.

He brought teaching about loving our enemies so that we could be like, or behave like our Father in heaven. This is a message about forgiveness and tolerance through grace to all. This message needs no leaders as Love is the guide.

Did we learn anything? Nope! Over the next centuries, driven by the same fear of maintaining structure and authority, the leaders twisted Jesus' words and others to fabricate the next set of "holy" scriptures to bring a message of exclusivity to the earth, further dividing God from His creation, yet presenting it as love, but with conditions, which is impossible.

What I want to share about what I learned about the history of Christianity is not going to be very pleasant for those who have invested their lives into their faith. Much of what I am going to share are things I learned that was never shared with me, but also purposely hidden, or ignorantly remained blind to it.

Because of the advent of the Internet, no one in leadership roles is without excuse as any form of study on any subject will bring with it information that offers different perspectives. If you really want to find that which supports your beliefs, there is plenty to build your case and reinforce your biases. But that is not how I approached this subject. I approached it with an open mind to allow the truth to step out of the forest of information. I wanted to trust in God alone, like David, by being still and knowing God within.

The Bible says that we can know God by looking at the heavens and within creation. Someone like Ken Ham has a huge investment into his beliefs because he does not form his reality based on creation, but forms a reality of creation according to the Bible. The infinite based on the finite. Creation is truly the hand of God at work, and it speaks volumes when we go and play in its backyard. Because Ken places the Bible above creation, he and others like him must work tirelessly fabricating, excusing and justifying to make creation fit into an incredibly small amount of information we have within the Bible about creation. That is not knowing an infinite God according to creation but knowing creation according to a finite Book. The same is true in knowing God alone vs. defining God by a few words found in scripture.

> *For since the creation of the world God's invisible qualities, His eternal power and divine nature, have been clearly seen, being understood from His workmanship, so that men are without excuse. Romans 1:20*

I may come across disgruntled in some of what I share about Christianity, but the information I share is only a tiny fraction of what I found that caused me great discomfort and shock as it continued to challenge my life long Christian beliefs. My life investment! I really hope you do not remain consciously ignorant but dig in yourself so you may know the truth. All my life when I claimed that "the truth will set you free," I believed I held the truth that others needed. Well, I found truth that exposed many of the lies of that once held truth. I am free today from the bondage of a religion purposely developed to create division.

As I stated in previous pages, the next few years were more typical and the vigor I once held slowly changed into experiences of epiphanies and synchronicities as I felt drawn to study all forms of science and ancient history. This was a time where between reading books, watching documentaries and reading information on the Internet, I would guess I read about 3000 books worth of information and maybe more. I followed my higher passion, or what you might know as the will of God leading me to the things I valued most within my heart. As the months passed, I could see that the things I was learning would not have been accepted or believed until the other things just in front of them were first studied thoroughly and digested. My hope is more in that you would be intrigued to come to God empty-handed and ask God to bring you on the adventure God designed just for you.

I know I have already shared a great deal on the subject of hell, mainly because that was the biggest hang-up of my journey, and also because I know it is the biggest hang-up of every church family whose doctrines embrace it as a literal thing. I was learning so much about love that the idea of the Creator punishing a bug no longer fit into the direction I felt I was being led toward. Call it being tricked by the devil if you like if fear leads your mind in that direction. A dark force in sheep's clothing perhaps? Trust me, I didn't just wake up, and the doubts of those things in my past training just go away. I was taught very well to be afraid of anything outside the doctrines that left me to a life blinded to so much more.

Questioning things now and then is still with me today but mainly because of the brainwashing that took place over 45 years of my life that are now only triggers to thoughts. Not because I am concerned within my present state of being that I could attract darkness to me, but because I understand more about what the darkness is and have no fear of it anymore. That is a subject all in itself, and maybe I will touch on it later.

The previous pages were more about a journey into a

darkness I needed to take to recognize who I really am, but also to address those things and beliefs in my life that I identified myself with. I found that the essence, the Spirit that lives within me lives within you and within everything. And therefore, my body is only a temple, a vessel in which my soul and spirit reside for a moment on this earth.

In the pages ahead, I am going to share a different journey from a new perspective of understanding about the deeper aspects of who we really are. To do that effectively, I have learned that I cannot just go to the full light or truth of what I know today as it would send you running. I honestly believe by the words Jesus used that he also only feed the people he spoke to with bits and pieces of truth that they could digest, and moreover through current cultural understandings which only further separate the truth of all Jesus wanted to share. In coming to this understanding I realized we stand on what Jesus said as the whole truth and live by it, and therefore, we stand on a false understanding of partial truths to the whole truth he held within his fullness.

I am going to share things as I feel they need to be said. As I share I am going to sound angry and very judgmental of the church because for a time I was very angry at so many years lost to something portrayed as good, even if it was meant in a well-meaning and loving way from a place of ignorance. If God is love, then the god portrayed in the Bible is an intruder disguised as the Creator to blind us in the name of righteousness. God is calling each of us to love one another, God is not calling us to worship Him. I promise that once we get through this chapter that things will begin to lighten up. In fact, I think you will be delighted you stuck with me through the hard times and faced some of these thoughts with me.

The years ahead of which I am covering are filled with doubt and fear, but also filled with greater peace and joy as I continued to follow the Spirit (the Holy Spirit if that makes you more comfortable) to where God wanted to lead me. I had learned by this time that I held nothing to my small understanding that could compare to what the Spirit holds to lift me up and surprise me with. If you like surprises, you need only give it all up and pay close attention to the synchronicities that happen all around you.

Wake each day with gratitude for life and smile in anticipation for new surprises! Sometimes my wife and I will just say to each other when together and things just seem to fall into place and right on time, "living right!". Not as in some form of holy self-righteousness that pleases an almighty judging god, but in frivolous fun and joy, and in being real and spontaneous! Frivolous is a great word for living within the Spirit! Frivolous!

I once was afraid to look deep into my heart and soul, afraid I would find darkness and decay that would expose the "joy" I only spoke about over my facade. Instead, I found Love waiting to show me a way to peace and happiness. Together we traveled through the darkness, together we worked on the decay, with joy we emerged from the tomb, saved from myself.
Matthew 23: 27 & 28

The order of the sub-titles in this chapter are not in any particular order. I am only wanting to share some of the things I learned that impacted me the most.

I am going to begin with a few well known hymns and one that was my favorite as I grew up in the church. I wanted to make sure I brought light to what is being promoted within the songs we sing in church.

Let's sing of our depravity

We grow up hearing a message of love, grace, and mercy but any mention of hell and eternal separation is somehow skewed and softened as hell resides somehow outside the control of God. If hell is within the control of God, then God is separate from Itself or demented. The message is either one of duality which can include fear and torment, or it is a message of love which allows and remembers no wrongs.

Softly And Tenderly Jesus Is Calling
Softly and tenderly Jesus is calling,
Calling for you and for me;
See, on the portals He's waiting and watching,
Watching for you and for me.
Refrain
Come home, come home,
You who are weary, come home;
Earnestly, tenderly, Jesus is calling,
Calling, *O sinner*, come home!

Why should we tarry when Jesus is pleading,
Pleading for you and for me?
Why should we linger and heed not His mercies,
Mercies for you and for me?
Refrain

Time is now fleeting, the moments are passing,
Passing from you and from me;
Shadows are gathering, deathbeds are coming,
Coming for you and for me.

Refrain
O for the wonderful love He has promised,
Promised for you and for me!
Though we have sinned, He has mercy and pardon,
Pardon for you and for me.

If you sang this song and knew it's tune it almost makes you cry just to think about how Jesus is softly and tenderly calling us to come home. Jesus is pleading, time is now fleeting, moments are passing for you and for me. O sinner! O for the wonderful love He has promised, even though we have sinned, He has mercy and can pardon us… *screeeeech...* Or what? If hell and torment are part of the Biblical doctrine and gospel message why is it skirted around in the message of this song? Shadows are coming for you and for me! From where? Who created them? Shadows!? This song makes it sound like hell and destruction are not part of creation, like God had nothing to do with it. It was just here. If the shadows the song is referring to is real, then God created it. What does that say about God?

I can see the picture in my mind behind this song. A mountain in the background with bubbling lava spewing out the top and sliding down through crevasses and over ledges consuming everything in its path! At the mouth of the opening several of Gods special fire protected suited angels taking the arms of those unwilling to accept the message and thrown in, as the man in a white robe is singing this song with a fifty-person choir behind him, joyous and compassionate looks on their faces as the drum of the song leads on. Behind the choir a large curtain hiding the mountain from those facing the man and choir where thousands of sorry looking dirty rotten sinners dressed in rags, men, women, and children, listening to a message about their sin and guilt and "O for the wonderful love He has promised." That is the whole picture here of the gospel message, and it is as far from love as anything can get.

Even though my wife and I left the church for almost ten years, I would still awaken now and then to a song in my head or hear one playing on the radio. As I listened, I was shocked by so many songs and especially the preaching from those that I loved to listen to on the radio for decades. Now I am hearing what was being said, this same message of love and mercy with hell as the unmentioned elephant in the room. Or hell and brimstone messages that were still sugar coated, again as though hell somehow existed on its own outside of the control of God, and God is the savior from this outside Menace, which you must admit is a little shady suddenly showing up in the new testament.

The Old Rugged Cross

1. On a hill far away stood an old rugged cross,
the emblem of suffering and shame;
and I love that old cross where the dearest and best
for a world of lost sinners was slain.
Refrain:
So I'll cherish the old rugged cross,
till my trophies at last I lay down;
I will cling to the old rugged cross,
and exchange it some day for a crown.
2. O that old rugged cross, so despised by the world,
has a wondrous attraction for me;
for the dear Lamb of God left his glory above
to bear it to dark Calvary.
(Refrain)
3. In that old rugged cross, stained with blood so divine,
a wondrous beauty I see,
for 'twas on that old cross Jesus suffered and died,
to pardon and sanctify me.
(Refrain)
4. To that old rugged cross I will ever be true,
its shame and reproach gladly bear;
then he'll call me some day to my home far away,
where his glory forever I'll share.
(Refrain)

This was truly my favorite song to sing at church. Back then I believed I was a sinner, I was guilty and deserved to be punished, what teenage kid doesn't? I was spanked enough as a child, so I must've been real bad and this only reaffirmed to me that I was a sinner. You grow up singing these songs with music that truly touches your soul, and then apply words of suffering and shame and sin and blood and sacrifice, and because of this one act by God nonetheless, for a world of lost sinners was slain. How can you not feel completely indebted to this God/man who saved us from eternal torment? At least until you realize that it is God who created it and that if he were all powerful, he most likely could have found another way. Like forgiveness could be an option for example.

Yes, yes, I know, he does forgive – but only those that repent, the rest who never knew him are somehow super wicked, men, women, children and infants, all wicked evildoers who deserve eternal punishment. Steve, you're so cold about it! Well, I say it that way to make me feel better about serving this "god of love". We cannot fathom punishing our own child for doing nothing, or for eating a cookie without asking. Go ahead, you have a five-year-old? Surely, she is bad for something. Grab her and spank her over and over and over. Even the thought of it should make you feel sick! You see, you hold a truth in your heart that knows that would be psychotic.

But that is not enough. If I believe in this God/man he will save me from himself, so I can live forever with him in "my home far away," a message in many song lyrics about heaven, a place of glory to share after I die. First, I am sure I don't want to be a part of a god who not only saves his own creation from himself, but died a painful death so people would say that their sins would magically be pardoned, but with strings attached because the people still need to believe without doubt that he died for them. Which of course is tough on those who live in all other areas of the world without access to the message.

There Is A Fountain Filled With Blood (Great title!)

There is a fountain filled with blood drawn from Emmanuel's veins; (need I say more?)

And sinners plunged beneath that flood lose all their guilty stains.

Lose all their guilty stains, lose all their guilty stains;

And sinners plunged beneath that flood lose all their guilty stains.

The dying thief rejoiced to see that fountain in his day;

And there have I, though vile as he, washed all my sins away.

Washed all my sins away, washed all my sins away;

And there have I, though vile as he, washed all my sins away.

Dear dying Lamb, Thy precious blood shall never lose its power

Till all the ransomed church of God be saved, to sin no more.

Be saved, to sin no more, be saved, to sin no more;

Till all the ransomed church of God be saved, to sin no more.

E'er since, by faith, I saw the stream Thy flowing wounds supply,

Redeeming love has been my theme, and shall be till I die.

And shall be till I die, and shall be till I die;

Redeeming love has been my theme, and shall be till I die.

Then in a nobler, sweeter song, I'll sing Thy power to save,

When this poor lisping, stammering tongue lies silent in the grave.

Lies silent in the grave, lies silent in the grave;

When this poor lisping, stammering tongue lies silent in

the grave.

Lord, I believe Thou hast prepared, unworthy though I be,

For me a blood bought free reward, a golden harp for me!

'Tis strung and tuned for endless years, and formed by power divine,

To sound in God the Father's ears no other name but Thine.

Once again, we are not just good people that make mistakes, but we are vile sinners! If you go to church, just look around you at all the young children singing along, repeating words like "unworthy though I be" pounding into their precious heads a message so damaging and degrading to a soul that is a part of God, magnificent, beautiful and filled with light they are.

Go ahead, look your five-year-old in the eyes and tell her she is guilty, vile and wretched, to make sure you put the "fear of God" in her so that she is scared to death of hell and torment and runs to Jesus for salvation. We do it in church and put lovely music to it and have our children sing these words over and over until the programming is set in stone. Surely, she is unworthy. But by the grace of God and the shed blood of Jesus pouring out all over the place from his veins to make the idea have a more fear filled impact, she may understand and hope like crazy that she will have enough faith, or hopefully be in the right denomination to escape the coming wrath of this god. Forget heaven! I mean that is great and all, but at least she doesn't need to have to go to hell. This is not really about heaven, it is about escaping the hell the god we love and worship created for us to spend eternity by default.

"There is no fear in love; but perfect love casteth out fear: because fear hath torment. He that feareth is not made perfect in love." *1 John 4:18*

Stepping out of the box of religion

I was careful in how I allowed new beliefs into my life, a subject we will get into as beliefs are what drive us, and for many what defines them. I would never again allow myself to be drawn into another box that would define God or me. Trust me, people have tried by vomiting out Bible verses after Bible verses, and it sounds like a resounding gong! I would much rather be hit repeatedly with a hammer, at least in that way the regurgitator could see the damage they leave in their wake. It's like having a conversation with a robot!

Once I stepped on the outside of my religion and doctrine where I could see that while I used to fight for my beliefs and doctrines within my faith system pointing out to the faults in the others, that now from the outside I could see that not only were all of the major denominations of Christianity in their own boxes of small beliefs but that the thousands of doctrines that split and made up these denominations were all in their own boxes as well, each one created out of having to be right. If love was in the forefront, we would see the unification of denominations merging with one another.

From the outside, I could now see the bias toward my own beliefs where there exists an underlying mostly unspoken understanding that all other denominations were at the very least not doing it quite right or completely failing the perspective or translation as it was understood by those of us who had it very well figured out. You might say that the more we had it figured out, the more in control we were, the less love we were sharing.

Because I found myself on the outside, I felt liberated once again to freely explore anything I wanted without the slightest hesitation of fear or guilt that was once there under the control of my religion, father, and family. I was in love with the Great Lover, and we were exploring the world together like I was just born for the first time!

Hell drives the need to be right

My study took me to many websites about the subject of hell. Most of the things I found were bias and filled with justifications. Meaning, it does not take long when seeking truth to find someone trying to make a point from their perspective and belief system. I know I am doing that here, but I am not trying to convert someone to follow something I believe in, but in helping to point out a few things to research yourself and by trusting in God alone to lead you to the truth you need to know within your heart.

As you research the subject of hell, you will find many people and their clever justifications are desperately clinging on to the only hope of salvation they ever knew because the grip of hell is so paramount in their theology. The unspoken idea of hell in their mind is just too real to them to question anything about what they been told and trained into, while at the same time speaking from an authoritative voice proclaiming God's mercy and grace.

I am sharing in this way because I was this person. If this makes you uncomfortable, please consider how others feel when approached by a person who tells them about the love of God. They all know full well you are accusing them of being wicked and sinful and going to hell. Those who sit quietly through your message are uncomfortable because they hold truth within their own hearts that is telling them that there is a darkness present. That fear is within their midst. As a Christian, I just felt good that I was being obedient to scripture and having to face these very uncomfortable moments. But I felt I was doing my job. It was about me more than it was them because we know we will face a wrathful god one day and say that we did what he told us to do. Like, little minions.

The biggest issue about hell and why I believe it is the main controlling factor used in the Christian life and even within other religions is because the fear of being wrong drives the person toward having to be right over all other attributes in life, even love because of the risks of being wrong are too high as it will eternally damn the soul. It is not enough to love another person to show the love of God within, and by these acts of kindness of true friendship, others will desire what we have that is beautiful to them and desire it for themselves. Again, the person who believes in a god of punishment is driven to be right out of fear. That's the bottom line.

As a witness for Christ, my message would always start out with the love of God and the "free gift of salvation." When rejected, my mind went to the result of rejecting this message, which is to face judgment and be cast into the lake of fire. Based on those last two sentences, which one is driven by fear? Well, you say, "Steve, that is not fear, that is the truth!" Ok, which of the two sentences above are driven by a believed truth that is driven by fear? If we are making excuses why someone is not worthy of our love, fear is present even if we deny it by the greatest truth in the Book.

If I reject the gospel message per the Baptist doctrine (which was my own), is it love or fear that drives the mind to need to be right? Yes, it is love that cares for our loved one who is rejecting the message, but that love exists because we want to save the loved one from the wrath of a punishing god. As long as hell and punishment exist in our mind as real and somehow a part of love, it will forever be the driving force to needing to be right as our eternal life depends on that believed truth.

> *"There is no fear in love; but perfect love casteth out fear: because fear hath torment. He that feareth is not made perfect in love." 1 John 4:18*

This verse is very clear. If we are in fear of anything, we are not made perfect in love. I lived in my fear of hell all of my life. How could I possibly see love for what it truly is when blinded by this fear that is sold as love?

Love is much more than just a word we use to describe goodness or a quality of God, love IS God. Love remembers no wrong. Love has no condition. Love Allows. If after reading those few words about love and are judging what I am saying by other verses, then that is called justifying your desire to be right. If you need to be right, then fear exists, and love is not made perfect.

Translation quantity differences on hell

What are the implications of 30,000 different denominations? Well, one is the splitting of denominations because of disagreements. Split after split after split. Most of these fights are over the perspectives of understanding of what the scriptures are teaching based on one of many English or other language translated Bibles. Today I use the Rotherham's Emphasized Bible because it is a direct translation of the Hebrew and Greek, which makes it read a bit funny because the author was not concerned about translating into how English reads, but in the English words that translate from Hebrew and Greek. This in itself was a big eye opener as compared to the KJV, the version my father was bent on being the best translation of the Bible. The reading between these two bibles themselves opens a whole new world to understanding why new denominations form and split and go their different ways. Most of us have no clue what we are even reading when taking the words so literally.

One of the biggest differences as it pertains to hell is that the The Latin Vulgate used by the Catholic church written in 400 has 86 mentions of hell in the old testament and 24 mentions in the new. The King James Version written in 1611 has 31 mentions of hell in the old testament and 23 mentions in the new. The Rotherham's Emphasized Bible written in 1902 has no mention of hell in the old or new testaments because there is no mention of hell in the Hebrew or Greek scriptures. Moreover, if you do your thorough research, you will find that most Jewish people never believed in a hell nor do they today.

How many denominations are there?

World Christian Encyclopedia (David A. Barrett; Oxford University Press, 1982) apparently estimated almost 21,000 denominations, and the updated World Christian Encyclopedia (Barrett, Kurian, Johnson; Oxford Univ Press, 2nd edition, 2001) estimated at least 33,000. "Denomination" is defined as "an organized Christian group within a country."
The Center for the Study of Global Christianity at Gordon-Conwell Theological Seminary estimated 34,000 denominations in 2000, rising to an estimated 43,000 in 2012. These numbers have exploded from 1,600 in the year 1900.

Side note. If you study the history of the church, you will find that about 300 years ago is when the Bible began to be interpreted more literally instead of metaphorically as it had been prior.

I was becoming more aware of the biases that existed in what I was coming across, and I moved on to the next articles or books until I found those few people who were more interested in sharing truths as they were. Most everyone has a bias which only reinforced my understanding of how a person within a denomination will always say his belief is the right one. I know I do, and also need to fight against having to be right but in seeking for the truth no matter if it proves me wrong. Even in the face of more than 30,000 different Christian denominations today, the believer will remain faithful and strong to their personal doctrines, mainly because of the investment of life given to this point. At the point where a person is in their forties and fifties and older, it is less about truth and more about investing in the justification of the current truth being held. The tighter we hold onto the justification of truth and our belief systems, the farther we get from love, the more dogmatic we become, the less connected to our true self, the greater the lie.

In fact, as a Christian, I claimed to follow a single truth that has authority over me. That I do not follow my own truth as that would be fallible. And yet just by claiming that my denomination within tens of thousands is the right one, is to say that my personal perspective of my doctrines is also my personal truth. In this one area, the Christian still claims the one truth, and all who are asked what truth is the right one will point to the Bible as the authority, while at the same time pointing a finger at their brothers and sisters claiming they follow the wrong doctrine and therefore the wrong god, revealing the naivety of the beliefs they stand on.

In my case I decided to follow a God I realized I never really knew to wherever He wanted to lead me, and in the process of that faith in Him alone, I dropped everything I had ever learned, much of it in my time in the garden. If the truth was the truth, then it would come back to me as such, and many things I once held as truth are true again to me today. However, they are not there out of childhood indoctrinations or followed blindly by song based propaganda and parental control of what I should and should not believe in.

The idea of more than 30,000 different Christian denominations really bugged me. It should bug you! I could not let this go. If someone told me there were only ten, I would possibly believe that nine were wrong. Maybe six of the ten still believed in original sin and salvation through blood and therefore, could still have some of their doctrines wrong but the main focus of belief in Jesus was on target with what I believed, and therefore only four billion people were going to hell - well in my current history. Ok, I could buy that if I was really invested in my faith and truly believed that four of the other denomination followers were messed up in their heads and wrong. The church has been fighting over this lunacy for centuries now with never a solution other than to create more separation instead of unity. The truth the church must proclaim make them grasp even tighter when loosening is what is needed for love to have its way.

I hold the right truth, so you're wrong

Division itself is one of the biggest implications that stood out to me. Not from where I was before because I was too ignorant and arrogant even to know to question why these splits were happening. Honestly, I didn't care enough to think about it. Why in the world is there division in the churches whose message is about love, long suffering, patience, grace, and forgiveness? What truth is more right over another truth to cause these splits? And what message does a split send to the world about its faith? This mentality alone confirms that God is not the people's source, but that He is a figment of the people's experience and finite understanding of form imputed unto the Spirit, while at the same time claiming with their mouth an almighty, omniscient God.

I think the biggest implication of tens of thousands of denominations raises a question about how I might know mine is the right one. If I lined up all the leaders of each denomination from around the world and asked each leader which denomination they think is the right one, they would each say their own is right. Who would've guessed! As I type this I have a smile on my face just thinking if that would actually happen, would they all be so stubborn as five years old children as never to question the implications of everyone being right and not realizing that that is impossible. However, not only would each leader say their denomination is the right one but would say that all the others are wrong.

I remember thinking at least a few times in my younger years that I was so happy that I grew up in the right denomination. I remember just being really relieved to think about where I would be if I grew up in the wrong denomination. I might go to hell and not even know it thinking I was right but really being wrong! I always thought there were only a few different churches and they were bad, and their people were going to hell. I'm not joking! And the funny thing is, is that while I type this, you the reader are possibly thinking this is your story, and you don't think this is very funny at all! Well, I really don't think it is funny as much as I think it is completely tragic!

Then there is the idea in so many denominations of whose understanding of truth and perspective and different bibles used, different years, different translations, and soon we discovered that there are hundreds of thousands of mistakes in the manuscripts where not a single one is the same as another. And there are 5,800 complete or fragmented Greek manuscripts, which are copies of copies of copies, and no original that anyone knows of. And why Greek and not Aramaic, the language of Jesus and the Jews of that time?

Are you sure you are grasping tightly to the right truth? If you believe in hell, this is a serious question? Your whole faith and foundation is based on the fear of hell and is most likely the underlying unaware reason you follow Jesus at all. I'm just saying that if you want hell to be a real place, then fear in hell is a real thing for you. Therefore, you had better be damn sure you are following the right scriptures and interpretation of that scripture!

Hundreds of thousands of mistakes

If you don't see the elephant in the room on that last topic, let me point it out to you. Because of my religious upbringing and belief in the Bible being God breathed, I was shocked to learn that there were over 200,000 differences recorded when scholars stopped searching with an estimate of at least 400,000 total differences, such as typos, words missing, words written in different order, chapters missing, pages missed, new verses added, and everything else that can go wrong with writing. As you can imagine, I began to question just how inerrant the Bible could be. As a Christian, I doubted what I was learning, and unwittingly forming justifications as to why to make sure my life investment, mainly in salvation remained secure. If I was wrong, then I was heading to hell. But my beliefs changed as I followed the truth. Am I now supposed to pretend that the facts and evidence of this history presented do not exist?

When I was younger, I just followed my father who claimed that the KJV was the best translation. So, like a good little boy and into my adult life, this was truth to me. The Bible was God's word and to even begin to question the thought of it not being so was to question who I was, and with hell being a real thing to me, I was possibly stepping into some very dangerous waters. Maybe the best thing to do is to just not even go near that question because I just cannot face life if reality was somehow different than what I was told and believed it was all my life.

You can begin to understand why thousands of Christian leaders all proclaim their denomination is the right one and all the others are wrong. I promise you, if you have not faced doubt to the point that it reveals the truth of your error, and then takes your very reality and throws it into an endless dark pit leaving you standing on a ledge of complete despair, then much of what I am sharing is most likely all being judged and damned for the unaware purpose of showing yourself just how strong your personal faith in God is. Trust me, egos don't get much bigger than that. Mine was huge!

So what is your excuse as to why a perfect God, whose message is to love and worship Him or be thrown into the lake of fire, would leave something so important to interpretation from non-agreeing copies of missing copies of mistyped copies into other languages from other languages, to a bunch of men, each with their own unique perspectives of what life is all about based on where they grew up, who their father was, and countless other things in life to skew a person's view of how they perceive reality?

Language translation

Let's take language translation alone. Let's use the word devotion. Think about your own life and the meaning that one word holds and how it changed and grew to mean so much more to you because of things that happen in your life, of how things you did in life surrounding that word affected certain outcomes, and then by the outcome and experience new revelations were learned. Now let's use the same word in Africa and all of its nations and tribes. Then China and its monks, then Jewish rabbis who speak Yiddish and/or a newer Hebrew and I could go on and on. How does this one word get translated to mean the same as it did two thousand years ago? You can multiply this times all the words used and their personal meanings times all the experiences of all the people of the world throughout their life and then throughout history.

To claim that we hold any form of correct meaning of any word that is to be completely understood the same way by another person as we articulate it by our experiences even within the same language is impossible, much less from Hebrew and Greek to English, thus the reason there are so many doctrines of "truth" today. The bottom line is that we cannot and do not believe in one authoritative truth if we hold on at all to any doctrine we deem the right or only one. That bias itself separates us from the One we claim to love. I held on to this also until I opened my grasping hand and found nothing but dry sand blowing away in the wind.

Literalism vs. Mythology

Taking a literal, historical interpretation of scripture only leads to a form of superstition that does little more than demand more details to further define and enforce countless doctrinal belief systems, over the infinite mythical depths of spiritual meaning and divine relationship found in the same words.

If what I was learning about the Bible and all its mistakes were true, then what are the implications of this? As I explained above, I could dig in and find everything I could get my hands on to prove the Bible right. But wouldn't that just be an excuse for being embarrassed for God not doing his job? But then that is what I have been doing all my life.

Maybe he is doing his job but in a clever and hidden way so that only a few intellectuals can find the answers and it has nothing to do with love. Or, maybe it's hope in establishing some law and order over people that lean toward killing and war and mayhem without something being written to guide them. But that doesn't sound very God breathed then. Or maybe the Romans saw how superstitious and loyal the Jewish people were toward their scriptures, maybe they created their own Son of God as their country was falling apart and needed to take control of its people.

I'm not completely against the Bible, which we will learn the further we move forward, but I do think for many it has become a security blanket for them instead of a hand pointing them to the God inside that is waiting to be trusted alone – to be our comfort - without the blanket. Today after understanding much more of ancient history and the stories found in early accounts of the genesis story and the flood and many other stories that found their way into the Bible from more ancient histories, I began to see and understand the mythology and how stories were conveyed in those days. In fact, I was beginning to learn that for a human with limited language to articulate himself about his experience about spiritual things could only be through symbolism and parables. How would you explain to someone accurately your feelings of falling in love? What literally is the quantity of love?

Understanding is not in the word spoken, but in the revelation the word is drawing from innate within the listener. The word may fail because the listener's journey in not ready to reveal the revelation as it relates to them. Revelations are truths and/or probabilities of truths that are revealed to each person's knowing from within their experience when the time is appropriate.

If we speak with the intent of conforming our own knowing onto the listener's knowing, we not only fool ourselves but may limit the spirit's movement in the listener's understanding of their personal knowing, and the word becomes smaller and defined. Therefore, share freely, accepting that your word spoken may not be understood as intended and that sharing our word may have much more to offer another than we presently comprehend.

When the Bible is taken literally, it completely loses the very essence of its power and purpose and makes it very childish. Did Eve really grab a fruit from the tree? Did "sin" enter the world at that very moment? Like - BOOM, or slithered in slowly? How about God walking in the garden in the cool of the day? Here is one I really love. God said unto them, "be fruitful and multiply." This was right after saying that the woman will cling to the man and become one flesh. Come on guys, are you telling me that without God commanding this that you would just look at your wife with a stupid, "so what should we do now look on your face?" But if that wasn't enough, if we take this all literally, is this the best God can come up with to guide humanity into the next thousands of years? Not something like, don't slap a lion, or don't step off a cliff! Or, Love one another – why not get this out of the way while things are still young and fresh?

The thing about reading the Bible metaphorically is that its message reaches the heart at the place the person is at in their moment of life. Well you say, we can't have that! How can you control anything with ideas like that? Exactly! The first thing that comes to mind when stuck in this mindset is fear. Should we be guided by a single truth? If we are not all on the same page, all hell will break loose. We need to control it! The western world knows so little of the eastern religions and practices and about their teachings of the truth residing within each person. The western mind cannot even comprehend an alternative because it has been told to resist everything outside of its belief, even when

Jesus himself taught many similar things that the eastern religions teach. Mainly about love and compassion, kindness to others, long-suffering, grace, mercy and forgiveness. Scary stuff when it comes from the eastern cultures! One would think that God didn't create these non-western peoples into their cultures, that they somehow exist beyond God's control or plan.

By trying to literally convey the experiences of other people's spiritual experiences we demand a spiritual truth through limited human language while completely devoid of the fact that our understanding through our own life and experiences will determine our understanding and interpretation of that truth.

Therefore, maybe instead of being dogmatic and therefore egotistic about maintaining an interpretive truth as "the" truth, it would be a better intent to convey spiritual experiences metaphorically for the purpose of the edifying of the lives and experiences of others to whatever end God leads them, thereby expanding on the truth.

It seems to me that we are more interested in proving a truth full and complete based on some original source, thereby making it stagnant and small vs. allowing truth to be a living thing that grows and matures with the uniqueness God created into every soul.

Perhaps the solid rock on which I stand is not a rock at all, but an ever moving and growing mountain that encompasses all of humanity where God is speaking truth into each of our experiences throughout our lives, thereby offering an endless flowering of experience to and from our neighbors.

Life should be lived frivolously

When I stepped outside this small box of beliefs, I began to look at each person in new eyes. They were all beautiful, unique and filled with their own life experiences and wonder, their own understanding of truth. You really want to control that!? Instead of being afraid of them, I was amazed by my own ignorance and arrogance. I no longer wanted to convert anyone to know what I knew, because I held nothing compared to the infinite knowledge and truths I could learn by getting to know and listen to more of God's people and their experiences within their relationship with God. The more I learned, the more I saw my depravity. The more I engaged with other people and studied the diversity of other cultures the greater God became to me, the smaller my box of beliefs, the more I loved life, the more I just wanted to live! Frivolously!

Today I rest in not being able to claim or hold or solve the whole truth. I really don't feel the need any more in having to solve and fine tune every detail of scripture to make sure it completely fits my doctrines. I no longer care about doctrines and having to prove mine is the right one, or better than the last one I was a part of or better and more correct than that church down the road from mine. I no longer worship any Deity or Lord or King or God, because that is of fear and nothing whatsoever to do with love.

It's not as though facts change a person's life long beliefs overnight, they typically don't. I would say it took me about five years of studying many things and reading between the lines from my own heart, and especially as I began to learn more about what love truly is as it revealed itself that I could let go of past beliefs. Today the thought of a place of punishment is completely ludicrous to me. Impossible! A "truth" I was taught and believed in completely has been replaced with a new "truth" based on more information of things I never knew before, but mainly through finding out what love truly is from the place within my heart. I do not rule out that there is still another "truth" that may change or alter my outlook on my current belief as more of life reveals to me more of life and truth. God is infinite, and yet we somehow think we know the answers to why we believe what we believe.

The inerrant word of God

The other thing I studied was about the Bible being the inerrant word of God. I touched on this in previous pages but want to discuss it in more detail. The Bible was written by way of channeling or spirit writing, visions, dreams or other forms that spirit communicates with man's consciousness. There are many people that have their opinions about this but scared of it so have no clue as to any of these forms of communication with spirit. I once believed that God reached out to each of the Bible writers over time knowing that one day the Canon would be composed as a guide to rule our lives. A complete speculation at best that we now act on by faith as fact. I think this alone is ludicrous as no manual of instruction is written over time. But "God is mysterious!" (The Christian cop-out line!) This is what we were taught knowing very little as to what really took place to put this book together and the intentions that were present. Years ago, we didn't even question where the Bible came from, it was just here and used as a way to help us spiritually, but the result was that it became a book of judgment on all those who did not believe as we believed.

With so many churches splitting over disagreeing doctrines and forming new denominations, among just very strange and seemingly contradictory things written in scripture, I was not ok with crossing these things off as misguided people or "God is mysterious" and just have "faith as a child", when what I was learning about the history of the church was not just misunderstood, but downright wrong and purposely manipulated to create and maintain childish adults who believe that worshiping a deity is not only ok, but perfectly normal, calling it devotion and love. How does love ask to be worshiped?

Please refrain from pre-judging what I am saying too quickly as I have much more to share and I have some corners to turn up ahead that will surprise you. When I say things like "faith as a child," it is not as though I am against this idea. On the contrary, I believe a childlike faith lives at the foundation of beginning to understand the fullness of love. Faith as a child from the Biblical religious standpoint I grew up in is misunderstood in my opinion as the Christian thinks it means that remaining in a state of childlike ignorance and unlearned of things outside the Bible is somehow pure, humble or noble and that becoming prudent is to step away from this faith. The church loves when prudent people remain close to home and study the Bible and books that promote its doctrines.

The church is very afraid of what is happening today because new truths that were once hidden or difficult to find about the church and its history are becoming readily available to anyone.

My experience with faith has moved from faith in trusting in words and in people based on the doctrines I placed my truth in, to that only of faith in God alone where truth exists within and tested against my intuition. A trust that God will make my paths straight so that faith in something other than God would actually be to not trust in God. The Bible has become this external object or form of which most Christians put their trust and faith overruling their intuition. Therefore, God becomes subject to the interpretation and perspective of a doctrine. And then argued about between tens of thousands of doctrines. God becomes humanized and small, therefore, making humanity small.

The Bible is a collaboration of great and wonderful ancient and not so ancient historical documents that can offer insight and guidance. But when we think we need to control it by inventing doctrines by which we teach others the meaning into one collective interpretation based on a perspective skewed by the culture and other factors, we bastardize it and remove the meaning it has for the individual. The relationship that it can provide to an individual and their relationship with God is removed, and then we wonder why God is not speaking to us today.

To the chief Musician, to Jeduthun, A Psalm of David. KJV Psalm 62:5-8

My soul, wait thou only upon God; for my expectation is from him. He only is my rock and my salvation: he is my defense; I shall not be moved. In God is my salvation and my glory: the rock of my strength, and my refuge, is in God. Trust in him at all times; ye people, pour out your heart before him: God is a refuge for us.

To the chief Musician, to Jeduthun, A Psalm of Bible before God. Psalm 62:5-8

My soul, wait thou only upon the Bible that tells me about God; for my expectation is from scripture that talks about him. The Bible only is my rock and my salvation about God: the Bible is my defense; I shall not be moved. In the Bible about God is my salvation and my glory: the rock of my strength, and my refuge, is in the Bible that tells me about God. Trust in the Bible about him at all times; ye people, pour out your heart before him according to the Bible: The Bible that tells me about God is a refuge for us.

I believe this Psalm is a great example of a man named David while being still and connecting with Spirit in his heart, wrote these words for the first time. Was David inspired by someone else's words? We call this God's word, so let it be God's word for David. These words can speak truth to our heart, but to claim it as more than David expressing himself about his experience that inspired him, is to lessen the uniqueness of David's experience with God, and miss our experience with God that has been quietly waiting for us to be still too enjoy.

I know the spirit is alive in my church!

But there is something alive and real in the church I go to, and in my relationship with God, you protest. Steve, you're wrong because I know it is more than just being afraid of hell. I know I love Jesus! I know God is love! And I know Jesus loves me and is real in my life! Yes, I believe in hell also and that God can cast out the chaff from the wheat. I don't understand how or why, I just know he loves me, so I worship him for saving a dirty sinner like myself.

God is alive and moving in very real ways within the church and within people's lives all over the world if he is omnipresent. Or is God omnipresent only after we are "saved," and as Christians, according to your doctrines? Can other people in other churches and even people in other religions find a relationship with a God of love without following your doctrines, or any doctrine for that matter?

In the church we used to attend, our doctrine was part of the deal, our songs of sacrifice, blood, death, love, lost sinners and worship were all part of the deal. Our family and friends are all there affirming us in our relationship, doctrines of original sin, hell, heaven, love, and forgiveness, all part of the deal. This is all packaged together to include the infant, to the toddler, the teenager and to the adult.

We are brought up in the packaged deal where the whole thing is offered as an accept-it-all or reject-it-all kind of way. If you didn't know God was packaged with all the rules and punishment, how would you know they could be separated? It happened in my own family I grew up in, and these same behaviors are still being carried out to the next generation and will be to the next if love is not embraced beyond truth. At the moment "truth of doctrine" is the ruler of many people's lives in the name of God as it was mine.

If you want a relationship with God, then you must also accept the doctrines of our church and follow the rules, recognize and admit to your imputed sinful nature, acknowledge that you are wicked and without hope on your own, believe in Jesus and his death and resurrection, and that he is part of the trinity as the Son of God, only then can a relationship with God exist, anything else outside of that is feelings that should not be trusted. How pharisaical have we become? The very Pharisees I pointed my finger at while standing with Jesus for having all their rules, praying in public restaurants to make sure everyone else knows and feels they are not as righteous as I, and proclaiming their righteousness before men, is the Pharisee I had become. And frankly, it is most of our churches today. If you think you're not, I would suggest that you ask a good friend to be very honest with you.

> *And when thou prayest, thou shalt not be as the hypocrites are: for they love to pray standing in the synagogues and in the corners of the streets, that they may be seen of men. Verily I say unto you, They have their reward. Matthew 6:5*

> *Pharisaical: practicing or advocating strict observance of external forms and ceremonies of religion or conduct without regard to the spirit; self-righteous; hypocritical. Dictionary.com*

Does love within a relationship really need all the other parts (the doctrines and rules) to make it real in a person's life? Do we really believe that wonderful loving Buddhists and Hindus who give their entire lives to loving their families and neighbors really go to hell because they didn't believe in Jesus? Is it possible that God just wants a loving relationship with all of his children of the world - "Red and yellow, black and white, they are precious in his sight?" Is it that they are all precious because Jesus loves them, but that he will reject them at death if they do not make a choice to believe in Jesus as the son of God?

I'm saying that because we happen to have a relationship with God within a specific denomination we adhere to, does that also mean a relationship with God cannot exist in another denomination or religion? This comes back to the tens of thousands of different denominations within Christianity. If I put the leaders and/or its people in a line and ask which one of them has the real relationship with God, will I only get one group of believers raising their hands?

I would guess that if I put the religions of the world together in one room and asked them if God and Love is present in their churches, sanctuaries, temples, synagogues, parishes, mosques, and others, that they would answer with a resounding yes. Is it possible that God is present in everyone's lives no matter who they are, but that some don't know it and others don't care at the moment? I know there are some that find this ok because they know there is love beyond truth.

But if you consider yourself a true conservative, Bible-believing Christian, then you can't let go of the doctrines that control you. You don't even know you are stuck in their trap because you are convinced that everyone else in the world is brainwashed, and you stand alone with your church of one hundred people against seven billion beautiful souls around the world created wonderfully in the image of the Great Lover, and call it the narrow road.

Do you have a great relationship with God, but live by your doctrines that support a love that can damn your loved ones to eternal torment if you don't intervein? Then you need to look closer to that relationship and question your view of love, because it is skewed and I pity your family and children who will most likely grow up following the same dualistic mindset into fear, frustration, and separation just like I did and call it being persecuted for Christ.

> *"There is no fear in love; but perfect love casteth out fear: because fear hath torment. He that feareth is not made perfect in love." 1 John 4:18*

Confidence in Confidence

Another thing I have thought about is confidence in our own confidence in our believing. If sin is damned and punished for all eternity outside of the presence of God, then sin cannot be accepted by God in any way because he is holy and righteous. But, we have a way of escape from God's wrath! We can accept Jesus as our personal savior because he paid for my sin on the cross. Jesus made a way for me to come into the presence of God by magically removing my sin through my belief.

However, how can I be sure that my belief in Jesus is one hundred percent? I know I have doubts, so that may drop it down to like ninety-nine percent. Yes, I realize that according to the Bible, Jesus paid for my sin, I get that! But I'm talking about my own personal confidence in my sinful and corrupt, non-trusting of myself, very broken confidence in my human belief in Jesus. I want to believe, and I am sure I do believe, but I am concerned that my confidence in my belief may be skewed and missing the mark.

The Bible says a lot about me believing in Jesus, which means it still falls on my shoulders to do the *work* of believing and sealing the deal. Jesus paid it all, by grace I am saved. But if I want to accept this but don't know if my confidence in my confidence in my belief is reliable, this is a big deal. I might get to heaven when I die, and God says, *"I'm really sorry, but you still wreak of sin because you had doubts about your confidence in your confidence in your belief in salvation and were not made perfect - not because of Jesus, but because of your failure to believe 100%. You were close, very close indeed, but too bad… depart from me ye wicked into eternal fire…"*

I know I am a little silly here, but at the same time, I cannot find anything in the Bible that covers my confidence in my confidence to believe as I think I may be expected to. I mean you either believe completely, or you fail and nothing and no one to tell you so until you die. How confident are you if depending on your own trust, which is fallible, in your belief in Jesus to save you from God's wrath, that you will make it? Who or what is verifying your confidence in your belief? You! I mean like once you're dead you don't get another chance! If you plan on living your life by fear of punishment and in need of salvation, then you really seriously need to figure this one out.

We preach this message to what we believe are sound minded people, but how do we know how sound minded they are, especially if part of the message is that we cannot put our trust in ourselves? Are you human? Trust in the LORD with all thine heart, and lean not unto thine own understanding. Proverbs 3:5 - This verse to me is an oxymoron as it related to trusting in the LORD for my salvation when the second part of the verse tells me not to lean on, or trust in, my own understanding. If we cannot lean on our own understanding, then who am I to trust that my confidence in my belief is sure?

What about your teenage son or daughter? Are they really mature enough to be 100% confident in their confidence of their belief? And what about someone mentally disabled? Or Hellen Keller? Surely there are many people who you would wonder if they were mentally capable of making a rational decision for their eternity, and then in no way ever really knowing it stuck. But these things do not fit into our more perfect paradigm of when we preach a hell and brimstone message from the pulpit. If the mentally disabled people enter our minds during these messages, we dismiss them from our minds with justifications and hope that God will be just in some unwritten way. All of this is riddled with fear! From inside we hold a truth trying to speak to us in these moments, but suppress the innate in us into a hidden place in our being so we don't need to face and deal with these less than fortunate people that God somehow made a mistake with.

Or, maybe salvation is not salvation as we understand it literally written in the Bible according to our doctrines. To understand something Metaphorically does not make the words false, but allows the spirit to speak to us where we are at in life. The question is, are we saved from hell or from sin, or from a wrathful god? Or maybe from our judgmental righteous selves for being unwilling to love our enemy as God loves us because a truth demands that I cast a member of my family to the streets that fails to meet the rules of my doctrines?

Anyone who adds to these words

When I grew up the thought of adding or taking away from scripture was cause for war! Well, among our family anyway as dad studied prophecy and we knew well the words written in Revelation 22:18.

One of my biggest moments in letting go of the literal and the inerrant was when I found out that someone added the last verses of Mark. Remember also that manuscripts of Mark are among the oldest known manuscripts of the new testament found. Later manuscripts show a revealing tale as it seemed Mark did not really end as it should have according to some scribes who decided it needed a better ending. The early scriptures ended at Mark 16:8, but it is the next verses that have molding many doctrines and certainly split some apart, and the ones I want to discuss.

I'm pulling most of my verses from KJV because that is the version most claimed most accurate and widely used to the fundamental Christian, where King James used medieval manuscripts (not earlier dated manuscripts) as the basis for its translation. Since 1611, older and more accurate manuscripts have been discovered, and they affirm that Mark: 16 9-20 were not in the older manuscripts of Mark. Either God forgot to put them in, or some man decided that God did not do his job well enough.

The Added Verses

9 Now when Jesus was risen early the first day of the week, he appeared first to Mary Magdalene, out of whom he had cast seven devils. 10 And she went and told them that had been with him, as they mourned and wept. 11 And they, when they had heard that he was alive, and had been seen of her, believed not. 12
After that he appeared in another form unto two of them, as they walked, and went into the country. 13 And they went and told it unto the residue: neither believed they them. 14 Afterward he appeared unto the eleven as they sat at meat, and upbraided them with their unbelief and hardness of heart, because they believed not them which had seen him after he was risen. 15 And he said unto them, Go ye into all the world, and preach the gospel to every creature. 16 He that believeth and is baptized shall be saved; but he that believeth not shall be damned. 17 And these signs shall follow them that believe; In my name shall they cast out devils; they shall speak with new tongues; 18 They shall take up serpents; and if they drink any deadly thing, it shall not hurt them; they shall lay hands on the sick, and they shall recover. 19

> *So then after the Lord had spoken unto them, he was received up into heaven, and sat on the right hand of God. 20 And they went forth, and preached everywhere, the Lord working with them, and confirming the word with signs following. Amen.*

Where do we even begin with the implications of these added verses? To start with, how does scripture change without them? How does this change the other gospel scriptures that were written years, and some decades after Mark? What in these added verses do most of the churches plant their foundation and doctrines?

Of course, we could just choose not to believe it. We could say things like, why would God let the scriptures go on for so long if it were not exactly as he wanted it? Again, humans justifying things to protect God's failure to be clearer. I did.

Verse 15. Isn't it interesting the verses I grew up on telling me that I need to go into all the world and preach the gospel, making me feel guilty for not being diligent in doing so, and then also making others feel like they're guilty sinners, got its origin in Mark years later? And then verse 16 where it specifically says to believe and be baptized to be saved, was a point of contention for years in my younger years and questioned in the churches I went to. And then to end the verse with, if you don't believe, you will be damned, opened my eyes even more to the manipulated scriptures designed to keep its sheep in fear and under the control of the church.

The manuscripts of John were written well into the first century with the intent to make Jesus a deity as well as show his divinity through the proving of miracles when there is no evidence at all of Jesus taking any credit for the healings that took place in the other gospels. Jesus was never about building himself up, but the people of the day believed in miracles performed by the gods and so making Jesus one of them was to give him divinity to prove he was God.

The reason I bring John up is because it is in John where belief in Jesus as the Son of God took place. Again, written decades after the earlier manuscripts, which were still written decades after the death of Jesus, and written in Greek. Why not Aramaic? That is the question you should be asking yourself.

The missing Trinity

Professor Bart D. Ehman who has a very interesting story on how he came to study Greek manuscripts and the road he was on to go into the ministry. He has learned through years of study of the manuscripts that he could actually see where changes to words were played with to change the meaning of the message. The doctrine of the trinity itself is not found anywhere in scripture other than in 1 John, verse 7. *"For there are three that bear record in heaven, the Father, the Word, and the Holy Ghost: and these three are one."* Which is a pretty explicit statement about the Trinity.

However, it does not show up in the early Greek manuscripts in 1 John. It's in the Latin manuscripts of 1 John which of course came later. The scholar to put together the first Greek new testament in 1516 was

Erasmus but did not include the verse because it wasn't in the Greek manuscripts that he had. The Latin theologians were of course very upset, but Erasmus told them it is not in any of the manuscripts that he had. But the theologians demanded that he add it as the Trinity is part of the church's doctrine that they taught. Erasmus told them that if they can produce a Greek manuscript that includes the verse, that he would add it... And so, they produced a Greek manuscript!

Once Erasmus received the falsified Greek manuscript from the theologians with the verse about the Trinity added, he also included it in the Latin version of the new testament. Moreover, because the verse was falsely included into the Latin version of the new testament, the King James translators also put the verse into the KJV when translating the Latin into English.

The justifications that we have amassed to cover the manipulation of history is staggering, and yet I honestly believe we have bought this whole twisted thing, hook, line, and sinker based on the fear people had from the power the early church held over its people, that only in recent years has begun to change because it is being challenged for its validity. I believe within the next decade, and possibly only the next few years, much of what is known and hidden at the Vatican and elsewhere will come to light and expose much of the lies that have controlled our lives for centuries.

The study into the history of the church was endless. I have shared only a few tidbits of the mountains of information available now as much of what was not available to the layman before is now coming into the light and available to research and study.

We know Jesus spoke Aramaic, and most likely not Greek. If you do your research, you will also find that some words spoken by Jesus written in Greek, cannot be reversed back into Aramaic because the Aramaic equivalent does not exist, so it is likely Jesus did not say these words.

Do you really believe that the leaders in power of those days in Rome where much of this all started had God and your best interest in mind? If you remember, the Pharisees had Jesus put to death. What makes us believe they suddenly stopped ruling over and controlling the people? Nothing about the beginnings of the church as we know it was without an underlining of power and control. Yes, many great people lived and died over the centuries believing in this, but unknown to a deeper part of their essence was a knowing in their heart, that something real existed in the relationship between them and their God. That is something we all have deep within your soul. My purpose in writing is to show you that a relationship with the Father not only remains intact but can become much more meaningful when we seek God within.

Sin must be punished

The word sin has changed today from its original meaning in the old testament, which was to miss the mark. Another way to view sin is the absence of love or the unawareness of love. Sin, however, has been used to describe evil and wickedness as though the fear that created these ideas are as real as love itself and has become an adversary to love as though there were two great deities of power.

Satan, the devil, also does not exist as a pronoun until centuries into the development of Christianity where they capitalized the s in Satan changing its purpose of the Hebrew symbolic meaning of spiritual adversary into a living super power. Can you see the very childish desire here that plays itself out in some video game? Our doctrines made the snake, Satan (in the story of the garden of Eden), who physically talks to Eve in the form of some lizard before God removed its legs – some believe. Do your research on symbolism understood by the ancient texts and scriptures. It will begin to shed light on how moving into literalism we destroyed the deep spiritual meaning behind the scriptures.

The biggest driving forces behind the main doctrinal points of Christianity are also taken from a few poorly and differently translated sources throughout the Bible. Invent a doctrine of sin and then a savior, who we will also make into a deity, and who will save the day in the end for only those who worship him. Wherever there is an external savior, self-responsibility can be shelved, which means we as sons and daughters of God in spirit are made null and void giving all our power away to the powers in control. We have become blind sheep by design.

You would think God would be clever enough to know that humans need things spelled out a little more clearly and in a step by step guide to prevent the continual splits that are occurring in the church for the last several centuries because the leaders lost control of the fear it held over its people. However, today we don't even need an authority to place its thumb on us because we now punish ourselves in their stead. The argument for or against inherited sin can be found and proven to support each side within scripture. I will point out a few verses of being born into a world of sin (dualism) vs. being born a sinner (evil doer).

One of the main verses used for this argument is found in Psalm 51:5.

Let's look at these from different biblical translations.

King James Bible

Behold, I was shapen in iniquity; and in sin did my mother conceive me.

New International Version

Surely I was sinful at birth, sinful from the time my mother conceived me.

Young's Literal Translation

Lo, in iniquity I have been brought forth, And in sin doth my mother conceive me.

KJV changes its translation enough so that a child is shapen, as in from conception to birth, but the later part of the verse is closer to the Hebrew; in sin did my mother conceive me. This sounds more like the mother lives in a world that includes sin (an awareness of) that the child was born into. The child is not a sinner.

NIV clearly takes the doctrinal belief of the child is born a sinner, and changes the words of the Bible to support the doctrine.

YLT is always more closely to the Hebrew translation, and I read something more in the line of a mother who conceived who lives in a world of sin, and a child who comes forth into a world of sin. The child is not a sinner; same idea as the KJV.

There are numerous Bible verses, in clear literal language, that affirm the innocence of infants.

The soul that sinneth, it shall die. The son shall not bear the iniquity of the father, neither shall the father bear the iniquity of the son: the righteousness of the righteous shall be upon him, and the wickedness of the wicked shall be upon him. Ezekiel 18:20 - Also see Romans 14:12

King James Bible
And said, Verily I say unto you, Except ye be converted, and become as little children, ye shall not enter into the kingdom of heaven. Matthew 18:3
Young's Literal Translation
and said, 'Verily I say to you, if ye may not be turned and become as the children, ye may not enter into the reign of the heavens; Matthew 18:3

Here we see that Jesus himself is saying that unless we become like little "sinners"? No, like little sinless children playing and having fun. KJV also likes to use the word converted here, which was for me a supporting word for the idea of choosing hell (not converted) or heaven (converted). Verses like this supported my doctrine I invested and believed in of hell and heaven.

I never gave thought to the verse pointing out the false doctrine of original sin. But there is more here if you look at the YLT, and what I also find in my Rotherham's Bible, and that is Jesus himself talking about the "reign of the heavens." What is this that is plural? Between these two translations alone, not only is sin not inherited because children are sinless, by Jesus' own account, but heaven does not exist as a single place. I will touch on this later.

Someone who was texting with me said:
"Sin must be punished. Isn't that common understanding? What do you want to do with the man who rapes and kills little children? What would you like to do to that man? If you tell me that he should not be justly punished, well then, you are being a hypocrite."

It is a common understanding of the religion of Christianity that sin must be punished, and as I hear this said, it helps me realize that this belief alone is based on what we humans exist within on earth and then impute these very ideas onto God (that which is not flesh). We cannot fathom that very evil men would not be punished after the death of the body. But we also cannot fathom that a little child who is only seeking to be loved but does not happen to know the "truth" would face the same eternal punishment. And why do we gravitate toward finding the best justifiable words to make out point?

Why not say,
"Sin must be punished. Isn't that common understanding? What do you want to do with the little girl who just wants to be loved but does not know who Jesus is? What would you like to do to that little girl? If you tell me that she should not be justly punished, well then, you are being a hypocrite."

However, I personally, and I know a growing number of people all over the world who can no longer fathom that love would punish at all because we are waking up to what love really is. What is it in a person that desires the punishment of anyone anyway? Where are grace and forgiveness? Can love be greater? If you come to this from the point of view that was taught in the church, then as fear creates the darkness in our lives, we can actually fathom that love can punish, mainly because our darkness cannot see love for what it really is. The soul is a part of the whole of God and is from God, and it is God. How then can God punish Itself?

"Sin must be punished."

I want to address this specifically. We grow up being punished as children in one form or another, so we understand the concept of punishment from very young. We do wrong, we pay the price. This is how life within form works while on earth. I say it this way so that we begin to separate the form from the spirit. If a man rapes a child, there should be just punishment for his actions in the flesh. But for all eternity? Is that just punishment? Of course not! What if we were talking about this person's loved one? Someone may begin to wonder who is worse, the rapist or the person that hates so deeply.

The texter continues,

"Sin must be punished. Isn't that common understanding?"

Just because the church has adopted this idea into its doctrines doesn't make punishing sin a part of how things work in the spiritual realm. Why do we want to punish the soul so badly unless within form (the flesh) we have not yet enlightened to view others as part of ourselves, as part of the whole of the Source of all? To suggest that a soul be punished eternally is to suggest that we are separate and somehow better than our brother or sister.

Salvation is coming to that place in our lives where we love everyone and everything, to love our enemies, to love our neighbor as ourselves. To turn the cheek. These are statements from Jesus bringing unity to the understanding of our consciousness. In fact, these are statements against the teachings of the old testament ways of living.

If you somehow skimmed right past that last paragraph because you heard those words a thousand times, let's reword them so we can see them in a new light…

- "I will love my **enemy** who converted to what I believe, so they are more like me and therefore more lovable to love."
- "I will love my **neighbor** who converted to what I believe, so they are more like me and therefore more lovable to love."

If you want to see bad people be punished after they passed on, then you are very fleshly sighted and might be surprised that others are not interested in the judgmental message you share about your god. If you understand that the body dies and you still want the soul to be punished for sins committed in the flesh, then you can see a little more, but your hate and condemnation meter is still in operation. You might say that you are your own enemy that needs salvation. Not from hell as though you are condemned, but from yourself for falling asleep to who you really are.

There is a great poem that was going around that says this well…

I was shocked, confused, bewildered
as I entered Heaven's door,
Not by the beauty of it all,
by the lights or its decor.

But it was the folks in Heaven
who made me sputter and gasp--
the thieves, the liars, the sinners,
the alcoholics, the trash.

There stood the kid from seventh grade
who swiped my lunch money twice.
Next to him was my old neighbor
who never said anything nice.

Herb, who I always thought
was rotting away in hell,
was sitting pretty on cloud nine,
looking incredibly well.

I nudged Jesus, "What's the deal?
I would love to hear Your take.
How'd all these sinners get up here?
God must've made a mistake.

And why's everyone so quiet,
so somber? Give me a clue."
"Hush, child," said He. "They're all in shock.
No one thought they'd see you."
~ Author Unknown

It is not in following a doctrine we believe is true that make it right, but in rising above the doctrines of our truth so we can see clearly the love that is always embracing the soul with compassion that our doctrines are condemning.

The same person texting with me said:
"They owe him a payment. But he himself paid the payment."

As in God created a world that would fail, so that he could blame his creation for taking the fruit he placed in front of them, so that he could come to earth thousands of years later as himself but more loving this time, to punish himself for the humans he allowed more power over his plan, to appease himself, so that through killing himself as a sacrifice unto to himself on a cross, sending himself into hell he made at this time in history, raising himself again to glorify himself, so that he could offer a free gift of salvation to his creation - but would add a glitch so that only if his creation would believe he is himself because he needs man's praise to help maintain his ego, then he would send them to heaven when they die, or they would send themselves to hell that God created, but has no control over, if they do not accept his free gift of salvation, which they can't because *"There is none that understandeth, there is none that seeketh after God." Romans 3:11*

> *"There is no fear in love; but perfect love casteth out fear: because fear hath torment. He that feareth is not made perfect in love." 1 John 4:18*

The same person texting with me said:
"You know, God is going to judge the world when he returns. We look at the world and the wickedness in it, and we say where is the justice?"

Yes, there are wicked people, but are there seven billion wicked people all over the world raising their children and working hard to provide for their families? Do we justify our damning beliefs a little easier by calling wonderful God loving people wicked just because they were born in a country we are ignorant about? Do we further justify our doctrines by focusing on the few that fit the wicked meter of our judgments while ignoring the massive majority who would love nothing more than to teach the proselytizer about unity?

Let me share another story to bring this a little closer to home:

God: Hi there Myrzakan! You are from the country of Kyrgyzstan, and five years old I see. It seems you had a short and very damaging life being with all those men! It's a shame at how you were used for sex, and that one evening they didn't stop until you were dead! Let's see here, hmm, well, I cannot seem to find your name in the book of life which means you must not have ever believed in Jesus.

Myrzakan: But God, I was born and sold as a slave into the sex trafficking world, you can see that for yourself. In fact, you created me there! The men raped me since before I could talk. Why am I being punished for what they did?

God: Has nothing to do with what you did or what they did, only that you didn't believe in the name of Jesus for the sins of Eve. I do not show here that you sinned yourself. But you do carry the sin of Eve for eating a fruit I put in front of her. This sin demands unending torment if not paid for. I demand payment you know!

Myrzakan: So, what these people did to me has nothing to do with why they're wicked?

God: They are wicked for doing these things only if they do not believe in Jesus. Some of them repented and said they were sorry and now believe Jesus is my son, and so are in my kingdom now because they killed themselves after what they did to you!

Myrzakan: Who the hell is Jesus?!

God: Exactly! Depart from me ye wicked into everlasting fire!

My journey helped me face these heinous division creating beliefs and psychotic doctrinal perspectives I had of a god that demands that sin must be punished. It was a loving God who revealed my own egotistic self-righteousness in having placed truth above love, the Bible and our doctrines above a truly loving God we have yet to embrace.

Love is made absent or weak where there is also doctrine or belief present. Love does not attach itself to the belief we want to attach to love because love knows anything other than itself does not exist.

Likewise, judgment of others justified by any doctrine or belief is not made of love because it exists only in the mind from a manifestation made out of fear and called faith.

Love will not claim partnership to something that does not fully allow. Therefore, compassion is all there is to offer.

Atheism and Evolution

Let's take a small journey into a time where after learning much of what I was learning about church history and found that because my entire identity and belief systems were summed up in my doctrines that I found myself empty-handed and really wondered at times if there was a God at all. Maybe this relationship I had on my journey away from my family was all some chemical in my mind giving me these feelings of joy and visions from a very active imagination. After all, I was scared and completely stressed out in the beginning!

I also wanted to really understand Atheism and those who embraced it because by this point I wanted to know more people and what they found important to them and what they believed. I was no longer interested in what I grew up into as that had completely let me down. It was something I was just born into because of where I lived on earth. When in Pakistan, Islam. When in America, Christianity. When in India, Hindu. When in China, Buddhism. This is not rocket science! It is only labels that have defined its people by its religions.

As I said earlier, I found atheists and agnostics also very refreshing and engaging because they truly wanted to be open and more real with themselves and others. In fact, it was in this place that I began to see the great facade that existed within the Christian believer by seeing it in myself. I could see all parts of myself and the facade I existed in and called it holy and righteous standing on a pedestal which was firmly resting on my ego. Honestly, as I look back at myself as a fundamentalist, I just am so sorry for ever opening my mouth at all. What kind of things did I say? What path did I send people on to become like me? God help them!

I remember having a few discussions with my son Jordan when he was staying with me during the time I was separated from my wife. He brought up Richard Dawkins. If I ever hated a man, it was Richard Dawkins, one of the most outspoken men of our day about evolution and science and has an insatiable hatred for the God of the Bible. Back then I was still working through my stuff in my life, so it was ingrained beliefs I had that made me still resist so easily. But Jordan showed me some videos of him speaking about the numerous myths that existed centuries before and around the time of Jesus that had many of the same attributes we have defined Jesus with. Like, deities that were a son of God, had a virgin birth, birthday on Dec 25th, died, buried for three days and rose again, and many other similarities.

As I write this, it was this that was at the forefront of much of my other study into Egyptian and ancient Sumerian histories which continued to reveal more of the puzzle of our history as we have come to know it. Learning about the Rosetta Stone found in 1799 opened my eyes to a number of things as well. Very interesting history in how the writing challenged the claims of the church about the gospels. But, like so many other things the church faced, the power of its leaders would have their way in maintaining control of the church by suppressing this information.

The more I listened to Richard Dawkins the more I saw a man desperate to reach a blind group of religious god believing people that were sucked into a fairy tale of superstition and very childish reasoning. Well, that was the way he saw it anyway. And yet, based on all I was learning and absorbing about so many areas in life, I felt Richard making his cases on less than all the evidence of things in life that have a voice of their own, which I will touch on shortly.

Life was not only evolution, science, facts, results and archaeology. I have learned that Richard among other atheist have investments in their beliefs also, and when pushed, they resist just like we all do. To think that I came from an ape was a very unsettling thought to me as someone who was told that I was created in the image of God. But I had learned to look beyond my comfort zone at things and stepped into places with both eyes open and willing to see whatever the evidence proved. I needed to keep dropping my biases that controlled my beliefs which in turn controlled my biases. The more I did, the more clearly I seen.

Atheists were the people that brought light to me and to much of the Bible's corrupt stories. Maybe symbolism can be found in some of these stories to see them in a more tasteful light, but all I see is an angry and jealous god bent on having his way or "off with their heads!" This is five-year-old behavior here! It is true that God was the one claimed behind the genocide of people and whole nations because of their wickedness. Killing men, women, and children, and even smashing infants on the rocks and are glad about it, found in Psalms. Revenge and slaughter and blood all over the old testament, and into the new. One atheist recorded that God was directly claiming involvement or imputed involvement (God told me to) of 2,476,635 deaths not counting the flood as recorded in the Bible. Satan, on the other hand, has killed 10 people in the Bible - but not without God's permission! Oh wait, there is one more, God kills Jesus - Romans 8:32.

Silly or not, this is what the Atheists are looking at and the reason they desperately want to help the people trapped in these belief systems while the Christians fight them back to prove a loving and forgiving God based on a book that clearly records a very unstable and controlling god. Noah and the flood is one of the biggest stories they contest. Not only because there are other more ancient stories of floods from many cultures that predate the Biblical account, but that fitting all the animals, their food for a year and taking care of all the manure over a year is mathematically impossible. Moreover, there is not enough water in or on top of the earth, or rain (which is just recycled earth water) to cover the highest mountains. These are facts known today about the earth that they work very hard on to try and show the Christian and Muslim they don't know what they are talking about. It is not only anger that drives these wonderful people, but a truly deep love for humanity and the earth.

Either way, all I began to hear was the noise of the arguing. From a distance, the Atheist and Christian are filled with the same irrepressible desire to prove and solve their personal agenda, completely void of compassion. When the subject is all about knowledge and facts, love simply steps aside and sits on the sidelines while the raging intellectual battle commences. This is what I call planting your ass at the foot of the tree of the knowledge of good and evil. The tree is a metaphor to remind us of the duality that exists in life, not something we were supposed to spend our time on to try and prove a winner. Intellectualism on either side has no winner.

Ken Ham, a fellow I grew up knowing because I loved dinosaurs and all animals, was very convincing to my young mind that the earth was created about six to seven thousand years ago just as we were taught by our church. As evolutionist continued to uncover more evidence to rock layers, etc. Ken was right there behind them working to prove them wrong with his findings. As of today, I am convinced that the earth is billions of years old based on so much evidence from multiple sources and from different disciplines. And that there were civilizations as old as two hundred thousand years and maybe more, that there was a flood, most likely many at the same time around the world caused by the earth shifting as it is again happening today, creating the ice age, what we see in the leftover of Antarctica. Do I think we evolved from apes? No, it wasn't evolution that created man!

Atheists exclusively believe in evolution as an alternative to Design and dismissing other options and possibilities. However, science and archaeology continue to uncover evidence of the origins of species, ages of newly discovered artifacts and other things in life that seem to prove their theories. After concluding that the Bible doctrines I grew up into and my faith was mostly a fabrication, I pressed on studying more about this world without God - well, what I would think at times. But there was a bias here also with these people that I was aware of that I was beginning to learn. It was less a bias for something that proves, without doubt, something within science or evolution, but more of hatred for Christianity, Islam and the idea of God. On the one hand, you could have very meaningful discussions about things, and on the other hand, they do not stand for anything that could not be scientifically proven as fact and resist. Investments! If I said that I had a vision, they would not doubt that I totally believed what I saw. But if I could not prove it through the scientific method by reproducing it, then it is a chemical of the body or mind, part of our genetic makeup. For them, truth derives from fact and nothing else. Period! If I tell some Christians I had a vision, they would tell me I have a demon tricking me with their lies.

Embracing the idea of Atheism, I was feeling the despair of thinking that I would not see my father or mother again. But I did realize that if death was final, then once I was dead, I wouldn't know any differently anyway. That was still disparaging to me as I wanted more than just this life. I felt in my heart that there was still more, I was just somehow hidden from it.

One of my favorite philosophers is the late Alan Watts who has such a kind and fun mannerism about him. I can listen to him for hours. Incredibly deep thinker because he has traveled the world and steeped himself into the diverse cultures and religions. He also touched on evolution and some theories behind it, and while he would not say one way or another about his personal thoughts, I knew enough about him that he was free of all these beliefs that control our minds. I was beginning to learn that when we invest in anything to believe in, that we are still in the flesh and remain enslaved and hidden from the spirit of love.

There was more to life than these boxes we build for ourselves. Life was about something bigger than the safety we have made ourselves to believe in. It was at the risk of life that reveals our true pathway ahead of us. Time and time again I found my path only by stepping through doorways into the unknown. The more I entered by trusting in God alone, the more I wanted the adventures that were brought into my life. Faith asks us to trust in the unseen before it reveals itself with surprising fullness.

The months that I studied and spent time researching everything about Atheism, I found out my son Jordan was also heading down this same road. At first, this was a bit disconcerting, but that moment passed, and I moved on with what I have learned to do, and that was nothing. Anything other than nothing would be control, and what control did I really have anyway, and what pain would it end up causing? If by my leading, the blame would become the tool for the failure. If I let my children fall on their face, they have only themselves to blame. Yep, it is amazing how much effort we exert trying to do God's job in guiding our children. Oh, you caught me! Here I am an Atheist talking about God. It takes a long time to move from one belief to another, and it is not by choice, but by the truth that reveals itself to us along the path of life. Yes, I know, as a Christian I believed salvation was just a choice and, BOOM, saved! But I think we are adult enough here to face the truth of how we think and believe in things as we look back on our life.

I engaged with Jordan and became an encourager to him as he traveled along this road. He helped guide me to both great and funny videos on YouTube that frankly really opened my eyes to just how blind I was in my doctrines.

We spent several weeks exchanging stories and things we were learning and things to check out. Here is an example of how love works and how it allows.

The initial fear in me (when I said this was a bit disconcerting), if I would allow that fear to guide me, it would bring me down a road I traveled many times with my children while trying to protect them from making the wrong choices. What is wrong with making the wrong choices? More importantly, what is right about making a choice to love my son without fear and conditions? I can tell you that the relationship I have with both my sons surpasses anything I could have ever hoped for. We talk about everything because they have zero fear of what I will say, and often encourage them in what they are doing. They know I will never scold them or tell them they're wrong. I do ask them to think about some things now and then, but they know I will not judge them for their ideas and thoughts.

This is what love looks like over a perceived truth I may hold. How could I depend my life on so much emptiness in the truths I was told about? Today, I hold very loosely to truths I run across, something I believe in for the moment because I know God is so large that I am no longer interested in defining truth just to satisfy some analytical or intellectual desire to solve a puzzle within a doctrine that isn't really there anyway.

Then one day, Jordan called me all excited to ask if I heard of a comedian called Duncan Trussell and the The Duncan Trussell Family Hour. Well, no I hadn't. He went on to tell me that he could get into Jesus if the discussions didn't need to be so clean. Like, it would be cool if those discussing things could swear and just be real. I told him I didn't have a problem with that, and if that helps him to connect to something then that's great! Not that he was calling to get my permission, we were way passed that, but he loved to share with me his new exciting things he was involved in and learning. What son or daughter wouldn't? Well, I think most don't because they've been shut down long ago. The good news is that even though I shut my kids down in the past, apology and becoming real about myself and my beliefs went a long way to restoring those relationships.

Jordan went on to tell me that *"Duncan Trussell is really into buddhism and talking about Jesus and shit but that he was just totally being himself and it was so cool!"* I'm trying to give you a little taste of how a conversation with Jordan would go. Well, soon he had me listening to The Duncan Trussell Family Hour and several of his guests who were amazing people shared their spiritual practices and adventures traveling around the world and much more. I enjoyed it because it reminded me of the time at Higher Ground where we could be very real and share and talk in a way that was most comfortable for everyone. Wasn't it Paul that said, "...To the weak I became weak, to win the weak. I have become all things to all people so that by all possible means I might save some. 1 Corinthians 9:22.

During my time away, and the transformation that took place in my life while going to Higher Ground, I studied a lot about Buddhism and found it extremely enlightening and powerful. I even special ordered an orange Buddhist robe from China I have used from time to time in my meditation. Something just popped in my mind… I asked Jordan one day if he ever talks to his friends about me. He laughed and said, *that they all know that I thought you were an ass-hole", but they cannot believe what I am telling them now. It was like my dad was a wanderer, then became a hippy and got into Buddhism without taking drugs!* I laughed too in hearing that, and it warmed my heart to know by just facing the things in my life, that I had won the hearts of my children back, and even their friends.

This summer I'm going on a trip to Canada to go fishing for a week with my son Travis and four other guys who will enjoy sitting around the campfire, playing cards and some I'm sure will drink, and smoke. Where swearing is a kind of right-to-passage to be among the gang. And while I never got the taste for alcohol, today I feel completely at home in the company of men that drink because they are just more real to talk with. We will all enjoy each other's company and be a part of and engage in God's beautiful creation.

I think for the most part evolutionist, and scientist are closer to God than most Bible thumpers are because they directly play in Its garden and universe with eyes wide open and with less judgment. If something is found false and they are invested, they do hang on a bit at times, but in time let it go for the new truths. They are like little children at heart touching things to see what they do and how they work.

If there is a God, it's going to be a whole lot bigger and a whole lot more incomprehensible than anything that any theologian of any religion has ever proposed. ~ Richard Dawkins

---

Reincarnation

My understanding of reincarnation is not as much in being born or reborn again and again into the earth plane as though death is very final, but that death is a moment in time to step away from the life experience for a time of restoration and celebration within the greater reality of our essence, who we really are on the other side.

Reading and learning about the life story of Siddhartha Gautama, who later would be known as the Buddha, (meaning enlightened one, a knower) I was amazed by someone with such incredible drive for wanting to know the meaning of existence, and later a life filled with teaching others how to find and experience a life filled with gratitude, joy and peace. The teachings of Jesus are very similar as it relates to loving others, and only differ in the words used. I found myself very drawn to the eastern teachings, as there was a simple letting go of beliefs and things that pull our western mindset away from the spirit of love with truths. In fact, a closer understanding and focus toward love than what I had known in the church. There was no damnation or judgment here other than what you bring onto yourself throughout life. And this too is addressed within compassion.

When Siddhartha Gautama was asked, do you believe in God? He remained silent because he would not acknowledge something of the Source of All to be spoken about from a human understanding knowing it was impossible. Some people believe Buddhism rejects the idea of God, and yet these followers embrace love at a much greater scale than what I understood within the teachings within my church. The Buddha did not reject the idea of God as we have defined it but stood in a place of humility as to not give it recognition to not define the Source of life, which is impossible. The Jewish people also believed this way and understood that to name something was to define it to our small understanding of life. They called "Him" YAWH, just by breathing, Yaaaaaa, Whhhhhh. And in this recognized Source without having to give "God" a label.

My research brought me often to Alan Watts (whom I mentioned already), one of the great philosophers of the twentieth century who talked a lot about Buddhism and his journey into eastern religions and philosophies. I learned a great deal from Alan and began to see life through very different eyes. There was such a great love that he conveyed, especially when he laughed, that I just wanted more, and wanted to know how I could have that also. Alan was one of those people you run into now and then that just seem to exude so much love and passion that it is palpable. Alan was one of many people I gained new insights from regarding the eastern philosophies. Other great teachers such as Barry Long and Gary Weber and literally hundreds of others had their own philosophies on life that brought me new understandings that expanded my view of the world and who we are.

Years ago, I had wondered about our short life. I wondered how a life of 60, 70, 80 years was even enough to begin to try and make sense of the world in which we lived. And when you grow up in the Christian faith the clock is of utmost importance, and even more so if something should quicken a person's demise for fear of their spiritually "lost" condition. And then it is on to eternity one way or the other. What was it in me that was wrestling with this? Why would I not accept the teaching of my youth without questioning things? Of course, I was told that the devil and evil demons were out to drag me into hell, so to have these outside thoughts was to question my eternal security.

When I was even younger, there were a few times where I felt and in some way believed I had been in some place before, or saw that scene, or smelled that scent, which we understand as Deja vu.

Of course, that would be placed right up there with other superstitions like, oh, I don't know, believing in some magic words or water or death to save a person's eternal status perhaps. Well, no longer believing that I was bound to my doctrines, I began to first research things about Buddhism as that seemed closer to home as Buddhism was somehow on the really evil list per my upbringing. It's amazing how fear of the unknown drives us to stupidity. Sorry, I don't know a better word to describe taking a strong stand against something when we know nothing about it.

As I studied more about the eastern religions and practices, the topic of reincarnation was a large part of their beliefs. I would soon find out that for many years, dating back decades, that thousands of cases were being recorded, books written, and documentaries produced sharing stories of young children who expressed stories of when they were a pilot in the war, or a child telling her mother that she would like to go home to her real mom who lived in such and such a place. Stories with incredible detail that got the interest of those who devoted their lives to this research and verifying that the names and places, pets, dolls, birthmarks, scars and much more all verifying these children's stories. Many cases of children meeting with siblings still alive who lost a loved one who was the reincarnation of the child. I strongly recommend looking into some documentaries or reading some books on reincarnation as it will open your mind to more expansive realities.

We doubt so quickly as Christians to such a thing as it is not a part of the doctrines of the church, or quickly justify it away with speculative coincidence feeling good about ourselves for having solved another problem, so we don't need to face more truth outside our own.

The tighter we hold onto a belief, the more blind we become to its control.

This of course in only the tip of the iceberg as there is so much more available to you to dig into, such as near death experiences. Near death experiences have exploded in the past few decades. You might say that something is revealing itself from the spiritual realm, or that maybe more people are willing to share their stories without fear of what their family or church members would say, or we have more sophisticated equipment to monitor this, maybe all of the above. I had my doubts for a while because some people would see Jesus, some mother Mary, others just white light and more. My belief and bias wanted it to be only Jesus. Many were expressing that they felt like they were finally home and most said they wanted to stay. But there are a few stories shared of going into great darkness with an evil presence. I didn't know how to explain this at first, but after studying so many different topics, answers to these things started to reveal themselves. I will get into that later, on the topic of consciousness.

There was not as much available on this topic with other cultures, but I did find some articles and videos with stories from India and of the Muslim people and their experiences with the loving light and encounters with historical figures related to their culture, but also some very shocking unexpected revelations to those sharing their stories and how it changes their lives. I did find it interesting that Jesus was one of the biggest encounters to the western cultures, but Jesus was also there to greet these people in their experiences in some of the eastern cultures also. I think there is something that has to do with our current beliefs and fears, but also what we may be expecting, and because love has no fear, it gently brings them back home at the level of understanding they expect before revealing more of the realm they are at.

I kept asking myself, are these all just demons playing a deceptive trick on me? Angels of darkness disguised as Jesus, mother Mary or uncle John, but most always changing these people's lives to be more loving and compassionate toward others as they continue in life. Because of how I was brought up, and verses in the Bible that point to such things as being demonic, I questioned what I was learning for several years while studying so many things. But then I would move forward anyway, trusting in God alone and not my fear of what I was told and taught to protect and lead me along the way. I kept remembering the verse that stuck with me from the very beginning that allowed me to venture into the unknown without fear… I was embracing love more and more along the way, and the fear in me was slower falling away.

> *King James Bible*
> *"There is no fear in love; but perfect love casteth out fear: because fear hath torment. He that feareth is not made perfect in love." 1 John 4:18*
> *Young's Literal Translation*
> *fear is not in the love, but the perfect love doth cast out the fear, because the fear hath punishment, and he who is fearing hath not been made perfect in the love; 1 John 4:18*

I found the philosophy of Buddhism very humbling when I learned the overview of their beliefs. Because they believe in reincarnation (as many other people and civilizations do all around the world), they also believe in karma, which is the debt, you might say, of a past life or lives that this lifetime offers the opportunity to overcome with love and compassion toward self and others. The followers grow to embrace a love for their fellow man, no matter who they are or what religion they follow, to know they will continue to reincarnate to help others find themselves and what they call enlightenment. But more importantly is that they know they will want to reincarnate because to do anything other than that would be selfish and not of love.

I found this in stark contrast to the Christian belief where we are here once to love others, but more importantly, convert others to our belief, we call the Christian faith, learn to live in humility and in gratitude toward God, while looking forward to being rewarded in the next life with streets of gold and mansions of glory, I guess to satisfy that earthly lustful unattainable feeling of finally being rich.

Based on those two outlooks on life and death, who is the less greedy and egotistical? Which really shows humility to their fellow man with nothing to gain? Who is really willing to do whatever it takes to make sure that every soul that is a part of this experience we have on earth comes to an enlightened knowledge of the One, the Creator, the Source of all there is? When I think about who I really am as called to be a Christian, I think of humility and loving others without reward. When does love expect a reward? We sing songs like "the old rugged cross, where I will exchange my efforts some day for a crown." Where does this place our attention when thinking about our fellow man? What does this make God into? There was a lot to learn from the Buddhist and their culture and their understanding of love as only being something you give away without the slightest inkling that reward was some final outcome for payment. The only reward was being able to come back into the earth and continue to help our brothers and sisters find enlightenment, to experience the Christ face to face every day and every moment.

Just typing the idea of reward here is appalling to me because it is placing a value on a person and soul. In fact, a teaching that would send a soul away from the presence of God removes love from the picture, which means that God who is love would need to separate Itself. To separate love or make it less than is to make it unholy and unrighteous and imperfect to use the Christian words here. This is impossible or love as we know it is not love at all.

This brought me to more things that brought more light to what I was learning and began to watch video recordings of people under hypnosis, which brought me to a fellow by the name of Dr. Michael Newton who recorded and studied more than 10,000 cases over the course of his career that began in the 1970's. In his book Journey of Souls, he tells a very interesting story about how he got into this very unexpectedly because one of his patients who lived with a pain in his side for much of his life jumped back into another lifetime before his current life during hypnosis. Dr. Michael Newton was typically skilled at bringing people back to their childhood to find traumas or blockages to address and did not believe in reincarnation. After the appointment was over, he started to make phone calls to France where the patient claimed he was a soldier and stabbed by a bayonet during world war 1. Dr. Michael Newton was shocked to find the fellow's name and other details were all accurate. This was the beginning of over ten thousand cases he would go on to record over the decades ahead.

There would be others also that started their own practices, and one woman by the name of Dolores Cannon has some very interesting cases and information, along with writing many books comprised of the information gathered from her clients during hypnosis. If you're interested in prophecy, then you will find it interesting that much of the information at times is closely related to prophecies found in the Bible. However, as I continued to gather the information I was learning that things have changed, and that prophecy as a fact is more of what superstition would like to make out of it, than what would be better-named probabilities because we can change their outcomes.

I realize that by sharing these things with such little detail that it becomes very easy for the reader to judge me for being naive and gullible to be sucked into such things. As I stated at the beginning of Christian history, this is all I have been doing for over six years, studying and absorbing the equivalent of 3000 books, and I'm being conservative. But as I stood somewhat alone with no real beliefs to stand on anymore, I was free to learn and discern what I was learning with the truth that has guided me toward love while pursuing truth. It wasn't as though I could go back to what I used to believe. Once the lid is blown off and all that I learned about the history of the church and everything else, I would not be real to myself to embrace what no longer is true to me. The person who grows up into their belief system and remains there strengthening it do not know of what I speak, because I didn't either until I crossed that line.

I also realize that I have been very hard on the church and the doctrines people have created out of the Biblical texts, but mainly to touch those few people who thought these thoughts and never could articulate them or dare to come out and share their feelings because everyone they know would be critical of their questions. I am also doing it to shock some and maybe make a few people angry one way or another to take a stand for or against love as it is calling each one of us from within. We must cross that line of fear and learn to love our enemies, so we may learn that they are our brothers and sisters in the One. You will find out shortly that I do attend a church where I enjoy the fellowship of fellow believers from many religions or none to gather in the name of Christ and love, to sing, to hear great messages based on scripture and to enjoy gathering in as a community in the presence of the God of love and compassion.

As I type this, I remember several years ago going through a very unsettling time of knowing I had no solid belief in much of anything anymore, but that I also found that wonderfully refreshing to know I was not living my life having to prove to myself this or that but was just enjoying life more in the present moments than before. I was learning something about love and that loving others did not require any form of belief system what so ever.

"He who has ears to hear let him hear."

I understood this as pointing a finger away from me in judgment toward others who did not believe as I did. Now I see it can only mean to die to the bondage of what I believe so I can hear what is being said.

Consciousness

My research on quantum physics has taken place several years ago but was very important to understanding a bigger picture that is floating around in my head. As with much of what I have written, I am trusting my intuition to bring to mind the things I need to write to express my thoughts. Consciousness is an important topic because a veil has been placed over our consciousness and the reason why we feel lost to the spirit.

While I had studied a great deal on things about quantum physics, and how it seems that consciousness in some way controls the outcome of our choices based on thought of consciousness, I still found it difficult to comprehend and moved on to other things completely. For me, this is the spirit telling me it is not time yet to completely know this. As my journey took me through Atheism and a bit of despair to think we evolved, we live, and we die, there was something drawing me back to science and more specifically the subject of consciousness. I wanted to know if all the things the Atheists were saying about consciousness, of it just being chemical reactions in the brain were true or not. They would point out that even when the brain is dead after a person recently dies, that there are things science have not discovered yet about ourselves that at the moment seem to suggest a consciousness outside ourselves, but really it is not.

I wanted to know more so I found numerous things of interest. One was of people who have had heart transplants. These people shared, with their family confirming, that their lives had changed in various ways after the surgery. One person said he never cared much about what he ate or how he took care of his body. After the transplant, he found that he only craves healthy food and now has a routine in place for physical exercise. It is a common practice not to tell the recipient of the new heart from whom the heart came from, but in a number of these cases, they were able to track down the donors to learn more about him or her. This fellow found out that the donor was a younger man who was very fit, ate healthy food and exercised regularly.

A white man knowing that these things happen with heart transplants was concerned when he learned that his donor was a young African-American man. He mentioned that he was concerned that he would suddenly probably like rap music. It turns out the man now could read music and could play the saxophone, and later found out that the young man was a musician and played the saxophone. The percent of these cases were about ten to twenty percent that has this strange phenomenon related to consciousness.

Another scientist by the name of Dr. Rupert Sheldrake did years of research on telepathy with dogs and cats and other animals. He shared that they found that dogs mostly, but also cats would come to the window or door, or wherever they came to greet their owner when the owner was on their way home, and it did not matter how far away from home the owner was. Further study showed that in many of the cases, that the moment the owner thought about coming home her dog would go to the window or door waiting in anticipation for his owner.

We all know of stories of people with near death experiences. There is more than enough information on this, and many of the people claim they either go into a light or hang around for a while and watch the operation from a higher perspective. Again, trust the spirit to guide you down your own path of excitement and interest to study these things and come to your own conclusions of what this is.

While these are only a few of the many things I researched, I was becoming more convinced that consciousness exists outside our physical body whether the body is alive or not. If anything, it solidified my hope that there is life after life even though I was taught this being brought up in the church, and something deep inside told me this also. When learning that I could no longer trust what I was taught, I put my trust in God to lead me down a road of information and then trusting that God instilled in me a truth meter that would let me know what to trust or let go.

On things related to life between life (LBL) hypnotherapy and the stories people shared about their past lives, I found this fascinating and watched hundreds of videos of live cases and began to put some more pieces together. Many of these people were greeted by loved ones and wept with joy while telling their stories during hypnosis. What I started to learn was that during past life or regression therapy is that it was as though the people were seeing events of the past, but not just still pictures, but being able to watch as the scenes played out.

However, in LBL hypnotherapy the people were actually engaging with their loved ones or others, even energy /

ghostly type energies they could not fully explain, and were communicating with them. Moreover, most of the hypnotherapist were able to ask to communicate directly with the others in this realm. Again, a great book to begin to look into this is Journey of Souls by Michael Newton. I am only pointing out that there is more going on in our world as it relates to consciousness and the science behind it that is exposing these things to us in greater numbers every year.

Is science really man's attempt to be as God, or in some way prove evolution, or to disprove the existence of God? When I grew up, I believed from all I heard within the Christian circles is that science was bad and was infiltrating the church and deceiving its followers, especially in the theory of evolution. But are we fooling ourselves by avoiding science as a possible resource to help explain spirituality? Is it possible that science itself has been given to mankind from the heavens to help us better understand who we really are, or even to help us break free from the veil that separates our form from spirit?

We have been all wrong! What we have called matter is energy, whose vibration has been lowered as to be perceptible to the senses.
~ Albert Einstein

Everything is energy, and that's all there is to it. Match the frequency of the reality you want, and you cannot help but get that reality. It can be no other way. This is not philosophy. This is physics.
~ Albert Einstein

Is spirit something hocus-pocus or an energy and vibration within a much grander construct of the makeup of everything we call physical? Everything that exists is energy and has its own vibration. A computer offers us a way to create amazing things that are useful, but pull the plug, and that world is gone. It is a form of non-physical using ones and zeros to create and develop the most amazing technologies today.

Is it possible that consciousness is really some mega computing type system that interacts with the physical realm? I ask because the study into quantum physics and the black matter or space that makes up everything inside and around everything are in reality nonexistent. It comes into reality and out again at such a high rate that we only see solid as reality. Everything on earth and in space is made of the same stuff we are, atoms and their neutrons and particles that are excited and bounce around disappearing and appearing making the atom almost completely space. In fact, if you took all the space out of all the space that exists on the planet, you could hold the earth in the palm of your hand as it would be about the size of a large marble. What this teaches us is that what we believe is real in our perception of the world around us is entirely something else. This gives a new light into what we call the sin of the flesh. What are we talking about if nobody is really there?

Much of this is my theory as I understand it today which means it is highly speculative. However, based on much of what I have mentioned above about consciousness and matter and reality, it seems to give some indication that there is more going on here than meets the eye - literally.

Speaking of computers, I no longer believe that there are really smart people who invent things like this out of nothing other than they happen to be really intelligent beings that evolved to this state. I am not saying there are not incredibly intelligent people, but I am saying that Bill Gates or Steve Jobs are no more disconnected from this consciousness than the artist who paints a beautiful picture, or the composer who guides his orchestra to play music that moves its listeners to tears.

Nicolas Tesla, for example, was a genius who worked on systems to offer the world free energy, and if you read his story, you will find that he was a very spiritual person who claims much of his ideas came from a core within the universe. Are these people demon possessed or enlightened by higher forms of consciousness? How are they communicating with this core, this consciousness, this spiritual realm?

"If you want to find the secrets of the universe, think in terms of energy, frequency and vibration." ~ Nikola Tesla

"The day science begins to study non-physical phenomena, it will make more progress in one decade than in all the previous centuries of its existence." ~ Nikola Tesla

"My brain is only a receiver, in the Universe there is a core from which we obtain knowledge, strength and inspiration. I have not penetrated into the secrets of this core, but I know that it exists." ~ Nikola Tesla

---

When Albert Einstein was asked how it felt to be the smartest man alive, Einstein's reply was *"I don't know, you'll have to ask Nikola Tesla."*

I'm not trying to make a point using a few men's quotes on energy, but I do want to bring attention to several of our scientists who knew there was something more to our existence than what little we understood and believed as matter, a beginning and an end to life on earth, and heaven was another realm. Now there seemed to point to something more that was in existence within our universe and a part of life on earth that was greater and ever present.

The evolution of human consciousness has grown into understanding that we are all part of a whole, part of a

Source. The old consciousness said that we are all separate and different. All through history and all around the world the indigenous people communicated with the spirit. The native American people knew how to communicate with the spirit. The Aboriginals of Australia known to be about 60,000 years old knew how to communicate with the spirit.

The Egyptians and Jewish people knew how to communicate with the spirit. Enoch knew so well that his vibration caused him to disappear from the earth dimension. (Although there are those that believe Enoch went up in a space-ship.) Krishna, Siddhartha Gautama, Jesus, Mohammad, Mahatma Gandhi all knew how to communicate and live by and within the spirit. But before we get too far ahead, when I speak of spirit I am speaking about a single source and yet I am also speaking of a vibration within consciousness that determines our level of "connection."

And Enoch walked with God: and he was not; for God took him. Genesis 5:24

History and knowledge continue to shed light on new truths. Is faith in a believed truth, a grasping for a place of elucidation? Is it possible that because we don't know what we don't know, that what we are sure about is not what we are sure about?

With One Voice

I saw a magnificent and glorious Tree, and it's roots covered all of the earth. From its mighty trunk Its branches reached out in all directions, and on them where every type of bird sheltering within the soft leaves ruffling in the quiet breeze. Some chirping, some singing and some just enjoying the symphony.

Within this sight and sound, I understood an intimation of unity and a feeling of compassion. But why compassion I wondered. Was there something wrong, it all felt so right? All I could see was the variety of sizes, shapes, and colors of those that made this their home at this moment.

Then one bird spoke to my spirit and said harmony could not exist before because in the past some of us trusted in stories of history as though they and it exist. But in time we came to realize that love and light only exist within the moment of compassion.

He went on and said that in the past we were exclusive and intolerant and called it special and holy. Only when we all decided to love one another did we see the true beauty and wonder in our uniqueness, and only within compassion did we see our true unity.

I am bringing this in here because it became a part of my journey in offering a more expansive understanding of God touching the lives of people in all religions, all over the world.

One of my favorite documentaries is called With One Voice produced and directed by Eric Temple. I watched this over and over as it presents leaders from numerous faiths and practices who share in the most loving and compassionate way from the heart about their specific experiences and faith. I remember how I was feeling, it was like taking a bath each time I watched it, and the dirt (dogma) was slowly leaving me as I soaked in the words of these loving people all who reveal a love and beauty that has always been present within me, but covered up with dogma and fear.

You see, when love it present, the idea that we need to believe in something goes away. The strictly indoctrinated believer can only comprehend a belief system. I say this again, I stand on the outside of my box of beliefs. The person following their doctrines can only understand that I am in some way just believing in something else and that something is false because they hold the truth. I am hoping as we continue through the book that you will begin to learn to place your faith, your full self, into the presence of Love, which is the Source, the Holy Spirit.

With One Voice. Many of these people have stories of their conversions toward the light, stories of how something of great love touched them and opened their eyes. Whatever it was that called these people into their field of ministry was of the same Source of love that I knew

I was also connected to and being called toward. This was a love that covered my truths that separated me from others I disagreed with.

I want to comment on many of these people who were a part of the documentary and special things they had to share as well as how they impacted my life. I strongly recommend that you watch this video once a week over the course of a month and when done watching, sit outside if you can in a quiet place to ponder on what you heard. Take a pen and paper with you and write your thoughts down no matter what they are. This is how we begin to see and face those things in our lives that are just habits and triggers, or that come from our very essence within.

Sadhguru Jaggi Vasudev, Founder, Isha Foundation

I get emotional just watching this man because there is so much love and wisdom that flows from his essence and seen in his eyes and countenance. As he shares his encounter one day while sitting on top of a mountain, his words touched me deeply as I have had very similar experiences of ecstasy, that as he says, *"that his body could not hold. It is not something you attain; it is something that you merge with, it is something you become."*

Wayne Liquorman, Advaita Non-dualist Tradition

This fellow hit me as most profound because he came out of years of alcoholism and cocaine just to get through the day. My vise was self-righteousness. We all seem to need to be saved from something we attach to ourselves and justify it in one way or another.

Wayne comments, *"on that day he was completely transformed, that it was a peace that passes all understanding."*

Marcelle Martin, Quaker, Pendle Hill Core Teacher

When Marcelle shares her story of looking up at the stars, and they no longer were out there, but inside of her as a type of oneness, I thought of when I was sitting on my porch that one morning and looking at my surroundings like it was somehow all brand new, like I could for a moment see into a greater dimension of reality.

Grandmother Killian Pitawanakwat, Anishinabe Kwe Elder

A native American who simply connected with Spirit through drumming and singing. There is so much we don't know about how God moves in the lives of his people in every culture and every land all over the world. Nature is a very important part of our lives, and we need to bask in the presence of our Great Mother earth often to get focused on what is important.

Joseph Goldstein, Co-Founder, Insight Meditation Society

While exploring Buddhism with a friend while in the Peace Core, Joseph's friend was reading from a Tibetan text and the word, "unborn" triggered something he cannot really explain, but his excitement tells the rest of his story as his life was completely reorganized at that moment as he said. *"What are most people doing? Worshiping the teapot instead of drinking the tea."*

Swami Karunananda, Satchidananda Ashram - Yogaville

The piece, the love, the unity, the light as She expresses was from a profound encounter she had while walking down the road as everything changed for her. Again, these were messages I held on to as they sounded like the experiences I was having at different times along my journey.

Sheikha Fariha al Jerrahi, Nur Ashki Jerrahi Sufi Order

She helped me see that even though the mystic paths live within the traditional religions, they go beyond it. It has been some years since I first watched this documentary, but it is love that I have been given a greater insight into that goes beyond the truth. For some reason people stop seeking at truth while love is still waiting to be discovered.

Brother David Steindl-Rast, Benedictine Monk

Brother David steps into a mystic world as he discusses the unity we come into through experiencing an ultimate reality. Reality? This too was something I explored and learned about that began to open my eyes to a closer look at science, and just what it is. He also reminds me of my father, and I think given time, my father would also come to embrace love as the missing element in our daily walk.

Ajahn Amaro, Co-Abbot, Abhayagiri Buddhist Monastery

Ajahn talks about that part of our being that is transcendent and utterly unlimited. Outside of time and form, outside any kind of duality. If I was beginning to see a picture of what it means to communicate with Spirit, these people were all talking about the same thing and yet from their own personal practice and faith find this place of peace, joy, and oneness.

Father Thomas Keating, Trappist Monk

Father Thomas uses language outside of my

understanding but stretched me as I listened to him over and over, and little by little the depths of his message was slowly breaking its way through my hardened shell of programming and self-righteousness.

A. Hameed Ali (A.H. Almaas), Founder, Ridhwan School

A. Hameed Ali said, *"Whether we know it or not we are always a part of the creative Source. We can't be anything else. Not only can we not be anything else, there's nothing else!"* While I heard these words, they're meaning eluded me for several more years as I was not at a point to know them in my current understanding. But I will explain in my own words how the oneness of all there is fits into itself, and nothing can exist outside this Selfness.

Rabbi Davis A. Cooper, Founder, The Heart of Stillness

Rabbi Davis said, *"There seems to be a direct experience with something that is luminous, expansive and has no boundaries. And there seems to be some aspect of the human mind when we are able to drop our thoughts and simply be with what is; there seems to be some kind of commonality that crosses over all traditional lines."* Nothing more to say.

Dr. Mohammad Faghfoory, Professor of Islamic Studies, George Washington University

An incredible soft spoken and warm man who follows his tradition, but goes beyond the words on the page as these others have as he allows himself to be guided by the Great Lover of his soul.

There are many others I have not listed here that share in the documentary. I highly recommend that you check

out this incredible documentary at...
www.WithOneVoiceDocumentary.org

Hillel a Jewish mystic who lived 70 years before the birth of Jesus was approached by a religious skeptic who challenged him to teach the entire Torah while standing on one foot. Hillel replied, *"what is hateful to you do not do unto others. The rest is merely commentary."*

I was more in love with the Creator after watching this documentary because I saw Gods hand working in every single one of these people's lives where before I held them as my enemy. If anything, it made my outlook on life fill with joy and my view of the world so much grander. I see God as no longer a judge and damning his own children to some outside existence, but allowing free will to express itself through countless personal experiences, all which help to wake us up to our true identity and essence.

I was beginning to learn that so much more could be said if only a few passages of scripture were among a book of empty pages, and when found would only say...

> *Therefore all things whatsoever ye would that men should do to you, do ye even so to them: for this is the law and the prophets.*
> OR
> *Thou shalt love the Lord thy God with all thy heart, and with all thy soul, and with all thy mind. This is the first and great commandment. And the second is like unto it, Thou shalt love thy neighbor as thyself.*
> OR
> *Thou wilt keep him in perfect peace, whose mind is stayed on thee: because he trusteth in thee.*

Is there more we need to know to live? Is the rest merely filled with commentary? And do we not intuitively already know these things? Maybe all the commentary should have never been recorded because it wasn't meant for us, it has become a stumbling block. I'm sure if we look hard enough for love, that we could find many other verses in the ancient scriptures of every culture and in the hearts of the people that love one another.

A Glance at Love and Truth

"There is no fear in love; but perfect love casteth out fear: because fear hath torment. He that feareth is not made perfect in love." 1 John 4:18

Over and over I tested love by letting my fear go when everything in my belief system, my "truth" wanted to control the situation based on what I was taught and knew. When Jordan came home with alcohol, at first my beliefs lashed out, later as I let go and allowed it to happen, he gave it up because it was a means for him of retaliation. Travis got into really crazy hard yelling rock music. I don't care for it myself but not because of some righteous reason anymore. Things of my upbringing wanted to stop it and tell him he was wrong, that it was not good for him. I was already amazed at so many things I was giving up and how by stepping away from the fear I was now having fun with the psychology of love, purposely looking for ways to witness its power. Within a few months, Travis gave it up all on his own, an experience from my perspective he needed to go through himself that had nothing to do with me, other than to teach me to let go of having to control these things. Later he was excited to have me listen to the next composing he found on classical music that is touching his heart.

But whether Travis returns to some music I think is strange, has no bearing on anything anymore. The only thing I can think of now as to why I wanted to control these things, was because I had my own facade of righteousness to protect. Meaning, it was less about the thing I was trying to control and more about how I appeared to others who may be looking on from their righteous position. It's all quite exhausting!

I understand there are those times when the kids are playing ball, and it goes out into the street or the first few times in learning how to mow the lawn carefully or ride a bike. The things in life that we watch over to make sure loved ones are safe and protected is of a different nature. I know there is a line there that may get crossed now and then between the spiritual and physical. But things pertaining to the spirit, to a child's will to do as she pleases may cross the line of the rules of the house, respect for her parents or when to administer discipline and what that should look like considering a bigger picture of love trying to manifest itself into each of our experiences.

But I put a lot of the misunderstanding of love on the Bible and the doctrines we invested in that have distorted some of its message about a God of love that can also punish, and punishment of torment and fire takes the idea of punishment a bit too far wouldn't you say? But no, "the Bible says it, I believe it and that's good enough for me." Ok, if that is your perspective, please put the book down or burn it if that blows your hair back. But you can see here that if God is love, and God can also destroy, then how could we ever understand what love is if we follow a scripture where the message clearly goes against everything we know to believe deep within our hearts about love, and how it relates to life within our own family?

Let's look at divorce. We get upset when Christians get a divorce because they should understand love better than the world. Why? It doesn't matter if you're a Christian or not, the whole of society is trained to demand their way to make it in life. The truth I hold from childhood is to protect my life because it is more important than compassion for others. Couples that have mixed religions in their marriages are especially in trouble if they plan on keeping the peace in the marriage. What must they do?

When Paul says *"Be ye not unequally yoked together with unbelievers: for what fellowship hath righteousness with unrighteousness? and what communion hath light with darkness?"* He is thinking the very opposite of Jesus. Now these are good words if you know that truth will be paramount in your marriage and overrule compassion. But I honestly question Paul's spiritual position as he seems to believe the world needs to have a finger pointed in its face in judgment of all the wrongs going on in a person's life. Paul is no different than the old testament war and control that fills its pages, and is part of the reason we understand a warped view of love today in the western world.

> *"If you love those who love you, what benefit is that to you? For even sinners love those who love them. And if you do good to those who do good to you, what benefit is that to you? For even sinners do the same. Luke 6:32*

Jesus is really stepping out against thousands of years of war and contention. Payment for wrongs was the way of life and war was a continuous result. While Paul is standing in his righteous judgment in the name of truth over the "sinners", Jesus, years earlier, was sharing love while having a drink with the "sinners". Jesus believes more in the spiritual essence of man where Paul is afraid of the flesh.

Thou shalt have no other gods before me. Exodus 20:3

Do you ever question or wonder just who this God is? Does this sound like a God of love and compassion? A Father to Jesus? Sounds like he has some real jealousy issues? *"for I the Lord thy God am a jealous God"* I guess so. But at least he's not a vengeful God! *"visiting the iniquity of the fathers upon the children unto the third and fourth generation of them that hate me."* Wow!

But let's look at these words metaphorically using love as the guide.

"Thou shalt have no other gods before me."
If God is love, then we can read this as the energy, vibration and flow of love that comes from God and is perfect, even to say that it is a part of who we already are so there is a melding of likeness, because it has our best interest in mind.

"for I the Lord thy God am a jealous God"
When we make choices that are in opposition to this love, we are placing importance on other things, other gods (stuff) to rule our lives. Jealous not because he is insecure, but that love is so powerful that in its perfect benevolent way, even within the allowance of our free will, gently finds its way back into our lives and brings us back into the oneness that we already are.

Metaphorically I can find love within the Bible and a much deeper understanding as it relates specifically to me which will be different to you because you are unique and amazing as a child of the Father just as I am. However, there is more than enough verses that are difficult for me to understand metaphorically, but if interpreted literally, then we should question who the writer was and his connection to spirit, and what spirit.

> *Be ye therefore followers of God, as dear children; And walk in love, as Christ also hath loved us*, (can we just end it there?) *and hath given himself for us an offering and a sacrifice to God for a sweet smelling savour. Ephesians 5:1-2*

Now I know I am not supposed to read the last part literally, but when I read this, it sure reminds me of old testament verses of God loving blood being spilled and the smell of burning flesh. How is this not a parallel and even far more psychotic to say that Jesus was "God's" son? Metaphorically, yes! But literally, there is no way. Jesus said that "I and the Father are one". I am beginning to wonder if the Father that Jesus is talking about is somehow different than the God that Paul is talking about.

Is it not obvious why we have no clue of what love is? You might say, "Steve you're just twisting words around for your own benefit." I was not the one to write those verses, and if you keep reading it only gets worse. Either this is not love, or love does have fear and torment and Jesus is a liar. What I know for sure is that what Jesus was teaching and what Paul was preaching were two very opposite messages. One of love without fear and the other from a place of fear and control. And because control freaks demand their truth, war and hatred are not far behind, and in fact war has never ceased until this very day because of demanded truths over demanded truths.

Love is made absent or weak where there is also doctrine or belief present. Love does not attach itself to the belief we want to attach to love because love knows anything other than itself does not exist.

Likewise, judgment of others justified by any doctrine or belief is not made of love because it exists only in the mind from a manifestation made out of fear. Love will not claim partnership to something that does not fully allow. Therefore, compassion is all there is to offer.

Life Between Lives

During an LBL session, the hypnotist gently takes his or her client into a meditative state and then asks them to begin to express what they see. These sessions typically last from an hour to over two hours. As they begin to describe things, the hypnotist will ask very common questions about the surroundings, what the person is wearing and to describe what they look like.

Going back in time

One person was a native to South America around the 1500's. He was being trained as a hunter and would be going out to hunt that day with two of his seniors who would be hunting for a wild hog. He went on to describe in enough detail as the scene played out to how this all took place and then in the evening where the village came together to celebrate the hunt.

I watched several where the person went back to those days where France, England and other countries were burning witches at the stack. These can be very emotional as some would describe being able to speak to spirit who were telling them to let people know that what people know about their doctrines and denominations is not true and designed to keep people in the dark as to who they really are. Some of these people were the so-called witches while others were friends who looked on in horror knowing their friends heart and what they knew about the love they wanted to share that was being destroyed by the church and its community unwilling to listen to their message, claiming it is of the devil.

There was a documentary that came out that I recently watched that showed one man who seen this as a business and so many people were accused as being witches and making pacts with the devil and were put to death. One of the stories was of an older woman who was not very attractive and lived by herself was accused because she just looked like a witch. If you find yourself believing that there were witches at this time in history that deserved their fate, watch this documentary on YouTube or from your local library: Witch Hunt: A Century of Murder Episode 1 & 2. I'm asking you to stop living based on what you been told and begin to do your research on things like this so that compassion may begin to replace the dogma that controls our lives. But don't just believe the next video, blog post, article or book, but to keep at it until you uncover the truth revealed to you from within.

I watched another LBL session where the person was from a blue water planet and believed to have been a type of whale in its seas. Others from different planets and forms, one who remembers running from a large dinosaur and escaping into a cave. Most of them went back hundreds and even thousands of years recounting the details of being a king or queen, in England or Persia, etc. One person described being a person in the crowd at a place where Jesus was speaking to a multitude of people and I believe even described what Jesus looked like.

Coming to the end of life

What I described above are the first parts of these people's journeys into past lives, but the next moments at the bedside and after the person passes, opens up a new reality we all have wondered about. What is it like on the other side? Who's there? Is it glorious? Read stories yourself in the book by Journey of Souls by Michael Newton, and/or go to YouTube and find Michael Newton or Alba Weinman, and from there so much more.

I remember one story shared, as the person under hypnosis was describing his life as a man as a Native American I believe. He described his life which was very noble and the loving relationship he had with his wife and children. If you ever want a good bedtime story, some of these are amazing. However, you must be patient as you wait a long time to listen as it takes time for the words to come out as the people are in a meditative state. Anyway, this was one of those that brought me to tears at such love for his children, as he talked with them on his deathbed, then sent them out of the tent type structure so he could talk to his wife alone. He described his love for his wife, and also that he was not afraid to die.

I would love to share all the stories that these people share because they are so amazing and wonderful, taking the listener into a realm only our fondest dreams are made of. One woman who was part of a group of wagons traveling through the west was attacked by Indians and an arrow pierced her neck. She explains the scene and then her death where she rises above as she continues to watch things unfold. Her husband is cradling her face sobbing and kissing her, she says. She stays around after the attack and watches her burial. During this whole time, she feels a pulling toward the light, but she can resist it and does until she is satisfied that she can do no more here.

A Spirit World

She like others describe their journey through a white space or tunnel which gets brighter the closer to the end they come, and then into a place where they are met by those they know and love. The descriptions for each is a little different, from ice or crystal looking castles to shimmering seas and white sandy beaches. Some clients express themselves in great detail and with eloquent language which of course brings the scene to your mind as you can only imagine something so beautiful in your dreams. Then it dawns on you that you must have seen it before yourself, over and over each time you return from your last adventure into the world.

In the spirit realm, they mainly speak to each other telepathically. Many other sources that I've studied show that as people continue to become more loving and compassionate towards others and more open and real about themselves that their "vibration" increases, and these people's reality begin to experience a new earth reality in the physical form and will communicate more telepathically here also. This seems to be by will as to how we open up to others, but touch seems to be very intimate in that communication is done through touch, which of course indicates that being in judgment of others or keeping secrets will expose these attributes in us.

What I have also learned, and again this is many recorded cases from people's experiences under hypnotherapy, is that it is not heaven as we were taught. I have also read cases where people indicate that they are in heaven and see God, the Holy Spirit and Jesus, and Uncle Frank, and mom and dad, etc.. But more cases point to a place where things are not perfect as in holy and righteous, but a realm where family groups exist and gather for a time. Even places for rehabilitation and schools to help educate the souls for their next earth entry. And not just earth, but the souls from other planets as well throughout the cosmos.

I realize as I share this people wonder if I have lost my mind, but I am only recounting to you things I have studied in many practices where the overall consists is one of unity. Everyone has different experiences as you would expect being that our experiences on earth are so different from one another. And again, I love this aspect as it increases my understanding of the One, the Great Lover who is all things to all people. The diversity and possibilities of uniqueness becomes staggering and wonderful. Would I really want to believe that life and spirit is one of conformity? No. Freedom, liberation and joy come from loving others where God created uniqueness's without condition.

Punishment and Rehabilitation

As I have eluded to earlier, there are those who go through rehabilitation as their life on earth may have been a part of some very cruel experience, or was the perpetrator themselves who got lost along life's journey. These souls are not always met by loved ones, but guides who take them through a number of processes to help them cope with the reality of what they been through or have done to other souls while in form.

Never in a hundred cases that I have watched personally or read about were the soul was ever punished for their actions, although it seems as though there were some that have done unspeakable acts while on earth go to a lower vibration existence often described as a darkness for their rehabilitation and take longer before they come back into the earth realm. Either way, the only punishment that exists here is the shame and guilt you take with you to work through from your past life. Many of the cases reported that they felt bad about having to report that they failed to complete their agreement. But no one is judging these souls as to why they did this or that in life. Never did I get the sense that any judgement whatsoever takes place. What I did sense is an incredible love and support as you would expect from a loving grandfather or grandmother who delights in his or her grandchild. There is a time to discuss things with your guides or angels of which it seems there is typically one who is the leader or in charge, and then other guides who help the soul work through their past life events and choices on earth.

There are also cases that I watched where people under hypnosis had other entities or spirits that existed within their own soul space, sharing space within the body. What we call possession. I grew up being told, demon possession. Over the years, I have watched a number of cases of church leaders working with people to rid the body of "demons" through exorcism. In each case, it was in the name of Jesus and a forceful presence of yelling and screaming from both parties. I grew up understanding this was the way and surely believed in such things. But then after watching numerous cases of both men and women who lead the hypnotherapy session learn of these additional spirits, he or she quietly asks to speak to the spirit, and then through conversation lead them to the light. Very interesting cases, even bodies moving and twitching at times, but always a very calm process.

These are not demons but souls of people that died and never went to the light for many reasons. But I could see where people come to this idea because these souls make a choice not to go back to the light, and based on their experience on earth can be very rough in their characteristics. These are souls who often were killed in various traumatized ways, or are younger and feel their life on earth was too short and therefore angry and want to stay. I was beginning to see where the church and those who are driven by superstition and it's teaching, with little information believe such things from a very fearful understanding, especially when the Bible, the Quran and other religions teach of reward and punishment, heaven and hell, angels and fallen demonic creatures.

Through study on the different eastern religions compared to things people would share here and there while being asked questions under hypnosis, is that there is an Akashic record that remains with the soul, and at the level you leave earth, so you return to work through more experiences to raise your resonance, your light, through compassion for others which in turn raises the vibration of the collective consciousness of groups and even the entire world. The idea of God being a source of love, a flow that energizes all that is, continued to paint a larger picture in my mind. God is not dictating events and things that happen in our lives sitting on a throne in heaven like Superman. We are part of this flow and through that in control of our own creativity and reality! God is the light and love that we play within form and have our being. We are always within the One. God is our eternal home.

To conclude on this part, I found that much of what the Bible teaches fits very nicely with much of the conversations of what takes place between the soul and his or her guide(s). They recognize that money caused them to be greedy, or just becoming distant from others because they were afraid to engage in life, or business owners who got caught up in power and control and the esteem it brought to them. All in their own words realized that they had become blinded to their purpose and often failed to accomplish their intended goals based on their agreements. In conversation with their guides, the guides would tell them that they were trying to plant ideas into their minds to guide them, but the souls were often to engaged in the world (the flesh per scripture) to hear. Some conversations that took place expressed the recognition of these ideas that came to them that helped them make good choices in their life.

Agreements and Contracts

In the previous section I brought up agreement a few times. I'm sure this raised an eyebrow, it did for me as I was hearing this over and over throughout these conversations. I was beginning to feel more empowered to think I did not just happen on earth, but that I was a part of a much larger existence. I always believed my choices would affect others and in fact could be felt for many years, and in fact could change the course of life on the earth after I'm gone. Hearing and reading about these things was both solidifying my understanding, but also expanding it as

I felt like I was much more a part of others who were on their adventures experiencing life for themselves while making choices for the betterment of all of mankind.

A whole new understanding of the verse in the Bible was unfolding to me, where Jesus is asking us to love our enemies. Jesus, being far more connected to this spirit realm, knew our enemy could very well be our soul brother or sister. I may very well have an agreement with a soul-mate of my past lives who would challenge me to face my belief systems. The implications by this point we're going through the roof as I continued to see a larger and grander picture unfold before me. Jesus was asking me to love those I hated because they were a part of my extended family sharing this life time with me to help me perhaps learn forgiveness and mercy.

Based on quantum physics and all that I learned about the singularity of all energy, the unification of energy, and that there is never a loss of energy but only a transference, the ideas that were beginning to build in my mind were that of a continues joy of the magnificence of what was presenting itself to me. I further studied the Bible scriptures and it was beginning to show me new understandings within the metaphors of scripture that were also beginning to teach a much deeper meaning to the words within their stories.

The children decide their parents

Well, it only makes sense then that if we have these agreements we make within our spiritual family that we also choose our parents. From the numerous stories told through hypnosis as well as many children recorded claiming they choose their parents, makes this a very likely reality. I did not decide to write this book on a few accounts of someone's testimony, or on one form of source that claim what they have experienced or somehow knew related to any one topic, but on many accounts within hypnosis, people who share their stories, researching very old resources in books, eastern religions and even Channelers sharing wisdom and answering people's questions.

While I am offering a number of ways by which information is gleaned to convey my findings, again I am asking you to research this information for yourself under the direction of what you believe is guiding your life.

I think there is more to Jesus' statement in mentioning that the children are like the kingdom of heaven, or reign in the heavens, (depending on translation used). What you will also find out is that children typically before the age of seven and others earlier is that they express themselves in so many ways that often alarm us. Well, you say (if you grew up in a strict Christian home), my children were perfectly normal and did not display any form of strange behavior like you're suggesting. From all I have studied on this subject, that makes perfect sense to me as the parents would quickly stifle the child long before they would allow these experiences to be expressed through the child. How many times does it take in a child's young life of being told they don't know what they're talking about, or you're wrong, before the child learns to keep her mouth shut?

My parents said that I never scribbled, and that the first thing I ever drew was a fish. I'm not real sure what the meaning of that was at the time, but I could be expressing myself while not even knowing my birth sign is Pisces. The fish is also a representative for the church because we were living in the era of Pisces, which was assumed as its own from very ancient societies. But I'm not going to get into astrology as I know almost nothing about it, mainly because I was raised to avoid it because it was evil. Again, fear of what we are told by others' fears, controlling our lives because we do not trust that God is present enough or in control of our spiritual lives. Hopefully by now, you will begin to set down these fears and begin to explore these things, trusting in God alone to lead you into truth through love.

Most of the stories through hypnosis were very matter of fact in that each of us are made up of spiritual groups or families. Those under hypnosis would explain that they would often stay for a time, to spend time with their families and friends, but that in time they would discuss the next mission, working out plans, and even the different places to exist. Then they would embark again as they enter earth once again as a baby. Those in the group would decide among themselves what was best in helping the others within their group grow more spiritually, or grow in love for themselves and others as we work to obtain enlightenment as Enoch did, the Buddha, Jesus and many others had over the centuries.

Reborn again on earth

There are the stories of young children who you can tell by their tone and facial expressions as they express themselves and talk about choosing their parents, that this is not a secret or strange to them. The idea of choosing their parents is so matter of fact, that they often wonder why their parents are asking these strange questions that are bringing this information out. It would be only cute if you found one here and there, but hundreds of cases start to paint a new and larger picture of evidence to this. Reincarnation is a part of our world and continues to make more sense as you listen to and read the stories. What I was learning was how deprived I have been from things in the world. I can travel the world on the Internet and find that what I am sharing here is very normal in the understanding of so many cultures.

One day I too stepped forward and said I would go. When I opened my eyes, it was my mother I seen first.

Well, if you wish to entertain the thought at all, the implications to contemplate are great and wonderful. Go ahead, after you read the next few words, set the book down and give some thought to what this could mean to you and how this can expand your understanding of things in so many ways. Think of your siblings. I was there with all my siblings (still am at the same time in spirit, which is our greater or ultimate reality), deciding in what order we would be born, who would be the miscarriage, stillborn or aborted baby. Who was coming into life disabled in some way and for what reason and to effect who? In spirit, the group already knows who the parents are, so what are the implications of recognizing the current earthly experience and belief system in place of that light?

I think of my sister Sai Lee who my family adopted from Korea when my father was on a job there to build a radio tower. My parents said that she ran up to them when they visited the orphanage several times and decided to take her home. What guidance is in play to make that all work out? Sai Lee was in the reign of the heavens with our whole group of family and friends making this happen. Why? What role was Sai Lee supposed to play and for what reason? Who is she supposed to impact by being born an orphan and what purpose of being adopted into our growing family?

I remember that my wife and I made the decision to have our two biological children. They would not be by mistake as so many are… or are they mistakes? Then there was the decision to adopt our daughter Alicyn from Korea, and so began the process of making this all happen. From our side, it seemed we struggled through this and that, certainly a lot of paperwork and requirements and waiting. And yet the implications and timing that took place that also included Alicyn's biological parents being part of the spiritual group and the role they would play as wonderful people who were just too pour to take care of her. What is Alicyn's role, and the role in our lives?

The roles we play

Much of what I was learning with this started to open my eyes up to many other things as I began to look at and into the lives of every person I read about or knew. The roles and occupations that we find ourselves in is endless. From the beggar on the street to the movie stars to the leaders of the world. Those that are starving around the world, why? This is not just some cruel out of control god we don't have answers too, but a God of love flowing in and through the most amazing orchestrated drama ever composed, where the actors are you and me as the creators of our experiences. Go ahead, it's okay to let your mind go on this. Let God lead you into your greatness so you may learn more of who you really are, magnificent and beautifully made as part of the Great Lover. What is the implication of the person who is rapped? Who was rapped and who was the rapist, and what in this experience and emotions do they want to learn about? What about the child who will live for only five years because she was born with a terrible disease? Just imagine with me the love that will rise from such an act? Not just on earth, but who is this soul in the heavenly realms? Magnificent!

> *For now we see through a glass, darkly; but then face to face: now I know in part; but then shall I know even as also I am known. 1 Corinthians 13:12*

Remember earlier I talked about Hitler. Let's step for a moment into the reign of the heavens, this place beyond the veil that keeps us seeing through a glass, darkly. Now face to face as the souls of those present in this group numbering in the millions. The age in time was moving from a darkness controlled by leaders who masked themselves under the righteous and holy umbrella of the church, teaching the world of its *God is separate, and reward and damnation* theology, into an industrial age which will create greed and control among the souls that will surpass anything the world has seen. The souls of the earth have completely lost sight of who they are as they enter the world, and completely lost the focus of their self and group appointed tasks and agreements.

And be not conformed to this world: but be ye transformed by the renewing of your mind, that ye may prove what is that good, and acceptable, and perfect, will of God. Romans 12:2

What is the will of God? If God is playing the role of being present in and through everything, allowing creation to express itself through us, and our role is to raise the consciousness of the reign of the heavens, then the will of God is also our will as we are a part of the Source of All that Is, the Oneness of All, The Great Lover, our heavenly Father. How do we transform the world toward Oneness? By the renewing of our minds to what is good, acceptable and perfect.

Now some may not like where I am going with this, but while I recognized Hitler and his cronies to be of the utmost "humanly" evil, I was now able to see Hitler through the eyes of the Great Lover as It plays its part of loving through allowing even the most heinous of crimes known to mankind soon to unfold on earth. We are the creators of our world and its outcome will be the result of our efforts to engage in love, with the encouragement of the love of God caressing us in its benevolent energy.

When the call came to what was being conceived as to what later would be called the holocaust, an incredible and mighty old soul stepped forward, with a thousand lifetimes of service marking his belt, fully understanding the ramifications of his soul choice. On earth, he would be born to Alois and Klara Hitler, and they would name him Adolf. Yes, Adolf's parents were present also among the group, along with millions of souls who would be born into German and Jewish homes. Those souls among the Jews and even the children who would be born into that time to parents who would face death in the camps, all knew exactly the role they would be playing.

Some would say that hell is too good for a man like Hitler. I say the heavens is worthy of such a soul who came to earth as a man to bring about so much pain that the whole world would rise up as one, united in love against such an atrocity to mankind, raising its collective consciousness.

Because of other resources I have studied, there is a place within consciousness that is dark. This goes along with vibration of sound and light. The other side of the veil is not heaven as we've been told. There is no indication through thousands of accounts that heaven is a single place as we in the church have been taught and believed, but countless expressions of heavenly places existing for those within groups of souls and guilds and angles and much more we don't know. Jesus, like others ascended out of form (the human biological form their essence occupied) before death of the human body. There seems to be levels of ascension or dimensions of reality that coexist as we grow and experience life on earth and quiet assuredly in other parts of the cosmos – and at the same time.

There are also levels of darkness, where vibration of life is lower than that of earth's, what is called 3D lineal existence or resonance where people who make choices to pillage, rape and murder others reside for a time of rehabilitation, but within that level of their resonance of being, whether in the soul only or taking part in the body on some other planet. This is not punishment as though God could ever be disappointed with Itself or what we would know as the Expressions of All That Is, but part of the laws that govern these realms for the purpose of edifying the soul's growth. And I am not speaking of laws like, thou shalt not… That is a human imputed idea to operate within form.

Do your research and give some deeper thought to the idea of reincarnation and a realm of consciousness where we select our parents. Do you have a purpose in life? Does life seem unfair to you, or did you choose it because there are things that need to change in your life. How are you impacting the lives of others around you, and who are they in relation to you? Chances are very high that the one you call your enemy is the one on the other side of the veil called your closest friend, perhaps even a past life lover or soul-mate.

God said to me, "Thank you my precious expression, for allowing Me to experience life through your experiences of life".

The Art of Channeling

Ok Steve, up until now I was just marking you off as some hippy type free loving freak who got caught up in some weird shit. But when it comes to channeling, this is totally of the devil and I want nothing to do with it!

Channeling or anything close to it like meditation freaked me out to, and I believe I was not guided to this information until I had a solid trust in God alone to lead me into it. I found that God was only love and by the definition of love cannot be anything other than love. The liberation that continued to free my life of its fears was driving me onward to new explorations of life and the wonders of all the magnificent and beautiful people who are just expressions of the Great Lover as I Am and You Are.

Mary and I went on a trip to New Mexico in October of 2016 offered through our church. One of our stops was to meet with Fr. Richard Rohr a renowned Catholic Priest, although he would be too humble to accept my statement as being renowned. The pastor of our church gave us small snippets of several pages of several of Richard Rohr's books to read so that our group of about twenty would be on the same page as to what we may discuss during our time together. On the plane ride there, I read the pages. Immediately after reading the information, a picture came into my mind of a willow tree. And these are the words I wrote down as they came to me in that moment.

The Source of all there is, is like a willow tree. It is in itself all that is, strong and sturdy. And within the winds of change, able to sway and bend with the flow of the season.

Its limbs are generations of historical personalities, with its leaves a unique expression of itself as each one of us, as ever expanding experiences toward unity and wholeness.

Yet there exists a great veil, like a cloud separating its awareness from itself. But the love that flows is ceaselessly calling out to its own leaves, nourishing the flitting and fickle limbs from its benevolent roots, a place where it decided to play a game with Itself. ~Steve Nyhof

Give some thought to where the art comes from in a small child, the girl that plays the piano by ear by the time she is five years old, the scientists who discover the same cure at the same time in various parts of the world or the inventor who realizes that her ideas are being developed across the world. What about the epiphany you had that one day, or the inkling you had that told you to turn right instead of left? What about the intuition you had one day that made you make a phone call to your mom? Maybe a dream of confirmation that your loved one is fine on the other side. We are typically completely unaware of all these things because we have been taught out of them by age seven by doctrines that condemn such ideas.

You walk into an art studio and are drawn to a painting that takes your breath away. What is there that is inspiring you in that moment? What is it that draws you to it? Have you ever played a game and got lost in the moment because you were having so much fun?

Is there such a thing as light and wavelength electromagnetic radiation producing resonance at an atomic scale that is in some way connecting your resonance with a consciousness of the same resonance? Can vibration actually cause the physics of form to hide from perception? Music is probably at the highest of connection we as humans come to enjoy. Things such as light, sound and vibration is what make up some part of us I do not understand, but somehow know that music can control my emotions. A sad slow song, to a happy fun dancy beat, to celestial strings that bring us into the heavens.

This is all considered channeling! Channeling is not something strange and outside as though new or indifferent to us, but that it is our connection to who we really are in a world we call home where all our intuitive ideas and inspiration come from!

You see, not only do we all channel, not only is it the very thing in which we should exist and have our being, but we unwittingly are channeling every day and all the time as we communicate with our higher consciousness (what we might call God, the Holy Spirit or the Christ) when something about us is heightened to make connection with It. Or lower within depression where we may connect with some lower consciousness. It is not an entity as in separate from God, or demonic, but levels of consciousness. It is the closest to making some connection to what I am trying to communicate.

Channeling I have learned is about as diverse as art or music or poetry, or all of them combined. It is unique as we are all unique and yet a part of the All as One. I think this is beautiful and again makes God a lot bigger to me and further out of my comprehension where it belongs.

Water is attempting to communicate something to us. Negative emotions prevent the water from crystallizing. Positive emotions allow it to develop into beautiful hexagonal shapes.

~ Dr. Masaru Emoto

Do some research on water consciousness by Dr. Masaru Emoto. Go to google and look at the beautiful crystal images that are produced by a beautiful song, a kind word or even just thinking about positive words. The information on water consciousness alone speak volumes to the importance of living in harmony with the world around us vs demanding a truth that creates negative and fearful emotions.

I know I have said this over and over, but it bears repeating because it is so important. From very young I can remember being told that we must not trust our feelings, and that knowledge was how we make proper choices in life. But I don't need to be intelligent or well versed on something to be compassionate. When someone is hurt, my innate within me goes into action. I feel therefore I act. My wife and children didn't need a husband and father pounding out words of wisdom and truth, they needed love and attention. Hey dad, look at this picture I just colored? I can say that is beautiful honey, or tell my daughter the "truth" of how it could improve. I was the dad that told her how to improve it... Who gives a rats ass if it is the ugliest drawing on the planet! Will it somehow destroy the universe? Are you embarrassed by it? Get over yourself! I think it teaches our children to be perfectionist so they grow up hating what they do when they fail, and what was left to feelings have been crushed right out of their precious souls! The essence of God within.

There is a lot more behind the science of consciousness that we can learn just by studying this subject of water consciousness. If you're not afraid of what this will reveal, the implications of this information is mind-blowing and I strongly recommend spending some time checking out Dr. Masaru Emoto.

One lady by the name of Tina Louise Spalding explains in an interview I found on YouTube that she was beginning to feel something wanting to write some words down, so she picked up a pencil and paper and wrote down some words related to the spirits that was trying to connect with her. There is far more to her story and you may want to find it. This all came slowly to Tina and in time she went to her computer and found that Ananda (what Tina describes as the nonphysical teachers) could type faster through her than she could on her own.

Tina channeled a book called "Jesus My Autobiography". Would it be too much to believe that

Jesus is still sharing his message today through other people? If he were, and it rang true, would you want to deny a message Jesus wants you to know in this incarnation of your life? It's a very easy read. Another book I am still reading as it is a similar book called "The Course In Miracles" channeled by Helen Schucman, an atheist by decision. In October of 1965 she started to write, a voice in her head telling her she can call him Jesus. I'm not going to be the one to tell you at what point along your path to read this book, and much will depend on your religious background, but I would strongly recommend that you let God guide you to this book when it is time as if you think what I am sharing is strange, you will find "The Course In Miracles" very challenging and without doubt incredibly insightful, far beyond human knowledge.

There is a great documentary I stumbled upon, like most of the things, called "TUNING IN: Spirit Channelers in America". Here you can learn a summery about some of the bigger names of Channelers and their stories, their backgrounds and how they came to feel they were called into this service to bring wisdom from the other side into our earth at this time. We have become completely lost to who we really are and spirit is breaking through our hard heads that speak of spiritual things across the pulpits or knocking on doors, but run and hide and call it demonic as soon as God is asking to be invited.

> *"There is no fear in love; but perfect love casteth out fear: because fear hath torment. He that feareth is not made perfect in love."*
> *1 John 4:18*

I watched many of these Channelers and listened carefully to their messages. Again, being brought up in the church and told that this was only of the devil and evil and sinful, that my programming more than my heart was questioning what I was stepping into. But the more I listened to their message the more I found the message to be one of love and compassion, of unity and oneness which rang true to my heart. If there were clever demons enjoying their deception by sharing a message Jesus shared about loving others, then these were truly some messed up demons that "Satan" would not be very happy with.

If this was wrong, then that would mean that the alternative was in the hands of the god of the old testament who was extremely unstable in all his ways. Once I trusted in God alone, the god of the Bible became clear to me that he was not the Father of Jesus, or of you or me.

If it is demons, then I am still waiting for the twist in the message. Perhaps they are just keeping me focused on loving God and my neighbors as myself so that I stop following a truth about a god that will condemn me to hell for not giving him my undying worship and allegiance. You will need to choose. Either a God of love with no strings attached and loves you unconditionally as love can only do, or a God who "says" he loves you and offers grace and forgiveness only after you give your life to him and bow down and worship him.

All that I learned about demons or what we would call "fallen angels", was becoming something else to me which I alluded to a little earlier, and will go into more detail further on. What I learned by listening to well over one thousand and counting channelings by maybe fifty or more Channelers, is that "the reign in the heavens", that this space of consciousness was also not perfect. I remember listening carefully to how things were said and thinking that no mistake could happen if this was God speaking because God is perfect. But then I also thought, that is my preconceived idea I am imputing onto this person and consciousness not knowing anything about it. Moreover, I found that some people hear the words in their heads and then convey in their understanding, where others (allowed only through permission) to give themselves over to having the consciousness (group or entity for human understanding) take over only that part of the person while channeling.

I started to learn that some were at this for many years, even decades like Darryl Anka, and Lee Carroll, two of my favorite Channelers. These people have perfected their skill where others I watched were just learning and stepping out to be heard. In the beginning, Tina Louise Spalding would jerk her head back when the connection was made, but today she has become more and more comfortable with the connection and smoothly goes into her channeling session.

What I am pointing out is that we channel every day within our joy and inspiration, and some from writing or allowing their guides, higher selves (consciousness) to take over for a time to share some wisdom to help guide their listeners.

But it can be different also. One group of scientists were messing around with sound systems and vibration levels and were able to connect with altered states of consciousness. One of the men in the group shared that he and his son were always excited to go to bed at night time because they met each other in their dream state and went on adventures together. How cool is that? But one testimonial is not enough to convince me, although by this time I have amassed so much info that together it was already painting a very large picture for me. I found that this is a very widespread practice among children who because they don't know better, just believe this is part of life and is to be expected.

The other thing I was learning from all these sources and information was that intuition, that which is a part of the "feeling" self is of greater importance, if not the very driving system that should be guiding our lives, and not knowledge. Like I said, I grew up being told feelings are bad and cannot be trusted. This is purely doctrine speaking as much of Jesus's teaching was about loving God and your neighbor, to caring for the poor, to giving up your life for your friend. These are choices of the heart. These things cannot be quantified or analyzed by the brain as they are of the very essence of who we are at the center of our heart.

Water has memory and carries within it our thoughts and prayers. As you yourself are water, no matter where you are, your prayers will be carried to the rest of the world. ~ Masaru Emoto

---

Every cell in our body is alive with memory. Water is alive with memory. There is no belief or system that is proven by the intellect that will ever offer the answers to the core of man's existence. Love will have its way, and I don't say it that way as if to strong arm something else, but that love is so powerful that after the darkness is finished screaming and kicking and flailing its arms, love will be right there, always was, never left, to embrace us with the deepest compassion and kindness we can ever know.

I am going to close this chapter with two scribed channels. One of Kryon's messages about creation, channeled through Lee Carroll. And a message channeled by John Smallman called "These are indeed exciting times!" I listen to Kryon almost every day to lift me up as he shares the love of God in such refreshing new ways. You can find Kryon on YouTube, and Lee's voice is one that deeply soothes and settles your soul as Kryon steps in to share incredibly celestial information.

Message from Kryon

Greetings dear ones I am Kryon of Magnetic Service. My partner steps aside and removes himself completely, he has to in order for the purity of the information to be accurate and true without a filter of humanism. The system is beautiful, it is a system of intuition which uses the human's intellect, the brain, all the language skills and yet without the filter. The God inside comes forward in beauty and benevolence, has allowed to speak. Using your language and the language which we are going to call and have in the past the third language. It has nothing to do with three languages. The third language is a metaphor, the three in numerology is a catalyst. A catalytic number would be that energy which then would change things that come in contact with it and that's you. What some of you will receive information even as I proceed that is completely different than the information that the voice will say.

There's an entourage here, it's not what you think. You talk about entities, you might even talk about Kryon as being a singular entity, it's not! It's not exactly a group, it's a consciousness that brings with it others who are also consciousness and fills the room with love. In a multi-dimensional way you cannot count what is here for that is a linear operation, but you can sense it, and that's good enough. If you're in love with somebody do they say "count it", they do not for it represents the essence of an emotion and energy that has no counting, and that's who we are. I present these things to you because I want to show you some things you didn't expect. I want to show you the glory and the grandness of you, far beyond just you. What if everything around you, everything, was a system? A system that was planned by your consciousness when you were not here. Listen to me! If you have God inside, to whatever that means to you... If you have the essence of the Creator inside, that means you were here before creation. I want you to use that part of you which believes that to stand by and validate a few of the things that I tell you.

What I'm about to tell you, and the story I'm going to give you, pieces and parts I have given before but perhaps not altogether and in this way, for the reason I'm doing it. There are times when I want to sit in the chair and just celebrate you! You're family! Human beings have a tendency to look up at the Creator and feel less than the Creator. Don't ever do that! For when you are not here in this earthly body you are part of the Creative Source that made the earth itself. And if you can understand and realize this, you're going to be able to change what you do in the body. You are valuable to the planet beyond belief. You have reason to be here even if you can't figure it out. I ask you yet again, do you have to know everything to walk forward? Really? And we say it yet again, you use faith every day of your life in so many mundane things and yet when it comes to your spirituality you stop and you analyze. You walk to your auto and you get in and you trust it's going to start and go. All of those parts, the workings of perhaps the internal combustion engine are not yours to know. You don't care, you simply go home. Why won't you do that with God? Why don't you trust the workings that you don't know?

I want to enhance this, I want to give you a bigger picture, and as I do this I want you to sit with me and go back in time. I want you to go back to creation. I want you to go back to the creation of the universe because you were there. You're not just an old soul, for that will give you an idea of how many lives you've lived. Go beyond that, peace of God (referring to the human) be a part of Creative Source, an old part, a part that had no beginning and no end. A circle of reality that always was and always will be. There is only one truth in the universe, and that is God exists. And all that is around it is imaginations and shades of the existence of God, for all around you, all you see, is God's creation. Everywhere you look with eyes that were created by God, you see God. But with free choice as a biological person, human being (said with great honor and love) you have a brain that is allowed to question and figure it out. And that's how I'm here. What I say today is not instructions, they're not revelations, not really. A celebration of what you might already know. Come with me to the beginning.

Dear ones if you want to know how the universe was created, I will tell you in some ways it always was. There was no such thing as the Big Bang your scientists will understand and know that. For the Big Bang is an idea of something from nothing and that is not the way it works. There are multiverses around you. Universes a plenty that are in multi-dimensions, even passing through yours. Do not try to locate them, find them or figure it out. It just is. It's part of a beautiful plan of balanced physics. When some of the dimensionality of the universe is in the multiverse, cross paths in a certain way a new universe is born. Yours was because of this, not something out of nothing but something that was designed, because other things were there and overlapped. In your case there were three overlapping as the catalyst created your "bang" and you came into existence. On purpose you were. It developed in ways you would not believe, faster than it should have according to what you figured out.

Time is relative, you cannot measure it by yours, you cannot even go back and look at light and decide how fast it was going, for it changed too! The actual physics that you enjoy is different in parts of the universe than here. How can you ever then take the measuring stick of what you know and apply it to something you don't? Therefore, the timing was different, the reactions were different, even what you see today, and you think you know about was different. But I want to tell you, what you didn't expect.

With the trillions of galaxies in this universe we concentrate on yours, and we never talk about the others, ever. For there are things going on in the others just as profound and beautiful and benevolent as yours, but you are in yours. It is so vast by itself you will never see all of it, unless you're on my side of the veil. It has wonders beyond belief, beauty, colors you cannot see in wavelengths that you only can dream about. It is the creation of God. Dear creator you were there and watched it. Time is not important because you don't have any problem with it. It is not in your dimensional reality when you're on my side of the veil, but you can still see the beauty and the light and watch it unfold. Dear ones your solar system is simply a pinpoint of light within billions of pinpoints of light, and yet here I Am with you.

I want to tell you about the creation of earth because it was planned. The seeding of your planet approximately 200,000 years ago which lended itself to what you call the Lemuria in 50,000 and beyond is brand new. I want to take you four to five billion years ago. I want you to watch your planet develop, and as you do I want to give you information. And the reason I do it is because I want you to see something, I want you to see a benevolent plan that has created the couch of consciousness and the garden that you inhabit. Something that was never an accident. Prepared in advance by the Creator Itself for you so that you will have an idea of the importance of the human being to us. How can I tell you things that you cannot know of or see or that you never discovered. I would like to remind you of something, the creation of earth as described in your most recent scriptures as the metaphor of a seven-day creation, these were indeed dispensations of creation steps of creation, not days. And look at the amount of verbiage given to the creation of earth as opposed to the creation of the universe or each galaxy or the trillions of other earths and stars. And why was it just the story of you. In that which you would call genesis, in the beginning it wasn't really the beginning at all was it? It was about you! And the reason that there are not volumes and volumes written about the creation of everything else is because everything else is different than you. You see you are created by design. Design! The Creator is the one who can put together the stars in a certain way. Control and create any part of what you would call that which is matter and math and physics itself in order to build that which it needs to build for you. Beautiful it is! God it is!

Picture the earth in its infancy, in its beginning. That is where the story started in Genesis, not with the bigness of it all, only a few words. About the universe and light, the sun, it's all about you, because the earth is designed. The first design dear ones had life occurring on the earth from two suns! Now you should know this. This is not verified, but will be, and is common sense. If you have a planet somehow rotating around a two star system of any kind, even if it's a complex rotation, you have double, double the chances for the beginning of life. The sun is the giver of life, it is the catalyst of chemistry combined with that on the planets which would then have amino acids, the electricity of storms, all then to create that which are the building blocks of the kind of life you know, with double the power of the sun, not heat, but the sun - two! It's going to happen quick! One sun was taken away. Now this is intuitive and you'll even find it in some of the prophecies in some of the channelings, but you'll find it in a very different way because it has gone to a way that humans like - fear!

But it was accurate, you lost a sun. Now there's a reason for this, and its twofold. Number one, so that life would not develop quickly, it had to come later, you had to sit and wait for it because this planet of free choice needed time for other planets to do what they did before you ever got going. And the second thing is, that all life that can travel from planet to planet in this galaxy knows that life will be found around two suns. So you hide. For the most part, you have remained hidden from the other life which is able to see you or touch you or travel to see you. And the few that do and have, do not necessarily talk to the others. There's no internet in the galaxy! What happened to your sun is it collapsed upon itself and gravity became great, much of it dissipated and the gases burned off, it never exploded, it simply collapsed. The collapse itself was traumatic, absolutely to the earth but there was no life on the earth, it didn't matter. Part of the earth was cooling, it didn't matter. The rest of it which was matter, and not much matter, became smaller actually than a planet and disappeared.

Some have channeled that that planet has a name and it's dark and it still rotates your existing sun. Some have channeled that it hides from you behind the sun, and that somehow in some way it's going to get a push to come around and destroy you soon. Now I want to ask you dear human being, with common sense, in this new energy, did you come all this way past a marker just to be destroyed? And so I want you to take that information and sort it where it belongs, into folklore, mysticism, and things that are not going to happen! Could I be clearer? The magnificence of what you've done does not then go toward destruction by a nameless planet that I will not mention. It comes at you from the dark with impossible physics that nobody can see. Here you are on a planet with technology that allows you to see small asteroids, to travel to them and land on them and you're expected to believe that a planet is going to come out of the dark, that nobody knows is going to happen or see, and your instruments can't pick up, and it's going to hit you and kill you! Common sense! Let it prevail.

But you lost the sun, the earth was hobbled at that point, life was tough, it was made tougher by the geology of the planet which kept erupting, it didn't quite cool as fast perhaps as others around it. Now it had one sun and that has something to do with it. It didn't have quite the gravity, did not have quite the friction that you would have otherwise in other ways that would create some kinds of the heat that you didn't expect. Just to say this, She didn't cool right, it's not like some of the others uninhabitable even by microbes. When life got its start it fizzled, didn't work, it wasn't balanced. It started again and it fizzled. It wasn't balanced, there was something missing. It fizzles, that is to say it dies because it was not sustainable. It was not

self-sufficient, the sparks of life were given five times. One sun, it's a tough call. Go ahead and try it, build a greenhouse, plant your vegetables and then cover it up with a tarp and let's watch what happens.

And then they happened over and over for whatever reason geologically you want to consider, and I will tell you there was intelligent design here. The earth would erupt, thousands of volcanoes would go off at the same time covering this planet with a dark cloud that lasted thousands and thousands of years! Nothing could grow, no life could happen, the sun was blotted out. The little sun you had wasn't there. Eventually it took place that the spark of photosynthesis happened and at the time that life started on this planet and plants started to grow and microbes started to move around.

I would like to give you information at that point in time, Orion, and "Octorious" (unknown - maybe spelled wrong) were alive and well with humanoids! Oh you are slow, that's by design. You had to be stopped from growing too fast because when you appeared and were seeded it had to be the right way with the right ones in order to get that which the magnificence of who you are and where you'd be. Controlled it was by the Creator itself. Even when you got going and things were good suddenly there was a collision and you had the moon, and you started over/ And then the volcanoes went off again wiping away eighty percent of the life that was There. Here comes the clouds, the beginning of animals, reptiles, disappearing completely starting over. By then the Pleiadians had the life force on their planet. The Pleiadians is a seven sun cluster. You see seven, you call it seven, that seven cluster is really nine. Some of the brilliance that you see from the earth that you call the sun's actually our sun's hiding behind the seven that you claim are there. The configuration alone allows life faster than yours. The earth is what you would call a planet in the sweet spot of biology, just far enough away from the sun, a sun which is a certain size to be the incubator that you needed for life but not a very good one at the time. The Pleiadians had more, not only that, there were three planets that rotated their suns which they could facilitate and eventually did as their homes, it's very different dear ones, this earth was by design.

Life finally got going and then the asteroids came and wiped it away yet again, volcanoes went off, and it was covered yet again. It didn't cool very well, dear ones it's still not cooled enough, you still have volcanoes going off. But it's now appropriate and okay. When life started to take hold as you know it today it was the beginning of the history that you know of. You don't know what happened before because there's no way to have recorded it, the molteness of the planet, the volatility of it wiped away every trace of what had happened. You only know what you can see that remained. If you had a way of interrogating the depths of the planet as it churned itself over upon itself you might actually be able to figure it out and you'd be shocked. It took so long to get going. One billion, two billion, three billion, three and a half billion, by this time there was life all over the galaxy that was humanoid and some of them had the Creator inside like you do and they had higher selves, and they were working on the puzzles that you were. And you were still microbial by design it is beautiful is it not how we held it back so you would not arrive too soon.

Now the irony in all of this dear human being is that you are not sitting here watching it and waiting for it, you see, you had planets of your own you were working on then. We have told you this before. This is what you do. What you are doing on this planet some of you are starting to remember you've been through before. That is the intuition starting to kick in and actually create a bridge between your consciousness and your innate and your higher self that starts to reveal what your Akash knows about you in other worlds. We do not encourage you to spend time with this because it will not help you now except for you to realize that it happened before and it turned out well. Why am I telling you this? I want you to know it was designed for you with love and benevolence and beauty for you! Some of you sitting there wondering who am I, why me, woe is me, with the lack of self-worth is unbelievably strong for a lightworker because you've been through so many negative things in so many lifetimes and you're expecting it to happen again! I want to tell you, this was designed for you because you are magnificent, this is the way it works and always has worked. You were able with free choice to destroy yourself, never get out of the playground but wisdom prevailed, and now you're in the twilight of an ascended planet by design.

Evolution. Now it gets different, here come the animals that are going to survive, not the dinosaurs, no more extinction, now we have to get going. And now we accelerate it and everything that you know about evolution is wrong! If you do the computations of how long it would take with the Darwin theory it would have taken eight to ten times as long. This evolutionary process to bring you to humanism was accelerated, massively accelerated, and not an average accident. When mammals started to occur and beyond the planet leading then to the primates, leading then to where you became in the evolutionary scheme, when this started to happen, dear ones, nature as you know it today was cranking out the things that you see in zoos today, and that is nature creates variety for survival. How many kinds of deers are there and rats are there or mice are there, all of the animals big and small for survival reasons had many variations and varieties, and by the way so do the primates... so did the humans! And occasionally you'll pick up a real tall one, or perhaps a real small one, maybe you'll even dig up one with a tail. That's not you is it?

Two hundred thousand years ago is nothing, nothing. If you compared the existence of your planet to a 12-hour clock 200,000 years ago, when the Pleiadians seeded you with the consciousness of the Creator is in the last second and a half, and it's right on time! By this time there had been eight other planets of free choice, billions of years had gone by, the Pleiadians were in their ascended status and had been for thousands of years, able to control physics move where they wanted to go, with the Creator inside of them, they were enjoying an ascension status partly biological mostly consciousness, difficult to explain, all multi-dimensional and beautiful!

When they came here, what they had to do in the first hundred thousand years, was to call out the other kinds of human beings. There used to be more than twenty, you see some in your biological records, maybe as many as 17, there were a lot more than that. Kinds of human beings all called down to one. Now I ask you right now, where do you see that in nature any other place? It was my design. It is counterintuitive to evolution, it is counterintuitive to nature. One human being was seeded so that one kind of human being could walk through what you've walked through, in beauty, in frustration, with free choice.

We've given you the rest of the story which we call the history of Earth. Now we gave you the history of the galaxy. A design that was elegant! You were out of the curve of chance, and we say to science right now, go prove it! For everything you're going to look at will not follow an average at all. It'll be outside of the curve a possibility and probability that things happened on

this planet the way they happened, and the reason is because it was designed for you. The beautiful meal called earth was cooked slowly and then at the last minute was accelerated, and the salt was put in, and here you are at the last minute and the meal is being consumed, that is to say is being lived by you and you are about ready to have the meal become the fruition of the consciousness of peace on earth. Does this put your perspective on another scale of who you are? What I have given you is absolute truth of the history of this planet designed, conceived, and built to be a planet a free choice, with one sun against all odds. And against all odds with free choice you just walked through the precession of the equinoxes, in 2015 which we call year two, your in the twilight of peace on earth.

Don't despair from what you see by those who deliver what they want you to see on the news! For the real news is that this planet is churning with change, and the change is not those who are presenting to you horror and hate! The change is that you cannot see, which is the rest of the planet starting to coalesce and react and decide that they want light. Slow it will be but don't fret. How long have you waited, how many lifetimes have you slogged through it to get to here? It's human nature that you'll wait a few weeks, to see a change, what about a few generations? You're going to be here and it's just going to get better. Every single moment that we channel to you, your biology has a chance to ring with the truth of who you are. And in that ringing with the third language is an energy of healing, awareness, beauty, solution to problems that are yours. Don't prejudge how you think it's going to turn out in your life dear human being because you don't know what you don't know.

The message today against all odds, the big gamble, wasn't really a gamble at all for here you sit having passed this marker. I want you to sit for a moment and feel the congratulations, the benevolence of the Creator inside, and would we say job well done, we mean it because you worked for it, and you earned it. And now I know what's going to happen next, you always have

done it, go do it! It's why we're here, built for you. The very cosmos knows your names... and so it is.

Message from Yeshua Ben Joseph (Jesus)

Humanity is on a roll! Yes, of course there are areas on Earth where great pain and suffering are being endured, but those areas are areas of great karmic clearance for all of humanity. Your progress toward a grand awakening is accelerating and intensifying. If you are not in an area of conflict, poverty, or intense suffering, then you are not meant to be undergoing those experiences. Your task is to be Love. Just by being, you are extremely effective in assisting in global healing and awakening.

Everyone on Earth at this moment – indeed at any moment – chose to be here at this moment in order to assist in humanity's awakening which has been ongoing for eons. However, as you have been told by many channels and spiritually enlightened ones on Earth right now, the awakening process has intensified and accelerated enormously over the last two or three hundred years, and is now approaching its culmination. These are indeed exciting times!

Do not be disturbed by the mainstream media news reports of disasters and catastrophes. These things have always been occurring on Earth and are part of the illusory games you chose to play when you made the collective decision to separate from Source. You CHOSE to play games that involved pain and suffering, and you FORGOT that you had made that choice. Consequently, you either experience pain and suffering or you see others undergoing it. Either way it is extremely uncomfortable because the illusion, as you built it, appears extremely real.

However, there is only LOVE! There is nothing other than Love! All that exists, exists within Love, which is Source, which is God. Choose the noun that resonates most harmoniously for you to label the Infinite and Supreme Intelligence that is Love, and remember that no word or label that you can think of or imagine can describe the infinite and indescribable. As humans you need words to communicate with one another – for instance "ice cream" or "chocolate" – but words are only very inadequate symbols and pointers, they are not what is signified.

Reality is completely beyond your comprehension as humans, but, at a very deep level of your beingness, you know that what you experience as embodied humans is not Reality. That is why so many of you are searching for meaning, because what you are experiencing as humans can never satisfy you. Experiences can distract you temporarily from your sense of abject aloneness, the state you chose to experience when you collectively constructed the illusion. You wanted to separate from God, Source, Reality, Love, the Infinite and Supreme Intelligence. And so that is what you experience so long as you continue to play the games with which the illusion provides you. Nevertheless they are only games, unreal, but intensely felt, and truly, you can cease playing them whenever you choose to do so!

Humanity's whole experience over the eons has been one of conflict between your intense desire to be separate and independent of Source and your intense desire to be One with Source. You are One with Source, separation is impossible, but because Source gave You Power equal to Its own infinite Power when It created You, You had immense imaginative potential and were therefore able to construct an illusion that seems intensely real to you in your limited human form.

To awaken is to release yourselves from the limitations you chose to impose upon yourselves in order to fully experience the illusion that you had so cleverly constructed. You are unlimited beings! The limitations that appear to restrict you are illusory! You have never lost the infinite Power that God bestowed upon You at the moment of your creation. You have just become so enamored with the illusion you built that you choose to believe it is real, complete with all the limitations it appears to impose upon you.

You will awaken because dreams and illusions are ephemeral and temporary unreal states. Like soap bubbles, they are easily punctured and then dissolve. You are in the process of puncturing myriad bubbles of insane beliefs that you have been holding tightly to yourselves in the intense fear that if you allow them to burst you will cease to exist.

You are eternal beings at One with God, and you are presently choosing to release your fearful and vice-like grip on the illusion. You have had enough! But, because you made it appear so real, you have great emotional and psychological difficulty in releasing your grip on it and of returning Home. You fear that there is no Home, that there is only the illusion, where you seek endlessly and fruitlessly for meaning, and so you cling on in terror, afraid that you will fall into an abyss of nothingness . . . but that is where you are at present! You are, as humans, living in an unreal dream state and terrified to awaken.

All of you presently incarnate as humans are on Earth to be Love in action, demonstrating Love in every moment and showing others how wonderful Love is. Those of you who have started to do so are enveloped in a vast personal energy field of Love that directly affects everyone with whom you are in physically close proximity, and then continues to flow out from your human center into the world at large. What you are doing is absolutely magnificent. No one else can do it. You are here to do only that, and daily ever more of you are becoming aware of this divine call to awaken and to awaken those around you who are more deeply asleep.

And although no one else can do what you came to do, neither can you fail to do what you came to do. Therefore do focus on the Love, the Tsunami of Love that envelops you all, because as you do so it expands and intensifies. There is no one presently on Earth who does not feel this vibrant and infinitely powerful energy field. But they still have a choice to make – either to accept and embrace It, or to reject and deny Its existence. Love never demands, controls, or imposes, It allows, and so all on Earth have complete freedom of choice.

Some will continue to deny and reject the Tsunami of Love enveloping them, and that choice will be honored. Nevertheless they will eventually choose to accept the Love that is offered them in every moment. Until then, if you meet some who appear to be in denial, unwilling to consider that they may be spiritual beings having a temporary human experience, do not proselytize. You have only words and labels, and, as I reminded you above, they are but inadequate pointers towards Reality. The only way to become aware is to open to Love which is the only environment that exists. No one can deny It forever, but they are entitled to the freedom to delay detaching from that denial.

Do not worry for them or fear for them, because there is only Love, and they will awaken. When they do their joy will be no less than yours, they will not have lost out because there is nothing to lose. Just intend to send Love to all, and rest assured that God looks after His Own, and ALL are His Own!

Your loving brother, Jesus.

Trying to live up to the ever-expanding expectations that only proved to bind me, I finally allowed years of anger, fear and false ideas to fall away, exposing the Light within.

It wasn't in the control mastered over the years, but in giving it up, and relaxing in what was always there that saved me. That still small voice, gently, lovingly showing me the Light within.

A Community of Love

The one you hate the most will be the one that will teach you the most about compassion.

People come from all over the nation and even from other countries to visit two cozy little lakeside towns known for their old fashioned and fun atmospheres called Saugatuck and Douglas, not far from where we live. A great vacation place with old fashioned early twentieth century hotels, vacation homes and quaint bed and breakfast places to take your friends and family. It is home to many LGBTQ folks who feel free to be who they are among those who live there and come to visit and enjoy it's unique and open spirit of community.

For most of my life because of my Baptist background, I judged these places and these people and was told to stay away because these people were wicked in the eyes of God. As the years passed that extremely judgmental spirit in me grew stronger and stronger around the "truths" I was taught and reinforced by stories of Sodom and Gomorrah and once again standing in self-righteousness behind Paul while he points his finger to all who are wicked and will not enter heaven. If I had not mentioned this before, during the time Mary and I were separated, I was slowly becoming aware as to just how judgmental I had become. I learned that while I was engulfed in something I deeply believed in as truth that I was also more deeply blind to its control over my heart and mind. Like they say, you can't see the forest for the trees.

About that spec in the other person's eye preventing him or her from seeing clearly... yeah, the plank in our own eye never goes away. There is always more truth to uncover. When you think you know you're right, that is when you can be sure you're not.

I stood strong in my beliefs and the truths I believed in. The stronger I stood, the more armor (justifications) I could put on for the fight, the more justified I felt before a god who I would please. Even though the Christian faith is about grace for salvation and there is nothing we can do to earn God's favor or please God, our actions completely denied grace as we lived each day pounding the truth into people's faces for them being "wrong". You might say that we never learned the difference between truth and love because we never really learned what love was at all. Truth was easy as the ego was happy to take the ridicule and persecution that Jesus said we would face and call it being humble and obedient.

A number of years ago my wife went to work in retail gift shops in Saugatuck and later in Douglas where she now manages a shop called Possessions. I can't say I was really happy about this choice she made. Not long after she would come home to tell me of conversations she was having with some of the men and woman who lived and worked there. Having conversations with women was fine, but even though the men were gay, it was not right to me and I fought the gut wrenching feelings in my stomach. I'm sure Mary would be able to share some of the judgmental words that spewed out of my mouth all connected to scripture verses I am sure, all in the name of truth.

The years passed and while I may have said hello to "those" people now and then, I'm sure the stench of my judgmentalism oozed out of my presence. Just before Mary and I separated, and learning something from the group at Higher Ground, she made a choice to look elsewhere for work, hoping to find something more than retail for a job. Well, you can image I was happy to be away from Douglas as that was a continue conflict in my doctrine. Of course I would call it a conflict to my soul or faith as those words hold more weight of righteousness making me feel more superior and holy.

A few more years passed, we had separated, came back together, and that time came where Mary was feeling more at peace with her life, our marriage and family had been healing and growing, and she decided to go back to Douglas where she felt most at home and enjoyed her relationships and of course those that visited from all over the country. By this time as you read earlier, I had learned a great deal about codependence, and I was more comfortable in my faith in trusting in God alone, but the feelings of that choice and move back to Douglas was still uncomfortable to me to say the least. I had not faced these fears yet.

This time having learned how to face my feelings I allowed love to step in front of me. I was not completely embracing love yet because I was still struggling with the truths of the Bible. The Bible metaphorically was coming more alive to me, but the old programming hung on to me like a life-threatening disease. Mary and I have not been to church for over nine years except for a time we went to a local church where an African-American woman was the preacher.

She was amazing and spoke with all the power and authority the Bible can deliver! But please understand, and forgive me if I do not say this as properly as I should. I grew up in a family where women were not to have any authority within the church, especially behind a pulpit. Moreover, I was only a young boy when my father told us that black people were the decedents of Ham (Noah's son) for being cursed. How am I supposed to know any differently? How do I come to experience the love of God when God can curse and damn his own children?

I say this so you may better understand how my stepping into a church where the pastor being an African-American woman was triggering all kinds of dogma in my brain shaming me for being there. Judgment was standing right in front of me pointing a long-crooked finger in my face, like a form with my father's face on it, staring me down like a demonic darkness waiting for me to surrender and comply to its superstitious and demented demands.

I am sharing this because someone like me needs to come face to face with the lies we have been typically unknowingly fed by our parents, whose parents fed them, and so on. The Bible is right when it says that the sins of the father are passed down to the third and fourth generation. It is time to break these psychotic ideas by helping those who are afraid to face these dark places in their lives by showing the compassion of the Great Lover, the One who loves without condition, by loving ourselves and others without condition.

Back to Douglas. On this one morning after meditating I drew a picture in my journal that came to me of the earth, a round circle. On the earth, I drew many little stick people all over the place, some by themselves and some in groups. Above that I drew a ball of truth which was broken and scattered all over the earth. Above that I wrote, "The Heavens" and show a ball of truth intact, whole and complete. This was a time I was trying to make sense of the truth that we can find all over the world by learning from other people and the truths that they hold. I was also learning that I not only did not hold all the truth, but I was learning I knew very little truth at all in my blind, know-it-all frame of mind. I wrote the following down next to my picture in my journal…

The truth of God scattered in parts all over the earth for all to find. As we come together and share our part of the truth with others and they share their parts of truth with us, we have more truth and know God more. God becomes big.

Some however believe their part of the truth is "all" the truth, indoctrinate it and use it to control others to believe as they do - or go to hell.

By this picture, you can see just how small God is to them, and why they live in fear. They are alone.

The next morning, I drove to Douglas to see Mary. When I got there, she was busy with customers and told me to go across the street and talk to Walter. Everyone in the area knows him as "Walter the Wonderful". A man in his sixties who has worked with Mary or in the other stores for several years. Walter is someone Mary holds a deep love for. I had met Walter now and then but my demeanor this morning was that of joy and I know I radiated love all around me.

I went to see Walter and I don't remember how we got on the subject about truth, but I was encouraged to find an incredible deep wisdom that Walter held in his spirit. A type of kinship that connected to me at once. He told me about a book he had read called, The Road Home: The Journey Beyond the Spiritual Quick Fix by William Frank Diedrich. Walter brought in a new book the following day, signed by himself to me, as a gift. I became very emotional just as I am now entering in these thoughts. I did not tell Walter about the picture and description I had written down in my journal, but Walter told me a story that is in the book which goes like this.

> *God wanted to bring truth to the earth, so he needed to find a trusting angel who could deliver it unbroken. An angel who was known for being clumsy eagerly stepped forward as he wanted to deliver the truth to the earth. Others laughed at him, but God gave in and handed the crystal made ball of truth to the angel. On his way down to earth, he tripped and the crystal ball of truth ended up breaking and scattering all around the earth.*

I was amazed to hear Walter share this story which for me was a wonderful confirmation of what had come to me several days before. What is called synchronicity, presented itself very clearly that morning. This was truly my first step toward befriending a wonderful man of whom I also hold very dear to me. In fact, much of my world by this time as I had invented it was already breaking into pieces, but now I was stepping into embracing those I used to hate as my new friends. I'm just telling it like it is. It was never me that hated anyone, it was my childhood programming that taught me to hate.

I believe it was the following year that Douglas put on a town party, closing off the street, brought in a band to play and enjoyed food and drinks from several vendors and a few local churches. I remember sitting on a rocking chair that was for sale next door to Possessions just taking in the scene. Unless you were looking into my face, you would not see my watering eyes as I allowed myself to take in the community that was before me. The music, a few people dancing and laughing, most mingling around tables that were set up, others walking here and there. It was perfect!

The sky was blue with a few wispy clouds and the temperature couldn't be more beautiful. I was truly losing myself into the bosom of God as I looked into the faces of Gods precious children not knowing really anyone, and yet they were all my brothers and sisters in this moment. On this evening, my reality shifted to how God looks upon his loved ones. I felt completely at peace and at home within the community. I think I may have felt for the first-time what Mary experienced and enjoyed all along.

There is a wonderful man I had come to enjoy listening to by the name of Bishop John Shelby Spong. If you read about him you will find that he has accomplished much in his life to embrace those that others would not because of the doctrines that took priority over their love for their brothers and sisters. I watched a debate between John Shelby Spong and Dr. James White on "Is Homosexuality Compatible with Christianity?" I had already by this time listened to many of Bishop Spong's messages on YouTube.

It was here that I came across this debate. If I ever watched a debate between truth and love, this was it. While Mr. Spong had answers to scripture from a more metaphorical understanding which encompasses love at the core, Dr. James White, a fundamentalists and literalist presented his case based on the truth of scripture as he would interpret them as facts. Six years ago, I would have thought Spong a heretic and agreed with White on every account. Today I see things completely turned around which is obvious by the words I have shared.

I watched this debate several times and realized that even if I turned the sound off (which I did), that the emotions in each of these men's faces said the full story of their position as the battle of truth vs love took place on a different plane. Yes, this was a debate about homosexuality within Christianity, but when you again stand back outside the woods, you can truly see a spirit of darkness at work playing with words to maintain the life investment that Dr. James White could not give up as his mannerism continued to show the anger and frustration that blinded him to the love that was being presented right in front of him. You could clearly see that Bishop John Shelby Spong had already given up his life investment long ago along his path to finding a love beyond truth.

Just recently I came across an article about a church in Phoenix whose focus is on the everyday needs of its members, many of whom are homeless trans youth. "We're about health and wholeness," says the founding pastor, Jeffrey Dirrim, as he points to countless toilet paper rolls for anyone to take. It was toilet paper week, and they had toilet paper. When I lived in Africa for over a year in the bush when I was nineteen, the one thing I appreciated more than anything else was toilet paper.

Ken Ham, a fellow I enjoyed when I was younger because I loved dinosaurs, ridiculed the Phoenix church saying "that we are seeing more and more frequently the total acceptance of homosexual and transgender behavior. Instead of recognizing sin for what it is, many Christians and churches, in the name of tolerance and love, openly embrace the LGBT community without ever exposing their sin and pointing them toward the one who forgives all sin - Jesus Christ. This is a compromise on Scripture's clear teachings about marriage and gender reaching out to others by meeting their physical needs is important and admirable. But as a Christian or a church, what is the point of meeting physical needs while ignoring the ever more important spiritual needs of every person? People need food, water, toiletries, a roof over their heads - but how much more do they need Christ?"

I am sharing this as another example of how a belief in truth over love compromises love completely. "In the name of tolerance and love", is said by Ken as though secondary to truth. If God is love, then Ken is placing God secondary to a doctrinal claimed truth. The original sin doctrine drives all the other interpretations toward a punishment of sin that must be paid.

"There is no fear in love; but perfect love casteth out fear: because fear hath torment. He that feareth is not made perfect in love." 1 John 4:18

What is Ken Ham afraid of? He is afraid of the family falling apart because he no longer trusts that his god is capable of controlling his children. I say control because in the mind of the believer, things are out of control per a book they believe holds all the truth above all other religions or practices. I also know they are afraid to love the LGBT community for love sake because I also did not know how to love the LGBT community while steeped in "the truth."

The less we judge, the greater the love, the clearer the illusion of fear.

Another step toward Love

Days after the Douglas party I was sitting by my computer and decided to do a little research on the church that had a food table at the party. I came across the church website and found that the church was the United Church of Christ. The name rang a bell with me because Bishop John Shelby Spong was a part of the UCC church. The pastor of the church is Rev. Salvatore Sapienza. I recognized his picture as he was also one of the fellows serving at the town party. I then navigated to their About Us page and watched some very interesting videos that hit home with me about how we judge other people that do not fit into our doctrinal view and group.

At that point, my phone rang and it was Mary calling me from her store in Douglas. She said, you know I have been talking to a few people who say that the UCC church in Douglas is a great place and that we should check it out. I told Mary that I was on their website at the moment and it looked like something I may be interested in too. This of course was eye opening to the both of us as we came to this same conclusion at the same time after being away from church for nine years.

So that Sunday we went to the service. If you ever had a picture-perfect idea of the white painted church in the country, this was it, only it was in town, with the foyer and front doors on an angle facing the intersection. The inside was as I would expect with stain glass arch top windows flanking the sides and wood floors that creak as you walk, and old wooden benches with its hymnal pockets. Of course, it isn't about the building, but it sure was cozy and quaint!

Pastor Sal gave me the impression of a very humble and meek gentleman. His voice was pure and clear, and his message was presented from a caring heart that deeply believed in a God of love. It was truly amazing to me as for the first time in my life from across a pulpit I heard the word of God preached metaphorically and with great passion and compassion. Everything I felt led to and studied in the last five to six years was now being presented back to me.

Mary and I left after the service and headed home. Mary said to me that if I was not comfortable we can check out other churches. I said that we had only just gone there the first time and so it will always feel a bit strange. An hour or so later in the kitchen Mary told me again that we could check out other churches, concerned that I am perhaps giving in to what she wanted and not what I wanted, (Mary of course knowing my family and background). With increasing emotion and tears in my eyes and a broken voice I leaned in toward her across the island and said, "you left Douglas to find something else, and later you followed your heart back there because God was not finished with me yet. God is calling me into this community and so I must go. This has nothing to do with my comfort." Mary was satisfied with my answer and happy I am sure as we are both very blessed now to be a part of this church and community. Pastor Sal and his husband Gregg have become very special to us, and there are not too many services that I can get through without tears of joy flowing down my checks. The presence of God and love is so real and palpable there within the people that I cannot contain my emotions.

We got to know so many wonderful people from the New Mexico trip we went on, but also being a part of the events and monthly potlucks at the church. I have really come to understand the importance of church community or any community and sharing our lives with one another.

This for me was a step across a threshold of my enemy. Jesus asked us to love our enemy and I think this is one of those things of what he meant as we must face the fears we create that are often found to be false. I want to take this moment to acknowledge anyone who is reading this book who has faced the hardships of the self-righteous who point their finger at your sexual preference. I was that person. I held a hatred for you without ever recognizing that you are no less a child of God than I am. I know this may sound egotistical, and may even come across superficial, but allow me to just say to you from the bottom of my heart, from myself and maybe that voice out there that knew they were wrong in what they said or did, I am very sorry for my behavior and actions and words that have hurt you so deeply. I am sorry you faced my judgmental stares over the years. I was wrong! I want you to know that today I stand proudly by your side as your brother in unity and in love.

We get caught up thinking we know the answers, even offering them in the light of kindness and caring. And yet when push comes to shove, we dig in to prove what we know, which then becomes a type of side-step to a present compassion that fails to be shared.

I sat there as the tears streamed down my face, listening to a voice calling me to the front lines. I was the man who had everything. I was the man who needed to be heard. I became the man that set compassion aside for my many justifiable truths.

I stepped through a door a few months ago of my greatest fear and found my greatest joy. It was a confirmation of how faith and trust is rewarded when compassion becomes the front runner to our striving. May I always make my choices using compassion for my lens.

Earlier I talked about reincarnation. While I never heard anyone share these thoughts in writing, hypnosis or a channel, I had come to my own conclusion that with many of the things that have been changing in the last fifty or so years with the consciousness of man, that those who are of the LGBTQ community are of the greatest and most honorable of the old souls who made very difficult decisions on the other side of the veil to engage in life being hated to stir up love and light within others.

These are those among the warriors of life times of being tested by fire and endurance, becoming the unstoppable storm. These are the mighty souls born into this world as men and women to challenge those who are judgmental from every religious background who places truth over love.

There is more than enough evidence documented in all cultures around the world that every single person living was at one time the opposite gender and gay to experience the results and to learn compassion for each gender and sexual preference. Oh yes, we were all gay at least once! Most likely more than once.

While I only heard this once in a channel, it rang true to me. It can take about two dozen life times for the mind to fully comprehend and embrace the new gender. Upon the first incarnations is when people feel most like they should be embodying the opposite gender than what they were born into.

Here are a few stories of this very example. You will continue to find more of these stories as more people are willing to share their incredible lives and experiences with the world. And of course, if you are willing to learn more truths that exist in the same world and reality that you occupy.

Mommy, Why am I Not a Boy This Time?

By the time Nicola Weather was five years old her mother was convinced that she was living proof that reincarnation exists. Nicola displayed the extremely rare ability of being able to recall her previous life. It started when she was only two and insisted that her toy dogs name was muff, and then just some of the other funny things that kids say like, "mommy, why am I not a boy like I used to be? My other mommy used to be called Ms. Benson and I was her little boy and I played with muff". These were all unfamiliar names to the child and Ms. Weather didn't know what to think, so she started keeping a journal of Nichol's unusual references.

Over time the clues began to indicate that Nicola was the reincarnated five year-old son of Mr. and Ms. Benson of Yorkshire England and his dog muff. Mr. Benson was a railway worker and warned his son not to play on the tracks, but one day he followed some friends and was hit and killed by a train. Nicola remembered her previous deaths so vividly she had a screaming convulsing panic attack when she saw a similar scene acted out on TV. Shortly after on Nikolas fifth birthday Ms. Weather drove them out to what Nicola called her other home. Nicola guided them straight to one of the four Terrance houses that match her previous descriptions, but there was no

Benson family there. Nicola continue to describe and guide her mother two paths and fields as she had played in before with muff. As convinced as ever, they went to the church registry archives and discovered records that indicated that on July 25th, 1875 John Henry Benson was born to Mr. and Ms. Thomas Benson a rail worker, and that he died when hit by a train at age five almost 100 years ago.

I Used To Be An African-American Woman!

Luke, a blond white boy has managed to convince at least a few people that he lived a past life as Pam Robinson, an African-American Chicago woman who died in a fire at the Paxton Hotel in 1993. Luke began to name his toys and things, Pam. Luke would say things like, "I used to have black hair". Or "I used to have earrings like that when I was a girl". Luke's mother was becoming more frustrated with Luke wondering where he is getting these ideas from, and who was Pam? Luke turned to his mother and told her that "I used to be Pam, but I died and went up to heaven, I saw God, and eventually God pushed me back down and when I woke up I was a baby and you named me Luke."

Luke's mother a bit taken back called her mother who remembered a book she had read in the seventies called, Twenty Cases Suggestive of Reincarnation by Ian Stevenson, M.D. Luke's mother decided to ask Luke if he remembered how he died. Luke looked right at his mother and said, "it was a fire" making a motion with his hand as if to say that he (she) had jumped off of a building. Luke remembers the city was Chicago, so they started their search for a building that burned. Luke's mother asked him what color his skin was, and Luke said, "well black of course!" They found that nineteen people had died including a woman named, Pamela Robinson, age 30. Pam had jumped out of a window to her death. They found a picture of Pam and then put a number of other fake pictures on the table also and had Luke see if he could pick out from the pictures anyone that he recognizes. Luke says, "I remember when this picture was taken" and points to the picture of Pamela. This story ends with Luke's mother saying that it seemed that after he got it all out, Luke never talked about it again and moved on with his life.

Two-Spirit, The indigenous perspective

If you were around in the late 1500's where the colonization of America began, and were yourself among one of the native people, you would be in honor of the Two-Spirit person because they were often placed in highly esteemed positions among the indigenous people. Native peoples of the Plains, the Great Lakes, the Southwest and California offer the most evidence for respectful two-spirit traditions. It has been determined that there were male two-spirits in more than 150 different Native American tribes, but there were female two-spirits as well. With over a thousand vastly different cultural and linguistic backgrounds, it is important not to overgeneralize for the indigenous peoples of North America.

I'm including this as another example of how truth no matter where it originates from removes the love that once existed in these situations, that in this case was highly respected and recognized as a great and wonderful gift from the Great Spirit. If a name like the "Great Spirit" offends you, then you might be offering praise to something less than the Source of All there Is, because that is what the Great Spirit is to the indigenous among us. God to the Christian, Allah to the Muslim, the Great Lover to me, the Father to Jesus.

> *But I tell you, love your enemies and pray for those who persecute you, that you may be children of "your" Father in heaven. ~ Jesus*

The Imitation Game

Mary and I watched a movie a few weeks ago called "The Imitation Game". It was about a man named Alan Mathison Turing who was an English computer scientist, mathematician, logician, cryptanalyst and theoretical biologist. Alan quickly became one of the government's greatest assets, with the cracking of Germany's Enigma code shortening the war by two to four years. Historians claim that Alan saved an estimated 14 million to 21 million lives. Alan Turing was prosecuted in 1952 for being gay. He accepted chemical castration treatment as an alternative to prison. Alan died in 1954 from cyanide poisoning.

The sheer number of homosexuals prosecuted in Germany a few years before and during World War II; between 1933 and 1945, was an estimated 100,000 men arrested as homosexuals, of whom some 50,000 were officially sentenced. Most of these men served time in regular prisons, and an estimated 5,000 to 15,000 of those sentenced were incarcerated in Nazi concentration camps. At this same time, over 49,000 gay men and women were prosecuted in England.

What on God's green earth would make, not only this many people choose homosexuality, but make anyone follow their innate desire for the same sex with such odds of possible prosecution and/or death? Because they are rebellious? Because they hate God? What insanely justifiable reason could we invent as to suggest that homosexuality is a choice? Why is the church not confronted with statistics like this, or use them while preaching about how much God hates his children? I think we need to take a closer look at the "God" we claim as loving.

Christians like Ken Ham, who are against the LGBTQ community are forced by their very public proclaimed ego invested belief system, believe homosexuality is a choice, and therefore a sin, do so primarily because the idea that God would create people this way would go against the Biblical teaching that they were taught and brought up into, and therefore make God a liar, which would then add question to the validity of the Bible's literal inerrancy.

What I have gained from the Alan Turing story itself is that a very old soul with the depth of technology came into the earth plane for the purpose of ending the war early. But far more importantly to stand up even after his death, as a human example to bring us past the focus on the flesh. In the Gnostic gospel of Thomas, saying 114, Jesus replies to Simon Peter…

> *114. Simon Peter said to them, "Make Mary leave us, for females don't deserve life." Jesus said, "Look, I will guide her to make her male, so that she too may become a living spirit resembling you males. For every female who makes herself male will enter the kingdom of Heaven."*

Simon Peters statement says a lot about the culture of his time, very male dominated, which is clearly felt in the

Bible also. Based on Jesus' response, he was possibly offering a little sarcastic humor to the male chauvinists present, but also bringing attention to the human essence, who we all really are and not our flesh or gender. It will be the LGBTQ community that will ultimately teach the fundamentalists of the world about the love of God. I owe a great debt of gratitude to those who despite my past have embraced a person such as I.

Embrace truth as paramount and you will never be at peace on earth. Embrace love beyond truth and you will find peace within!

Research these things for yourself and come to your own conclusion of what is happening all around us in a world so much bigger when we face our fears and take our blinders off. And maybe before you even think evil against your brother or sister in your heart about why they are wrong or sinful or glare in disgust at the person you disapprove of, take a moment to wonder if he or she was your sister or brother in a past life. Maybe even a lover or best friend or partner trying to teach you something about yourself.

Every human on earth is a child of God, a part of God, a part of Love just like you and me. And when you travel back across the veil, when your days on earth come to a close, there will be no one there to accuse you or punish you for your behaviors and deeds. However, I believe you will face yourself and need to deal with the choices you made so that you might continue to grow and heal your soul. I promise you, it won't be a lack of knowledge or righteousness or some ultimate truth that will come to your memory at that moment, but the lack of loving the enemy that was placed into your life by your own plan. What happens next is completely up to you.

The world has never been more lost of its love because of clinging on to a hope of truths some will die for, misunderstanding they are completely giving into the desires of righteousness over compassion, therefore stepping into the same darkness they claim to fight.

As long as truth is demanded over truth, an intolerant fear remains in control, and love as part of its nature steps aside allowing our free will to control the illusion we created when we lost sight of love long ago where we once remembered Its benevolent power.

So how does love prevail?

By loving the enemy. It is only our fears that manifested separation from love in the first place. Dying for truth never worked and always separates. Love is always there waiting to show Its unexpected outcome through compassion.

The following fictional story is a summary formed around my current beliefs, some possibilities and likely probabilities, based on hundreds of sources and their sciences, history, religions, theories, and philosophies found throughout the world.

The ideas behind this story in no way reflect the theories, philosophies, religions or beliefs of those whose names I have shared throughout this book.

The following is a fictional story about a grandfather and his two grandsons who take a trip to their cottage in Canada, find a hidden treasure, and then have a conversation around a camp fire where the three of them discuss a number of things related to God and creation, and of course how love must find its way to front and center in our lives.

The Hidden Treasure

On a cool sunny Spring day, Grandpa Reed took his daughters two sons fishing at their cottage on the Batchawana Bay in the south of Canada which shares the bay with the north side of the upper peninsula of Michigan. To the northeast side of the bay is a small snake-like river called Batchawana River that winds north into the wilderness where Grandpa Reed enjoyed fishing with his father who owned the land before him. Back then they would put up a tent, but years later Mr. Reed built a cottage just off the road called Memory Lane and sold off some of the other lakefront properties to people who were also looking forward to relaxing in the peace and quiet the place brought to a busy life.

The younger of the two boys is named Tyler, who was just eleven years old, has curly wild blond hair and deep blue eyes, loves fishing even though he finds it hard to sit still for more than five minutes. His older brother Jared is sixteen, is tall and thin, brown clean cut hair and bright blue eyes like his mother. And while more laid back than his brother, fishing was not really his thing. However, he did enjoy the stories that his grandpa Reed shared as they grew up around the fires they often enjoyed in the evenings on the sandy shoreline in front of their cottage.

The morning of the next day after arriving at the little white freshly painted cottage the evening before and having a good night sleep, the three got up early, had some eggs and toast for breakfast, put their fishing gear in the small aluminum motor boat and headed several miles across the bay to Batchawana River. The skies were deep blue with large fluffy clouds and a bit on the cold side with very little wind, but the ride across still required a thin jacket. The area had torrential rains just days before, and evidence of that was seen at the mouth of the river as they entered and commented on how muddy the water was. But that didn't stop the avid fishermen who continued upstream for about a mile winding around until they came to the bend where they would enjoy the next few hours catching their favorite fish, rainbow trout.

It seemed Gramps had that magic touch, without a doubt from all the years he had been fishing, and he was the first to hook what seemed like a big one. Jared lost his cool demeanor as he was searching for the net and almost tipping the boat over. Tyler who is typically a bit fidgety was surprisingly calm when he saw the fish surface the water and with wide eyes said in a very monotone voice, "We may need a bigger net." Gramps just said, "Nonsense! Jared, get that net over here! This fish is coming home with us!" "Tyler, watch out!" Jared yelled while trying his best to straddle the seat and keep his balance at the same time. Mr. Reed reeled the fish near the boat, and Jared put the net right where his grandpa wanted it, scooping the fish up and dragging it over the lip and into the boat where it did what most fish do, flip and flop in their new compromised environment.

Mr. Reed asked Jared to grab the fish through the gills and lift it out of the net and into the fish well. Jared, still bent over and holding onto the net looked up at his grandpa and slowly shook his head and said, "I'm not touching that thing" looking back at the fish! Tyler stepped forward calling his brother a baby and grabbed the fish as though it were a baseball mitt and lifted it with a grunt with both hands out of the net and dropped it into the fish well and closed the lid. They all sat down a bit winded and started to laugh and talk all at the same time while not one of them listening to what the others were saying.

The sun was now getting a little higher in the sky and warming the once chilly morning. Everyone put their lines back in the water looking forward to the next surprise. Jared took his jacket off and tossed it into the front next to the tackle box. About ten minutes had passed, and while there were a few nibbles, no one was getting a hit. Then a flash caught Tyler's attention from the corner of his eye, and when he turned to look, he saw nothing. Shrugging it off he went back to watching his line and paying close attention to how his grandpa was doing it. Gramps was slowly reeling in, and all you could here was the sound of his reel, tick tick tick… tick tick tick…

Then Jared said, "Did you see that?" Both Tyler and Mr. Reed looked over at Jared with an inquisitive look in their eyes. Tyler with a little more interest wanting to know if he did not just see things himself. Mr. Reed said he didn't see anything shaking his head and going back into his normal fishing posture and telling the boys to keep it down. Tyler quietly told Jared that he saw a flash of light a moment ago which caused Jared's eyes to widen with question. "That is what I just saw!", Jared whispered. Mr. Reed shook his head and told them the sun is most likely reflecting off the water, but Tyler and Jared were not buying it, this was different.

Tyler searching for clues and not paying much attention to fishing at the moment pointed over to the bank where there looked like a hole with sediment spilling on the outside as though the rain had washed it out exposing the top curve of a hole. Jared said, "I don't see it" looking to where Tyler was pointing. "Under that large fallen tree, just over there," Tyler whispered. Mr. Reed shifted in his seat rocking the boat slightly when both Jared and Tyler saw the flash of light again. "Did you see that!" They both said at the same time. Jared asked his grandpa if he would take them over to that sandy bank over there, pointing to where the tree had fallen. "There is something there, and Tyler sees a hole in the side of the bank." Mr. Reed agreed as he was more interested in making sure the boys had an adventure but also because they already had their fish for supper tonight, why not. They all pulled up their fishing lines and headed for the shore just fifty feet away.

Jared and Tyler existed the bow of the boat onto the sand and headed around the fallen tree to where Tyler clearly seen a hole and flash on the side of the small embankment. Mr. Reed got out and pulled the boat up onto the sandy shore. Tyler peered in and because it was dark could not see much of anything. Jerad told Tyler to be careful, "You don't know what is in there." "Gramps, do you have that shovel with you?" Tyler called out. Mr. Reed handed Jared the shovel who handed it to Tyler. Tyler began to dig the sediment away from the bottom of the hole so the sun could shine in. Then when Tyler stood up, suddenly with surprise in their eyes, they could all see something bright and reflective in the sun. Now Jared got in there also digging with his hands to clear the opening. "It's treasure," Tyler yelled out! Jared told him to be quiet, "It's most likely a large stone or something." While Mr.

Reed was not saying anything, he too was a bit curious as to what this might be.

When the opening was large enough, they could all see a corner of a box of some kind. Tyler again said, "Told you it was a hidden treasure!" "We don't know that, here grab that handle there and pull." Jared said. But it was too heavy and didn't move. Mr. Reed's interest was now driving him too and asked Tyler to hand him the shovel. After clearing more away from the hole and the area around it, they could all get their hands on it and pull. It moved! Large smiles on their faces as they looked at each other. They pulled harder, and the box gave up its stronghold and slid out of its sandy grave.

The box was made of some hardwood, almost black, but had four metal straps that were nailed with small headed nails into a number of circular designs and into the wooden boards that made up the chest. The straps were fairly thick and showed very little rust on them. The boards, however, had decayed quite a bit, although it appeared that there were no visible holes. Two large, what looked like padlocks were fastened securely on the center two of the four straps. However, there was no hole to place a key, only what appears to be some form of hieroglyphs. The three of them dragged the chest to the boat and with great effort managed to lift it into the boat and position it into the center between the two fixed bench seats. Knowing they were too excited to find out what was inside the chest, fishing was off the schedule for the rest of the day, and so they headed down and out of the river and across the bay, back to the cottage.

It was close to noon when they arrived back at the cottage. The clouds were thinning, and the sun was warming up the day. They hoisted the chest onto the shore and dragged it up and onto the porch of the cottage that faced the bay. Mr. Reed asked Jared to go to the shed and bring him the electrical cord and small cutting grinder. He asked Tyler to bring a few chairs out to the porch from the kitchen and then to go and get the fish and clean it on the table around the corner of the porch where the water spigot and hose was coiled up on a hook. As Jared returned with the tools, Tyler already had the chairs on the porch and was running to the boat for the fish. "This was going to be the fastest fish cleaning he had ever done," he thought to himself. As Mr. Reed was cutting through the steel bands just over the padlocks, Tyler was filleting the rainbow trout which would give them about fifteen pounds of meat to grill and enjoy that evening.

Snap! One of the steel straps let loose. Everyone breathed in heavily, looking at each other with a half-smile and a glow in their eyes and suddenly a little nervous. Mr. Reed asked Jared to make up a few sandwiches and bring them all some juice from the fridge. "And don't forget to wash your hands first," he yelled over his shoulder. Tyler was just finishing and washing things away and would put the fish in a plastic bowl filled with water and placed in the fridge for the evening meal. Mr. Reed took a few large bits out of his sandwich then told the boys with his mouth full to "co an i oh ah hai" pointing to the chairs, then continued cutting into the second strap. Jared and Tyler backed away and sat on the chairs and began to stuff their own mouths as they too were very hungry, and then taking gulps of pop to wash it down as they watched on as Gramps was grinding through the second strap in anticipation.

Snap! The second strap gave way and the chest lid popped just enough to let some dust out of the cracks. They again all looked at each other as their hearts began to race a little wondering if they should stand back before opening the lid, you know, in case something is alive in there! Well, that it what Tyler was thinking anyway. Mr. Reed slowly opened the lid with a few creeks as the metal and wood resisted to give up its secrets. "Books! Books?" Tyler said as he dove in grabbing at the books and moving them around hoping for some gold coins or something of value! Mr. Reed reached out his hand as if to tell Tyler to stop, knowing the books were ancient and needed to be handled with care. "Oh man!" Tyler said, disappointed after all this suspense getting up and walking inside to plop down on the couch to play on his Gameboy. Jared was also a bit disappointed although he was not saying anything. However, he did notice that Gramps was really taken by these books and his curiosity made him sit back down in his chair as he watched his grandpa's face seemingly filling with delight as he blew the dust off one of the books and opened its cover.

Mr. Reed was in the military for years after his training and rising up through the ranks, and then stationed in Nevada at a place known as Area 51 back in the 1970's. His full name and rank in the Army was Lieutenant Colonel Casey Reed, which gave him access to highly sensitive information. He never said much about what he did there, but the boys were soon going to find out some of their grandpa's deepest held secrets over the hours ahead.

Jared glanced over at the open book in Gramps' hands and noticed it was written in a different language, more like markings, so he too got up and headed into the house and decided to text a few of his friends about what was going on and to find out what they were up to.

Mr. Reed continued to look through each book in the chest and spend the rest of the afternoon with the boys hanging around the cottage. When evening came, and the sun was beginning to set, they all pitched in to prepare the fish and vegetables on the grill and grabbed some homemade bread the boy's mother sent along with them for their trip. They all loved the flavor of trout and nothing was better than fresh trout grilled to a perfect golden brown with Gramps special seasoning recipe. They all sat on the porch to eat around a small table and asked their grandpa what his thoughts were on the books they found. Mr. Reed said that he was able to understand a few of them as one of his expertise was in deciphering codes and that required symbol recognition and the study of numerous ancient languages.

Both Jared and Tyler stopped chewing for a moment on hearing this as they were a bit shocked to have just learned this about their grandpa. As they continued to eat, Mr. Reed told them that what they found was truly a great discovery and he was sure that those in power would love to get their hands on it, and in fact shows some evidence that based on what is written that some of these books may have been left here, possibly by mistake from Beings outside of our planet. Jared choked and coughed on some bread and then took a drink trying to compose himself again while Tyler chimed in to respond to Jared's unspoken reply "What did you just say, Gramps?"

Mr. Reed looked at both boys closely in the eyes as if to measure them up as being mature enough for what he was thinking of sharing with them. Both boys swallowed and said nothing. Mr. Reed asked them to clean things up while he would begin to build a fire in the fire pit down by the water's edge. The sun was by this time just setting on the horizon, and the sky was ablaze with beautiful colors reflecting on the few clouds that still remained. When the boys had things cleaned up and put away, they headed outside to where their grandpa was sitting on a log and poking around with the fire to get it going.

The sky was turning a dark blue, and a few of the brighter stars were beginning to shine. The moon was not visible yet but would be within a few hours. Jared and Tyler sat on their own logs forming a right-angled triangle between the three of them around the fire pit. Gramps had several books with him from the chest which he was treating very respectfully, almost sacredly as he had them laying on a very nicely folded blue blanket next to him.

Mr. Reed picked up one of the books that seemed different and more elegant than the others as it had several leather straps and what looked like golden clasps that held the book shut. On its heavy cover was a raised round symbol with two thick ropes that circled a single vertical twisted bar of sorts that Gramps said looked similar to the Uraeus found in Egypt, but different. Mr. Reed opened the book and found the first page which was filled with colors and symbols, but also lettering that he understood and could read. He said that this was an account of the beginning before time ever existed but that the book was strange somehow because when he opened to the last pages earlier that day found that it was also talking about things in our modern times. Not from a prophetic standpoint, but as if someone had updated the book just a few years ago as the ink seemed fresher than the other.

Tyler and Jared looked intently at their grandpa as he said this to find out if he was joking or not as the chest seemed to have been buried for many hundreds of years, maybe thousands. When Mr. Reed began to study the first page, Tyler and Jared glanced at each other to reaffirm that each of them heard what their grandpa just said. Jared didn't buy it but was interested in what the book contained, while Tyler was thinking to himself that this truly was a treasure better than gold and must be worth a lot of money.

Gramps said that on the inside of the cover it said that this was…

> *An Account of the Arcturian Council. A Ninth Dimensional Collective Consciousness who were placed in charge as the Overseers of the Records of the Universes whose Galaxies contained the Planets where the Most Amazing Games were ever Played.*

Tyler and Jared looked at each other with a funny question on their face when they heard the word "game" come from such a book. Mr. Reed looked up and stared into the fire for a moment as if something clicked in his mind. He was thinking about the three top militaries of the world, USA, Russia and China and the leaders of great power within the major religions who actually control these powers. Mr. Reed had information about the Vatican in Rome and the artifacts and tens of thousands of books they controlled from very ancient times that were hidden from the public knowing they would completely rewrite history as we knew it.

Jared rubbed the bottom of his nose and moved a little sensing that his grandpa was concerned about something, but also that there was a lot more going on behind this man he thought he knew. As Mr. Reed looked down at the book on his lap, Tyler took a sip of his pop which caught Gramps' eye. "Tyler," he said, "would you go grab me a nice cold beer from the fridge for me please?" When Tyler returned and handed his grandpa the bottle, Gramps popped the top off on the corner of an upright log and took a swig. "Ahh, that's better," he said. Jared and Tyler just looked at each other and smiled as their grandpa looked down at the book again and turned the page.

The Eternal One

Before the Beginnings of all Beginnings, there was only One Consciousness, and that of The Eternal One whose nature has no utterance, for language would become a Created element of Sound. We refer to It as the One Sole Spirit, The Self Generator, whose Energy and Love and Light cannot Diminish or Increase as It is Perfect within Itself and inextinguishable. The Eternal One remains nameless as it can never be defined. It has no Beginning or End, and Its meaning is known only to Itself. Love is at Its very Core and is the Essence that Flows throughout and within, and would soon be unleashed into what would be called Creation.

Jared chimed in before Gramps took his next breath to continue. "This sounds like the genesis story I recall hearing in church, but it sounds different to me. I thought God created everything. I thought God was this "Eternal One" that this book is referring to." Taking another sip of his beer, Gramps said, "Yes that's right. Sometimes depending on what language we grow up into, we think we are the ones that have things right. However, like this, it is just another name that people call God. Let's continue and see where this takes us." Turning over the first stiff yellowish aged page and continued to read.

The First Creation

The Great Circles of Eternity was yet to be thrown forth, known within the substance as the endless Ages of Expressions of Itself. The first Creations were put forth as Spirit from a breath establishing the rules by which all things would have Their existence within Spirit and within Form. Creations would create Creations of Itself and multiply throughout an infinite Cosmos within The Eternal One. Everything made was Itself the Essence and Expressions of Itself, and though understood as separate in various Forms will always return unto Itself because the Expressions are The Eternal One and can never be Divided.

Mr. Reed stopped reading for a moment to look over and at Tyler and Jared, but only to digest what he was reading. Tyler asked, "How does creation create creation? I thought only God could create things." Gramps asked, "So how do you think God creates things?" Tyler thought for a moment and said, "I don't know, kind of like speaks or thinks things and poof, there they are. Kind of like a magic trick, only for real!" Gramps smiled and nodded his head in acknowledgment, and said, "You know, science has come a long way with heart transplants, and I know the first brain transplant is about to take place on a human." Mr. Reed thought of what science was doing with humans already taking place for years under the secret programs within the government. With that, both boys eyes widened with question on hearing about a brain transplant. Jared said, "For real Gramps?" Mr. Reed nodded his head and said, "There is something in the idea of this that makes a person wonder if there is something more to this idea of Creation creates Creation."

Jared said, "Referring to '*Expressions of Itself,*' the picture that comes to mind is of a ball, round and complete all in itself and the air inside is the expressions, all of creation including the planets and the universe. Only that God is the ball, everything is encompassed within the ball." Gramps smiled in affirmation and added, "Very insightful Jared, and the parameter of the ball is infinite, so it is impossible for God to be outside of Itself." The two looked at each other for a moment while that sunk in. Then Mr. Reed looked down, turned the page and continued to read.

The Consciousness of all Expressions deriving of Itself exist and are governed as The Eternal One but through the Creations will, through Creations designs at will, within and by the power of Vibration and Love and Light and Sound which govern over the Collective Consciousness and degrees of Knowledge and Wisdom that will ceaselessly grow and mature throughout Eternity through each Expression as Itself and of Itself. Everything within Creation will always remain a part of The Eternal One as it is impossible for Creation to become anything other than Itself.

Gramps turned the page and continued to read.

A Spirit of Love

The first Spirit breathed into existence from The Eternal One was also the first Expression created out of everything that The Eternal One is. The Eternal One is Love, and because Love can hold nothing back unless It becomes something else, the fullness of Love was now complete and whole within the first Expression of Itself. The first Spirit was now the second Consciousness of the collective of two as One, complete and whole and perfect as The Eternal One, for It was and is The Eternal One.

Mr. Reed looked up at the boys to see if they had any questions. They were silent and just taking in these celestial words while staring into the fire. At the moment, the words did not seem to make any special impact on their young minds. He smiled looking back to the book, turned the page and continued.

The Cosmos

The first Spirit spoke within a resonance of perfect Harmony as It thought of Its First Creation, and Universes of Space were thrown into their Frequencies of Vibration and Love and Light and Sound. Each becoming Spirit themselves and knowing their place within the Cosmos. Each one complete and whole and perfect as the first Spirit, as The Eternal One, as they were and are all One and within the One. The Expressions of each were alive unto Themselves, and Their Consciousness were as One, complete and whole and perfect as The Eternal One, for they were and are The Eternal One.

Jared added a few more logs to the fire. Mr. Reed paused for a moment considering the implications these words held compared to his present view of the universe and God. He turned the page.

The Collective

The first Spirit spoke within a resonance of perfect Harmony as It thought of Its Second Creation, and a Trillion Spirits made of Frequencies of Vibration and Love and Light and Sound were spread to the infinite Spaces within the Cosmos. Each one an Expression of The Eternal One, the first Spirit, and the Universe. Each one complete and whole and perfect as the Universes, as the first Spirit, as The Eternal One for they were and are all One and within the One. The Expressions of each were alive unto Themselves, and their Consciousness were as One, complete and whole and perfect as The Eternal One, for they were and are The Eternal One. To these, the first Spirit shared the will of The Eternal One which was Its own and the will of Each. They are to do as they please within the Cosmos, for the system of Love was in place, and the order that would govern was set forth into each Expression and the Collective Consciousness.

As Mr. Reed finished reading that page, the boys could see the emotion in their grandpa's face and the tears that welled up in his eyes that reflected the dancing flames of the fire. Tyler said, "Gramps, are you alright?" Mr. Reed nodded his head blinking a few times to clear his eyes and looked up into the faces of these precious grandchildren of his. He was just thinking of how big and wondrous God is and how he is connected to these boys in ways he doesn't really understand but somehow knows. He said in a broken voice, "I was just thinking about how much I love you two young men!"

Tyler was a little unsure how to react to Gramps emotions as he pursed his lips and crinkled his nose to keep himself from crying while looking down on his folded hands and twitching his fingers. He never seen his grandpa get emotional like this and with the tattoos he has on his still strong arms, always thought he was the toughest of the tough! Jared said in a quiet voice, "We love you too Gramps," while poking a stick in the fire just to avoid eye contact. None of which was missed by Mr. Reed as he smiled and returned to the book to continue.

Tyler interrupted his grandpa and asked, "Can you hold off a minute, I have a thought but want to run and get another pop," as he turned to head toward the cottage. Jared called out, "Get me one too please." Gramps yelled out, "Please bring me another beer," looking over at Jared and taking a deep breath. He said, "What do you think so far of what you heard?" Jared replied, "Pretty crazy shit, ah, I mean stuff Gramps, giving him one of those, sorry looks which only made Gramps smile and shake his head. "I heard a lot worse in my day young man! Gramps said."

Tyler returned and handed a pop to Jared and a nice cold beer to Gramps. "You had a thought you wanted to share?" Gramps asked as he took a gulp of his beer. "Ahhh," said Tyler, "that hits the spot," mimicking his grandpa and setting his pop on the log next to him that he was sitting on. "Every now and then my friends at school talk about aliens, and of course most of us think they would be something scary and strange, but after hearing what is said in that book, I think they might be similar to us." Gramps looked at Jared who seemed to be interested in what Tyler just said, asked Jared what he thought. Jared just said, "I don't know, what do you think?" looking back at this grandpa and taking a sip from his pop. Mr. Reed breathed in again and said, "You know, I know of things that the governments have all been very careful not to indulge information on, but I think Tyler is onto something when he thinks they are like us." Not real sure how to take what his Gramps just said, Jared asked him point blank. "Do you believe there are aliens out there somewhere on other planets?" Gramps looked him square in the eyes and said, "Not only do I know they exist on other planets, but they have been visiting the earth for thousands of years, in and out of our dimension of reality."

Gramps moved his gaze over to Tyler who was wide-eyed with anticipation eager to hear what Gramps might say next. "You know there are aliens, Gramps," Tyler said moving and knocking over his pop. Jared was waiting for Gramps reply. Gramps took a moment to think about what he would say. "Since the 1950's governments from all over the world have been collecting evidence, and as of today there are more than one hundred thousand UFO cases on file, most of which have recently been released into the public domain from a number of governments. But, for the most part only a handful of people dare to put their reputation on the line for talking too much about it, but even so, more military officials are coming forward in the last few years and sharing their information."

Jared drilled in a little harder this time leaning forward a little, "Gramps, have you ever seen an alien in person?" Gramps smiled, shaking his head and said, "I have not personally seen an alien" and took another swig from his beer, then looked down at the book in his lap and turned the page. Gramps knew this was getting a little too close to revealing secrets he signed numerous contracts over the years agreeing to remain silent about. Mr. Reed said, "let's keep reading as it seems we are getting into some interesting information here." Tyler and Jared glanced at each other for a moment both knowing that Gramps was hiding something that would totally change people's view of the world.

Creation Creates

Both Spirit Light and Spirit Form is governed by Vibration and Love and Light and Sound. Form is made of these same Attributes inside the DNA but of projections of a governing Holographic system created to have Their Expressions within the Collective Consciousness of each Spirit Creator which vibrated on Their own frequency and therefore hidden from one another, but known to all. Each of the Spirits within the Collective imagined Their own celestial Universe with the power of Love that united all the Spirits and Their Forms as they would breathe them into existence through thought.

With an explosion of Light and Sound, the Cosmos rang with an Orchestra of Benevolent Harmony of Tones that Sprang forth into Life, each Spirit of Light and Spirit of Form, each one Unique Expressions of Themselves and The Eternal One.

There is no Hierarchy in the Heavens, nor is The Eternal One above another for All is as One and of The One. The Expressions of each were Alive unto Themselves, and their Consciousness were as One, complete and whole and perfect as The Eternal One, for they were and are The Eternal One.

It was almost completely dark now, and the stars filled the cloudless sky with billions of stars. The crescent moon was also rising now into the heavenly scene. Mr. Reed, looking up into the sky, told the boys to look up as he pointed out some of the different constellations that were so clear from this place on earth, one of the reasons Mr. Reed's father came to love this piece of land.

He said, "After hearing what we just read, makes you feel pretty small knowing that this is only one of a trillion universes, and who says God stopped there?" Tyler, still looking up, added, "And yet even though we are small in form, we are a part of God!" Jared, now looking at Tyler and then Gramps added, "We say God, and yet now that single word means the One of every expression - us, all people and everything." Mr. Reed looked deep into Jared's eyes, just nodded slowly in awe of the depths of the understanding Jared and Tyler were grasping.

Mr. Reed looked over to Tyler and asked him how he felt about that. Tyler said, "Pretty great!" Then Jared remembering what he learned at church said, "But what about sin? I thought that sin separated us from God," looking back at Gramps with a question in his face. "I mean, I have done bad things and surely said some things that were not very nice. So, I feel bad at times when I look back on those things, you know?" Mr. Reed nodding his head looked at Tyler and asked him what he thought about what Jared was saying.

Tyler shrugged his shoulders and said, "yeah, I guess that sounds right, but based on what you have been reading, maybe there is more we don't know. I mean, like, it doesn't seem like these 'Spirits and Forms' could ever sin." Gramps nodded his head affirming both boys for being very honest about their thoughts. He said, "Let's read on and see what's coming up next. Maybe your questions will be answered." Turning the page, Mr. Reed continued to read.

Filling Creation

Throughout the next trillions and trillions of earth years the Universes were filling with Galaxies and Stars bursting to Life and Planets that over time from molten rock and minerals slowly cooled, and the Spirit and Consciousness of each gave Life to the smallest Micro Organisms as they began their journeys into every type of Creature, Great and Small over Millions of Years that would Swim and Walk and Fly, and others that can only be Expressed in Light and Vibration.

This was the Design of each Spirit overseeing Their Universe. The Foliage and Water and Rocks and all kinds of Spirits and Forms, Hidden and Seen that Existed on Them had Their own Spirit of Life in Them. On the Surface or in the Heavens or within had Their Life and Breath and had their Being. Each one complete and whole and perfect as the Universe, as the first Spirit, as The Eternal One for they were and are all One and within the One.

Jared said, "So Gramps, what happens to these beings when they die? So far I do not hear anything about when they die." Mr. Reed said, "There is an idea that many people all over the world believe in what's called reincarnation. Even the people of Jesus' day eluded to the idea when they thought Elijah's spirit had returned in the form of John the Baptist. That does not just happen unless that perspective already exists within their community and belief system. This is a belief that the body returns to the ground and the spirit goes back to where it came from. Then the spirit returns again into a new body born as a baby into a new family. There is decades of study that show that the spirit always remains in the spirit realm, the heavens, while also within form, in a body. Some people believe that the body never needs to die to go back to spirit. Like Elijah - poof, gone! He just wanted to go back home. I believe Jesus also ascended prior to his death on the cross but also knew how to stay around by manifesting a body. Maybe there are souls that go hang out as a whale today and tomorrow just go back home, and the whale may or may not even know." Tyler said, "Wow, that would be cool," smiling at Jared who was clearly thinking of his own adventure! Mr. Reed returned to the book and continued.

Ages of Development

Throughout the Ages, as Beings advanced within Their own Galaxies at different paces on different Planets using the Materials and Physics that were similar to each Planet, and also different from others became the Building Blocks of Civilizations who Advanced in Science and Technologies Creating all Forms of transportation, electrical and water systems, agriculture and even teleportation systems.

Others created flying vessels that could change Vibration and Frequency to appear into and disappear from different Dimensions within the same Star System and even to different Galaxies. Still, others would learn how to travel by thought alone. Throughout the Ages, the Flow of Love Manifested Itself within the Spirits and Forms giving the fill of Abundance to every Desire which was the Desire and Will of The Eternal One.

Mr. Reed took another sip of beer while looking at Tyler and knew by his inability to sit still when he wanted something. So, he asked him what was on his mind. Tyler said, "Based on what you just read, there are aliens or 'beings' from all over the universe, and they must have spaceships." Gramps said, sure seems that way. Tyler's mind went off into space. Jared was currently texting one of his girlfriends while Gramps continued. "When I was younger, I believed as my father did that God created the universe and all within it, and earth was the only planet that had life. But there is too much evidence that is pointing to life outside of our planet. NASA has pictures of unnatural formations and objects on the Moon and on Mars. This is no longer a secret and part of the public domain. And the Mars rover wheels are decaying indicating that there is some form of bacteria or living organism.

You guys with me here?" Tyler looked down and over to his grandpa completely missing what his Gramps just said, "Um, based on all that you are reading, it seems everyone and everything is a part of God, and yet when I look around me it all seems so separate." "Individual," Jared added pressing the 'send' button on his phone. Tyler agreed, nodding his head. "Gramps, how do you see things in the world?" Mr. Reed said, "I think as we get older and begin to step beyond the things we know and been taught, there is something inside of each one of us that is seeking for some kind of truth to who we are. We are born into this world and grow up and old... like I am. For much of our lives, we just get busy with our lives and families without asking why. What is this all about? And yet perhaps in some underlining way we are always moving down the paths that are leading us to more truths and more love."

Jared said, "I have been thinking about this a little now and then at night when I can't sleep. I feel kind of lost and wonder who I am sometimes. It's like I am being kept from something, like I am not free, but not free from what I don't know," his voice trailing off as he stared unblinkingly at the flames of the fire.

Then there was silence among the three of them, all now staring into the fire, memorized by the flames for a moment. Then Mr. Reed said in a soft voice, "Maybe the separation we see around us is only part of the illusion we are to experience. I know I have learned a great deal throughout my life about myself. I also know that we are all just made up of particles of the same stuff the stars are made of, and most of it is space… nothingness. And yet at the same time, because we are a part of the same stuff, we are all part of one thing." Jared said, "We are learning about quantum energy and physics in school and what they are talking about is much of what you are saying."

Mr. Reed said, "In the Bible, Jesus talked about the kingdom of heaven was not a place, as not here or there, but within. That kind of makes us and everyone a part of God don't you think?" Jared said, "But what about sin Gramps? Who cares about the heavenly places when the Bible also says that all have sinned and fall short of the glory of God? I don't want to go to hell when I die because I didn't do something right!" Tyler was quiet and looking down at his feet. Mr. Reed said, "Well let's think about that for a moment because I too grew up in the same church and once believed these things." That statement caught Tyler's attention and heightened Jared's.

Mr. Reed continued, "Like I said a few minutes ago, as I grew older, other thoughts came to me that caused me to question what I was taught. The Bible does say that verse you mentioned about sin, but it is in the doctrines of man's interpretations and perspectives of what they believe that we grow up into and believe as part of the one ultimate truth. Has your mom let you go to the church across the street from ours? Both Jared and Tyler shook their heads, and Jared said, "No way! She says they don't believe in baptism the way we do and so are misguided and going to hell." "Exactly!" Gramps said in agreement, recognizing once again to the blatant foolishness in what we cling to as humans. "Tyler, what about you? Are you afraid you're going to hell?" Tyler looked at Gramps for a moment and then down into the fire, "I just cannot believe a God of love could send anyone into a place of fire and torment. But it says so right in the Bible and Pastor Jenkins says it's true, so who am I as a young kid going to question that?"

Gramps smiled as he remembered all too well the hell and brimstone preaching he grew up with, and Jenkins was no different. "Tyler, what does your heart tell you about a God that can cast His children away?" "Scary! I think I really don't want to know Him," Tyler replied. "But He is a God of Love Tyler, don't you want to know this God of Love?" Gramps purposely trying to drive a point to the contradictions within its literal message. Tyler, a little unsure of what his grandpa is asking said, "Well, of course, I want to know God is loving, but I cannot ever image for a moment that you Gramps would ever hurt me, like throw me into this fire here," said a little angry and frightened at the same time as a tear left his eye, turning to look down so no one would see.

Mr. Reed did not need to see to understand the emotion he just heard. But he stayed cool and let the boy soak in the moment as he continued. "Tyler, I could never in my wildest dreams ever even have that thought run through my mind," but the statement fell on Tyler's deaf ears because he was too afraid of hell to know to believe anything else, and his grandpa knew it. "Tyler, look at me. For only a moment, I give you permission to set your beliefs down so that you, who are perfect and filled with love and compassion, can reply to my next question. Ok?" Tyler nodded his head. "Tyler, what does your heart tell you about who God is?"

Tyler waited a moment before responding as he was thinking about what he really wanted to believe about God and the stories he heard about Jesus. "I want to know God is loving and could never hurt anyone like I know Gramps that you could never hurt me. I feel safe with you, and I want to feel safe with God…" Tyler's fears returned as he thought about what he has been taught, "but I am just not sure I can trust Him, how can I really know that He will not send me to hell?" At this, he began to whimper and wipe tears from his eyes, but he did not want to leave because he trusted his brother and Gramps not to criticize him, and that made him feel safe.

Jared, feeling a tug to fill the dead space with some words said, "I feel like God is loving, and Jesus seems really cool in how he handled himself, but even Jesus talked about hell." Gramps jumped in on that and said, "Jesus talked about Gehenna, the city dump in the valley of Hinnom, where years before people used to sacrifice their babies to Moloch. Jesus was saying that if you live outside of love, outside of loving your neighbors, be in judgment of others, hurting and stealing from others, or just not being compassionate, then you are Spiritually dead and are like the dump where things are thrown away because they have no value, they become useless, where the fire never dies, where there is gnashing of teeth because of anger and blame of others. Meaning, living within a place in your heart and mind that causes yourself and others pain and suffering. You become like chaff among the wheat that is better if blown away then to be a part of the joy of the group that wants to live in harmony, within the unity of love. These are metaphors used to speak uniquely to each person who has ears to hear."

Wiping the tears off his face with his sleeve, Tyler said, "So there is no hell Gramps?" "What does your heart tell you, Tyler?" Gramps said. "That it can't exist," Tyler said. Gramps nodded with a smile, "I think you are growing up and beginning to see things as an adult should when they set their fears aside." Tyler suddenly realized by what Gramps just said that he did in fact set the fear of hell aside for a moment to share his deeper truths he held within but never dared to say.

Jared, not wanting Gramps to get off the hook so easily, and because he also believed hell was real said again, "Gramps, what about the verse that says, all have sinned and fall short of the glory of God?" Mr. Reed replied, "First of all, sin is a word that we made up to address the dark side of humanity that exists on earth that refers to the duality of life. Push and pull, up and down. It gives us a place within form, our body, to base things on. Good and bad come from these same opposites but through fear, that which is absent of love invents ideas that God is angry at sin, and therefore we are somehow wicked and undeserving of God's love, that we deserve punishment. To fall short of the Glory of God means that while we are in the body, we have become unaware and lost to who we really are, spiritual expressions of God, we are part of God! How can we be bad unless God is also bad? That is impossible! What is possible is that while within form, in the body, we can choose to do as we please and in that do things to other forms, other people, and even things like spilling oil in the ocean or cutting down complete forests to make a few bucks. Yes, there is what we call sin in the world, but what it is, is the acting out in ways other than that of compassion to people, animals, and the environment, all of which are our spiritual brothers and sisters. Many Christians don't seem to care much about the earth or environment because they believe it is all going to be destroyed - again because they are taking the Bible completely literally. There are many literal and historical things in the Bible, but that does not mean it all is. Most is symbolic and should be read and understood metaphorically as there is no other way for the Spirit to communicate with a literal, linear world."

Jared commented on that last statement, "But I thought the Bible was the inerrant word of God Gramps?" I will ask you the same question I asked your brother, giving you permission to set your beliefs down for a moment. What does your heart tell you?" Jared said, "Well, when I am at church and listening to Pastor Jenkins, he makes it sound like it is all true and clear, and I seem to understand it as he says. But then throughout the week, as I am away from hearing the message, too many thoughts come to mind that don't fit into what the Pastor is saying. It's like I know that something does not make sense, but I also don't know what makes sense either… does that make sense? They all chuckled in how that came out, but also in agreement realizing that it made perfect sense. Tyler got up and put another log on the fire and Jared poked it around a bit sending sparks into the sky like little stars heading for home.

Mr. Reed replied to Jared's statement, saying, "We have been reading some stuff that say some different things about who God is." "The Eternal One!" Tyler threw in.

"Yes," Gramps agreed, glancing at him with a smile. "That we are in a way all part of this Source of energy, of everything. As I read these words, do they speak truth to your heart, looking at Tyler and Jared? Jared nodded and said, "It is almost like we don't know some things, and when we hear something, it either feels right or wrong to us." Tyler said, "Gramps when you were reading the previous pages, I felt like I wanted to be there watching things happen! I felt very good about all of it." "Honestly Tyler, I think we were all there at the creation of things, we just don't remember," Gramps replied. Tyler stared up into the night sky just pondering the thought.

"Jared," Gramps said, "tell me more about how you feel about learning things that seem to fit with your heart." "Well," Jared said slowly frowning his eyebrows a bit as if he was really thinking deeply about what he wanted to say. "It is almost the opposite for me I think. When I go to church, I am told how to believe and not to trust myself. What comes to mind is the verse, 'trust in the Lord with all thine heart; and lean not unto thine own understanding.' So, I believe I should trust the Bible because that holds the only truth and because I am a sinner, well, whatever that means, that I should not trust in my own understanding. Which makes me wonder how I trust in anything! I don't know."

Gramps looked at him and said, "Jared, you are a precious child of God. Breathe and slow down a bit and forget anything you been taught for a moment. Tell me in your own words without thinking you need to recite verses. Just dig deep within and share what you feel in your heart." Jared visibly relaxed on his log and said nothing for a moment. No one was in a hurry. Jared said, "I feel I have some understanding and truth that I somehow know but cannot always explain. It's like a thought comes to me, and I know it completely as truth, but then it's gone, and I cannot even tell it to myself in words to help me remember, but like there are not words sometimes to share what is on my mind. I'm getting all confused now aren't I?"

Gramps put his hand over his mouth and said, "**The force is great with this one me-thinks**," sounding like Darth Vader. They both looked at Gramps in shock, and then they all burst out laughing at how silly it sounded, especially in how grandpa looked.

"Jared," Mr. Reed said, "I'm going to go back to your verse. 'Trust in the Lord with all thine heart, and lean not unto thine own understanding.' The next verse says, 'In all thy ways acknowledge him, and he shall direct thy paths.' Trust in the Lord, acknowledge him. Do these sound like verses telling you to trust in the Bible, or in God?" Tyler butted in, "I thought to trust the Bible was to trust God, it's the same thing?" Gramps gave a look to Tyler that said, really? "What do you think about those statements Jared," 'Trust in the Lord, acknowledge him.' "Well, like I was saying before, I think I know things inside that are true." Gramps jumped in, "And could we say that the Lord being inside you, as Jesus said, the kingdom of heaven is within you, that we being a part of God hold God within us? To acknowledge him is to acknowledge yourself because God lives within you. God is not somewhere out there, pointing into the night sky, as though separate from you, but he is also out there and within at the same time. The Bible says that God is omnipresent, that is everywhere and all at the same time. Separation is impossible if that is true."

"Now here I am bringing up verses, but I do it because it rings true to me. Here is another, 'Be still and know that I am God.' Many people in the church are afraid to be still and know God. Or being still is sitting somewhere and reading their Bible, and I'm not going to say that is wrong, but it is still a diversion from being still and alone with God without any other form of distraction. They do not want to listen to their own hearts many times because they may not like to know what it is telling them about themselves, or most often, too busy and unaware of God within trying to speak to them. We should take a break from form, the flesh as the Bible says, and be still within Spirit and allow our awareness of the Christ consciousness that indwells us. To listen carefully because God is still speaking. To make the Bible all important is to give attention to form like anything else, which is of the flesh. The Bible within itself often keeps people from experiencing their spiritual self when the Bible's purpose should be to point us to having an experience with the Spirit."

"Christ consciousness Gramps," Tyler asked? "Yes, many people believe that Christ is Jesus' last name, or a little less childish, that the Christ came into the world to save us as though he would be a person they were waiting for, again thinking very literal about these words. The Christ is an ancient word also known as the Chrestos and Christos, from Latin Christus and Greek Khristos 'Christ.' Meaning benignity, kindness, usefulness, etc." Gramps continued, "the Christ was always here from the beginning as it is within and is the consciousness of God. Christ is the relationship we have in our spirit to God. The conduit. The telephone line. The Christ has come into the world, but we are hidden from it, unaware within Form, but our spirit seeks to find it within the kingdom of heaven, which is where Tyler?" "Inside us?" Replied Tyler. Gramps nodded and smiled and looked over to Jared just to see if he was following.

Jared said, "This is making a little more sense to me now. Like you say, it is more on the spiritual side of who we are and makes it more unique to who I am personally. Maybe that is how God becomes more personal to each of us." Gramps smiled in amazement to the understanding of both these young men. Jared piped in again, "So are you saying that I should listen to my heart and not the Bible?"

Gramps twisted an eyebrow and said, "Yes and no. Yes, always listen to your heart if what you are hearing is good for you and good for others. But the Bible is filled with great words of wisdom, like, do unto others as you would have them do onto you. If the voice inside you causes harm to yourself or others or causes you to fear, then you need to question where that voice came from. Right? If wrong, it is most likely your own understanding. The Bible also says, 'There is no fear in love; but perfect love casteth out fear: because fear hath torment. He that feareth is not made perfect in love.' Does the thought of hell cause you to fear?" Both boys nodded with of course on their faces. "So, therefore, hell is not of love! Does love make you think of hell?" They both gave a funny look like, that does not even make sense! "The Bible, when interpreted literally, has more contradictions than any other book I know of because it was never meant to. Our doctrines and beliefs invented this idea. But the Literalist will fabricate all kinds of things out of nothing or use other verses that help his or her case to keep God holy and righteous. They live in fear of losing their investment of their lifelong held beliefs, so they try their best to put love and fear into the same box.

We must live daily within Christ, that is to remain within the heart of God who is within our heart. Jesus said I and the Father are one. This was not because he was claiming to be God as the church has made him out to be, but that we and the Father are also one, as in everyone and everything while appearing separate in form, and yet are really all interconnected and united within The Eternal One," tapping the book on his lap. Mr. Reed could see that what he was sharing was a lot to take in, but that the boys seemed to be at peace with it at the moment, so he took another swallow of beer and returned to his book.

Creation of the Soul

Up until this Age, Spirits existed as They wanted within any Form or without Form, or moving into other Forms. All Spirits have the Breath of Life within Them which remain within Spirit and within Form. Then The Eternal One spoke, and the Soul came into Being as Its own Expression which would exist United within Spirit and move within and without Form.

The Soul has the power to Divide into any number of Soul Expressions without diminishing the Whole of each Expression as It was the Whole. Souls will keep a continuous record of everything It Experiences within a Higher Consciousness so that over time and through unlimited Existences as Expressions within and without Form, It will grow with Knowledge and Wisdom. The Soul's purpose is to find Its way back to The Eternal One where It will Find Itself United as The One.

Jared said, "I didn't know the spirit and the soul were different things." Tyler said, "I think it is cool that the soul can be in multiple places at the same time! I wonder if I'm also in Sparky?" Jared shook his head a bit condescending, "Tyler, animals do not have souls, and the way Sparky lays around, I doubt he even has a spirit!" Mr. Reed chuckled and chimed in, "I'm not so sure. The original Hebrew communicates this a little differently than most translations and does not make that distinction. But who really knows." Mr. Reed continued reading. Both boys were thinking how much fun it might be to be a bird or an elephant or a fish.

Into The Darkness

There came a time within the greater and more evolved Planets and Its Races of Beings who were by this Age traveling throughout the Galaxies having Mastered Form and Matter, Biology and other Incredible Feats of Science and Technology.

The Eternal One decided It wanted to Experience Separation from Itself through Its Expressions. It was not as much a decision of The Eternal One as much as it was a Collective of Higher Consciousness as the Expressions, those Beings that were of common stature, evolved to walking upright and more Intelligent among Their Peers that wanted to Experience Separation from Love, from The Eternal One, from Itself.

The Oldest and most Wise Souls agreed to this Experiment and Adventure. New Planets and Atmospheres were formed within specific Star Systems from the Creation of Their Collective Conscious thoughts, specifically Designed to remove a portion of Their DNA upon Birth, not Born from Their Mother Planet anymore, but from the Creatures Themselves who evolved over time and into Beings of Their own Expressions whose portion of DNA would also be removed, passed down and through the preceding Beings. Born as Offspring and Nurtured into an Unawareness of Love. A portion of DNA left would cause the Beings to desire for The Eternal One. This will feel like a Darkness, becoming Lost to Itself, an Emptiness and an Illusion. The Eternal One wanted to play a game of Hide and Seek with Itself where It would be Born countless times through Expressions into the World unaware of Itself, open Its eyes and ask, Who Am I?

Jared took a sip of his pop and said, "So Gramps, from this is sounds like other planets or star systems, or whatever, before this time did not have the same issues like sin and separation. This actually explains a lot when it talks about a darkness and being lost. The other thing I get the feeling about is that Spirit is in some way scientific like there are physics to it somehow." Tyler turned on his log to get more comfortable, facing Jared a little more. "What I mean by that is that, like, we as humans already have learned so much about biology and physics that we are only just short of actually creating some of the parts that make up living tissue." Mr. Reed also sat up a little more, impressed with Jared's understanding of science. "I totally understand what you're saying Jared, believe me, I understand."

"How about you Tyler," Gramps asked. "Well, it sounds like there were many places like earth, maybe even still are." "And what is earth like Tyler," Gramps asked? "Well, you know, like we been talking about where we think we know something, or don't know and believe we do somehow, but is hidden. But that there are goodness and badness that exists. Some people help the poor while others steal from a store. We say that God is in control, but I don't really see that when I look at things, like when a person is born blind or like how my best friend is sick with a disease that he may die from. Somehow deep down I know God loves me, but tomorrow a shooting could happen at our school, or our house may burn down, and I will feel like God is not there. Earth does not sound at all like the first pages of that book where it seems the beings live in peace and know God so fully."

Mr. Reed being very impressed with Tyler's insight asked him, "So where do you think sin came from?" Tyler thought for a moment and said, "Well, in the Bible it says that Adam and Eve ate the fruit of the tree God told them not to. However, that has been bugging me because it does not make sense to me that because they disobeyed God on that, that everyone now is sinful and going to hell if they don't get saved. That just does not sound like how God or Jesus would make things work, it's just all twisted… I don't know, it doesn't make any sense." Gramps was impressed with Tyler's last statement as he knew it came from a place in his heart and not his head like his first statement was.

Gramps asked them both, "So what makes sense to how things work?" Jared said, "Sin might be another word for being lost then. But not in a way that needs to be punished for being bad, but that… um, but that we need to find our way to being found." Jared, shaking his head, "That came out wrong." Gramps jumped in, "Let me try and see if this is what you are trying to say. The Bible says that we are born into a world of sin, this does not mean we are sinful, but that we were born into a world of duality and free choice. Meaning, unlike how many planets most likely operate in complete harmony and don't even know of such a thing, on earth and maybe others we have the freedom to choose good or bad because there exists a different dynamic that caused us to be hidden from the fulness of God. It's like you said Jared, you know something to be true but cannot articulate it into words. Something is hidden. And because God is perfect and complete there is nothing missing from us other than our own present state of lost-ness. Which also means that to be saved from this lost condition is in finding out who we are by seeking after God. Maybe as simple as loving others reveals who we are. And when we die, we go back home to Spirit wherever that is and then later come back to continue to grow."

"So, the Bible is the way to find God," said Tyler. "Yes," said Gramps, "it is a way to help us on our journey, just like any other religion in the world teaches its people to seek after God or Source or The Great Spirit. The problem comes when they stop at the very childlike literalization of their scriptures and never grow up into seeking God within and trusting themselves to be enough, believing that the God they have been learning about lives within each of them, in all of us. I'm not saying that people in the church do not have a relationship with God, everyone does at some level of awareness. I am saying that for many, the truth of their doctrines has become so important that they have stepped into a place of fear thinking they need to cling to their truths, and the love that was once there leading them into the heart of God from a very young age has been replaced with truths that do nothing more than scare people away because of the judgements they contain."

Mr. Reed held up a finger and said, "hold on a moment, I need to use the bathroom, so give me a moment, and we will continue when I return." Tyler turned to his brother and asked if they should call their mom. Jared said, "No that he had texted her not long ago and let her know that we would be up late and that we were having a campfire and talking with Gramps about God. She was happy to hear that and said that she loves us and to have a good night." Tyler added, "I don't think mom knows what Gramps knows," with question in his eyes. Jared agreed, shaking his head, "But mom loves lots of people at our church and us, and I think no matter what you believe, loving others without judgment is what is most important. I think that is what Gramps is sharing with us." Tyler replied, "But she doesn't want you to visit your friend Pete's church down the street." Jared nodded in acknowledgment to his brother's statement.

As Mr. Reed approached, he said, "That's better," as he returned to his seat setting down another beer on the ground next to him. "Well let's see," Gramps said, "seems the next pages are… Yes, the book is listing all the planets by name that have undertaken… dual consciousness... Here it says… Oh! I'm sorry, do you guys have any questions?" They both shook their head and said no. Mr. Reed turned the page and continued to read.

Dualistic Experiments

These are the accounts of each Planet within Their Solar systems that have undertaken the process of Duality of Consciousness. Consciousness in and of Itself is of the One Consciousness. Duality is the Illusion of Separateness, or the Hiding of the Whole for the purpose of learning how Soul within Form will function and act without Its Awareness of Itself and then given Freedom to Choose within an Environment Designed to change.

Gramps reading forward a bit, "…more about what we learned in 'Into The Darkness.' So let's see here," Gramps began to page through the book, "so the Garmatelis, Myrmote, Ziour..., boy, some of these I cannot even pronounce, no, no," turning more pages, "The Pleiadians Star system…" still paging through and in a low monotone voice shared without thinking, "I have heard of the Pleiadians in some of our briefings in the military, I believe many still live within the earth…" Tyler and Jared looking at each other a bit wide-eyed and disbelief to what Gramps just said, and then back at him with more interest. "Let's see here," Gramps babbled on, "no… Daro.. Daridra, whatever… Ok! Here we go! What I was hoping to find," smiling as he looked up at the boys...

The Milky Way Galaxy

The Accounts of the Milky Way Galaxy. Time is unknowable for time is always changing over the Ages. Time is also an Illusion within Form. From within the Heavens, We, the Counsel of Duality, stood on the Shores of a celestial Plane Envisioning the Greatest Adventure ever to be Created within the Cosmos. Many of the Old Souls standing with Us had already been through many Planetary Adventures, and Some were also in the mists of Their Adventures on other Star Systems at this same time but willing to Embark on another wishing to grow wiser.

As a Collective Consciousness, we agreed to Our Vision, and the Galaxy Exploded into Existence and into Its own Mineral based Biological Holographic Dimension and Vibration. The Stars found Their places and the Planets began their Ageless Journeys around Their own Solar System. Mercury, Venus, Earth, Mars, Jupiter, Saturn, Uranus, Neptune and Pluto and Their Moons were all put in Their places, turning within Themselves and Orbiting around Their Planets and Their Father Sun. Nibiru was placed into Its Own orbit as the System required a Nemesis to disrupt perfection Creating Balance starting at a

Planetary Frequency.

"So, Gramps," Jared said, "when it is talking about old souls, do you think we are old souls? I mean, after what you said about reincarnation, we could have come to earth many times already!" Tyler was deep in thought to what Jared just said. Mr. Reed said, "I think you are beginning to put the puzzle together young feller!" Tyler said, "So then that would mean that everyone on earth are old souls? That's a lot!" Gramps said, "I do not have an answer to that. With so many different beings in the galaxy, it could be that while they are old souls from other duality planets, that they may be new to the earth, but I am just speculating just thinking about this now myself."

"And also," Jared added, "I never heard of Nibiru! I have studied the solar system in school and learned a lot about the planets, but Nibiru is not one of them." "Well," said Mr. Reed, "back in the mid 1800, there were astrologers that believed there was another planet out there because of something seemed to be tugging at Uranus and Neptune. There are also some very ancient Sumerian texts about a planet on a highly elliptical orbit that travels 3600 years around our sun. Today many astrologers believe we are beginning to see it at times behind our sun. The planet is also called Planet X, as well as Nemesis because it can cause gravitational pulls to the planets and even earth, which at this very time is even tilting more on its axis than ever before recorded in modern history."

Tyler said, "Are we going to be in trouble, Gramps?" Mr. Reed said, "No. I think we will be just fine although there are a few people who believe it will get a bit colder and those living on coastal properties may need to move further inland. But this is normal and part of the cycles of the planets. What I find interesting is that NASA just found a ten-mile diameters object that is admitting more light than all the stars in our galaxy combined, and they don't know how it can give off that much light as the power of it defies all known physics. We are only just beginning to learn about space as we go deeper and deeper into it." Jared said, "The more we learn, the smaller I seem to feel, you know like we live on this small blue dot out in the universe." Gramps nodding his head just taking that in while gazing up at the stars. "So, what's next Gramps!" Tyler blurted out, breaking up the moment. Gramps looked down and said, "well, let's see here," turning the page.

The Accounts of Planet Earth

The Earth was without Form, Molten and spinning for Ages as It cooled. For One and a Half billion Years the Earth cooled to make ready for Life to fill Its Lands. Mountains rose from the deep molten core, vast Valleys sunk in Their places. Volcanoes spewed forth their Lava covering Its Land with Smoke and Soot hiding the Sun's Light for another Age.

Then when there was only Darkness and Calm, and the Heavens were Clear and Pure, The Spirit moved upon the seemingly lifeless Sphere and Touched Her Essence. Her Spirit Sprang to Life and She became a Living Being onto Herself. Mother Earth would bring forth Life from the Womb of Her Essence, from the Beauty of Her Procreative Energy She gave Birth to the Biological Particles Designed with Their DNA by the Spiritual Systems put in place Eons ago.

Jared seemed to enjoy this part of the book more as it related to things he was learning at school. He said, "So I know our school teaches evolution, and that sure sounds like what is going on here with its millions of years, but Pastor Jenkins says that the earth was created about six to eight thousand years ago. I have talked to my friends on both sides who seem to have information for both, so I am not sure what to think about it."

Mr. Reed said, "Well, centuries ago we did not have the information we have today. I grew up believing in the six days of creation also because it was what I was told. Being in the military has afforded me access to information that is not known to the public, to the world. Based on what I have seen and learned, like the newly discovered civilization found by our satellites about one mile below the ice in Antarctica. Excavation has been going on since 2001 and archaeologists date it back about 50,000 years."

Jared and Tyler were both intrigued but asked their grandpa if this was information they should hear. Gramps said taking a sip of his beer, "There is a lot of pressure from the public now demanding that the governments disclose things that have been hidden. The US military holds information that is really about 60 to 70 years ahead of the public technologically. The highly-classified people excavating these sites said that it looked like the cold hit them in a moment as they died immediately. Within were several different races found which were fully intact, even beings with elongated skulls and some beings that were over fifteen foot tall. Many of these have been removed leaving only those that looked most like humans to take photos of the area because they want to offer the public more evidence to the age of the earth without shocking them with life that defies what we been taught about Adam and Eve being the first humans to walk the earth."

Jared and Tyler were both studying their grandpa's face closely to make sure he was not just telling a fib. "I'm serious," Mr. Reed said nodding his head and taking another sip of beer. "I know this raises all kinds of questions in your heads which we can talk about tomorrow when we head out again to go fishing. But for now, I want to try and get through the account of the earth yet tonight." Jared and Tyler nodded their head in agreement, and so Gramps continued to read.

The Akashic Records of Earth was put in place and would record and hold the Ageless Vibrations of every Living Thing that would Swim in the Seas, Crawl on the Land and Fly in the Heavens. Over millions of years, Mother Earth continued to bring forth Life after It's kind but also Branching off where Appropriate to sustain Life in Perfect Harmony throughout the Earth. At one point, the Souls of Its Creation began to enter the Spirits of the Creatures of the Earth to experience Life in All Its Forms. Some have even entered Flowers and Trees, and even the Rocks of the Mountains, while other Parts of Them were Great Birds sailing on the Winds of the Heavens.

Tyler giggled and said, "Jared, that would be a great place for your soul to spend some time, in a rock!" Then he laughed while the others shook their heads and smiled. Jared sad, "Well, if this is true, then spirits are what give life to creatures, but the soul is somehow unique on its own." Mr. Reed nodding his head in agreement. Tyler asked, "Gramps in church all the creatures were made after their kind, but here while it says the same, it also says that it splits off to create harmony, what does that mean?"

Mr. Reed said, "In evolution, we theorize that in some cases depending on the circumstances that arise, some species changed into something else. Some whales for example still have bones where rear legs would be and yet no fin or evidence that it needs them at all. In fact, they are not even tied to the skeleton anymore, but just out within the muscle tissue. It seems to me that at one time in the life of its kind it was first another that had rear legs and walked, possibly on land before it went into the sea. This is very interesting because most theories say they started in the water and moved onto the land. Just the opposite." "Wow, I didn't know that," said Tyler. Jared also shook his head not knowing that either. Mr. Reed said, "All you need to do is dig for more of this information. Most people are comfortable with what they know, so have no interest to learn what they don't know. Especially if what they could learn counters their beliefs. Let's continue." Mr. Reed turned the page.

The Consciousness of Karma

As Life continued over the next several Billions of years, The Spirit of Lucifer, Who took on the role to bring Challenge to Freedom of Choice to the Expressions within Form, was sent into the Earth Plane to offer the Alternatives to test Their Character, but never beyond Their capability to Endure. Lucifer became known in the Spirit World as The Eternal One's Highest Esteemed Companion, for It offered Love an Adversary as a Backdrop to Love, an Illusion of Darkness for the Light to Dispel and Shine through.

"Hold on now there Gramps!" Said Tyler. "Lucifer is the Devil! Satan! How can God call him a great, esteemed, whatever... companion?" Mr. Reed looked over to Jared and asked him if he had an answer to that question. Jared said, "Well, I agree with Tyler, I thought Lucifer and a third of the angels were cast out of heaven because he tried to become greater than God."

Mr. Reed said, "The Bible says that the Devil goes around like a lion looking for someone to devour. Jesus said to Peter, Get thee behind me satan. The Bible translators took the Hebrew and Greek meaning of this word which was a metaphorical idea of an adversary, not in the form of a being or fallen angel, but in the idea of a spiritual contention, to offer an alternative to a better choice allowing man to grow spiritually, and then capitalized the word making it a pronoun, a being, literalizing the meaning which completely removed the spirituality of the writers purpose. Was Jesus talking to Peter as Satan? No! Peter was saying things that were contradictory to what Jesus believed he needed to do. Peter may not even ever said those words to Jesus, nor Jesus to Peter, but the writer wanted to bring about the conflict that was going on within Jesus' heart."

Mr. Reed continued. "This is a representation of the conflict that goes on within our own hearts as we make decisions for our lives. For Jesus, this was a decision of life and death and Jesus chose death as a witness to what extent we must love others, and that he was telling us that the body is only temporary. When read literally, we only have a childish story that brings in the form of an equal power against God, which is impossible and silly. Moreover, we bring emphases to an evil creature and our minds go away from the struggle Jesus was facing, when the story is not about an evil at all, nor is it really about Jesus.

Metaphorically the story is about you and me, and who we are spiritually while in the body, and how we live within life and the choices we make that will impact ourselves and our loved ones. Literally, it is something that happened two thousand years ago, and repeating it over and over and over to try to keep it alive is death itself. The Bible can come to life when we apply the messages to our lives today, at this moment, in this moment and in this moment. Sorry guy! Kind of went off there."

Jared shook his head and said, "No, I think that made a lot of sense to me. I don't know that I could repeat it, but I know what you are saying, and that really helps me see the Bible from a different perspective." Tyler said, "So was Peter Satan or not?" Looking at Jared and then to his grandpa. Mr. Reed just shook his head and said, "No," with a smile. "We will have to go over that again when you get a little older. Let's continue, shall we?" Looking down Mr. Reed turned the page and continued to read.

> *The Science of Consciousness within Form on Earth became a Sliding Scale between the Reality of Love and Light and the Illusion of Darkness. Belief systems would be Created from the Minds of the Fearful that would also become the Reality to Form. The Brain would be Split in Two, One to Control the Biology of Mind and Physics, and the Other to Guild The Spirit away from Form. This will be a continual Duality within man, a Push and Pull between the Flesh and the Spirit. While on Earth within Form, Life will be shortened when the Flesh is desired, causing disease and pain and suffering. And Life will be lengthened and at Peace and Joyful when the Spirit is desired.*

Jared chimed in, "So this is kind of what you were just saying, Gramps! That this contention, this push and pull, the good and bad is all within who we are in our body. Right?" Mr. Reed said, "I think that is exactly what the Bible is also saying when it talks about satan. Even the story of Job is a great example of a metaphorical account of humanity. Life, or satan the adversary comes at us from every side, and sometimes it takes everything away from us. The question to Jobs strength lied in the idea that he would not give way to the flesh as the spirit was for him the only real truth of his life. It is a story that tells us to endure, to live in the world but not be of it, do not give into the thinking that the flesh is in some way more than just an illusion, it's not! We are here on the earth for a time to experience duality, to gain knowledge and increase in wisdom for the edifying of the soul, that part of us that is real and perfect and always within the heart of God.

Tyler said, "I never liked the story because my Sunday school teacher said it in a way that made it all fine. She said that even though Job lost all his children, God gave him more children smiling while she talked as if that was a good thing! As I thought of mom, she would be crushed to lose us, and never completely happy again just because she had new children later! I don't get it," looking back to the fire and pondering on his thought. Mr. Reed said, "That is a great point and very deep insight to something more that is going on in your heart, which is rejecting the story as literal because it then contains fear. Literally, it is a sick story of God having fun together with Satan while testing Job and allowing Satan to destroy these children and give Job a disease."

"However," Mr. Reed continued, "metaphorically, the writer is telling us that even when things are taken from us in life, more will be gained to us within our spirit because of the experiences we encounter. That we will grow through trials, and what seems like God as a deity and provoking his subjects to anger. God is not testing us, but we as expressions of God wanted to learn greater things through the experiences lived within form. Your Sunday school teacher only knows the story as literal because that is how she was taught the story. And so, in telling it from that point of view, the kids learn to combine pain and love together giving further value to believing that God can punish. Furthermore, they never learn the deeper meaning behind the story. As you learn to hear messages of the Bible you can begin to understand them at a much deeper level and apply them to yourself where you're at in life." With that said, Mr. Reed looked down again and continued reading.

Karma will be the Scale of where the Form is at throughout Life and when passing from Life, Shedding Its Form to return to dust, and entering the Heavenly Realms. Because of the Desired and Conscious Experiment being played out on Earth within Duality by Old Souls, or Old Expressions of The Eternal One, the Consciousness that They take with Them into the Spiritual Realm will continue to Exist at that same Level.

Within the Spiritual Realm, there will be much Praise and Celebration to those who finish doing better than where they started. For those who finished poorly, Praise and Celebration for participating still takes place, but They enter the Spiritual Realm in a Lower and Darker Plane where They still hold to beliefs recorded by the Akashic Records and are able to take the time They need to re-energize with Their Spiritual Family before returning to Form, born again as a baby, specifically Designed by Themselves and their Spiritual Family to Live Their Life once again to the fullest.

Jared asked his grandpa, "So what is Karma, the book mentioned that Lucifer was somehow related to Karma." Mr. Reed said, "First of all, Lucifer is a consciousness, not something that possesses a form, nor is It blameworthy as though it does anything to you without your consent. 'Satan' has become a deity and spirit of sorts that Christians blame bad things on in life. Lucifer is related to duality, to offer choice." Jared said, "Gramps that makes some sense to me, but I still don't get it."

Mr. Reed replied, "Let me give you an example. You work hard for $400 because you plan on going on a weekend trip with your buddies to go fishing. As soon as you hold the money in your hands, you have a thought about the Play Station you really want. Neither of these things are bad, but one is going to let your friends down. Lucifer plays the part to challenge you toward growth. If you would choose the Play Station, 'Satan' would be blamed for twisting things and 'making' you 'sin.' 'Sin' being the choice to be absent of love. But if you choose your buddies, Lucifer will have actually done Its job as intended. The bottom line is that you alone are responsible for your choices. Does that make sense to you?"

Jared said, "It does, and it sure sheds new light on Lucifer, or 'satan' who is seen as a wicked creature that wants to drag people to hell and hurt God. But now I can see that it is within form, our existence on earth is the experience of free choice because there is duality." "Wow!" Gramps said, "I could not have said that more clearly!" "So, what about karma," Jared asked.

Mr. Reed said, "Karma is a name that is used to measure our spiritual life on earth. What we do for ourselves, what we do for others. If you lead others to find the love that exists within them, to find God, then you have not only helped raise the consciousness of that person, but that also raises the collective consciousness of the world as a whole.

When you die and then return to earth again in your next life, you may find yourself in a better situation in life. If you hurt others or kill, your karma consciousness goes down, again also taking the collective consciousness of the world down. We can think of the dark ages as we call them. Because of so much war and bloodshed, much because of religion and the importance given to living righteously according to a set of rules and scriptures and governed by the church. This is the idea of karma according to a number of eastern religions." "What if someone takes their own life, Gramps?" Jared asked.

Mr. Reed looked at Jared with great compassion in his eyes knowing of a friend of his that recently took his life because of turmoil in the boy's family. "I know how we grew up and all we been told about things like this from the church, but I am here to tell you that God is love and there is no fear in love, which means it is only of goodness and compassion and kindness. I think people who are depressed have allowed the vibration of their essence to lower into a dark place, and so there is more for that soul to work through on the other side." Jared just stared into the fire while listening as tears welled up in his eyes, missing his friend. "I miss him, Gramps! I really miss him a lot." "I know you do Jared, we all do," Mr. Reed said.

Mr. Reed continued, "The thing I see in the writing we just read is the idea of entering the spiritual realm at lower levels. Knowing God is love, allows the creation, Its expressions to choose what they want in life. But that in death, the experiment is not over, but a kind of time out to refresh outside of the body because the heart of God is the heart of all souls who like God are in love with their brothers and sisters who continue their journeys on earth as they work to bring light and love to their fellow brothers and sisters."

Jared jumped in, "Based on doing bad, for those people that do wicked things in life, are they punished in the lower spiritual realms? And I thought God could not allow evil into His presence, how does that work?" Mr. Reed replied, "I was also thinking the same thing as I read what is written here. I think the church gets the idea of hell and punishment mainly from the doctrine of original sin." Tyler asked, "What is original sin Gramps?" "Well, as we talked about before, it is the idea that because Adam and Eve sinned in the garden, that all have sinned. But I think we are learning that sin is a man-made construct created out of our fears. And then because we are human who demand justice and punishment for wrongs against us in the body, something Jesus gave up the right to, we impute these ideas onto God, and therefore distort the meaning of love."

"Back to your question Jared. Because sin is not real or is real only within form, it is not a reality to a God of love. Death itself is an illusion and science itself is coming to this same conclusion. We are eternal whether in form or in spirit. That is our true nature. We cannot be anything other than that. Therefore, I also cannot even imagine that there is punishment as that would suggest that we are somehow less than God when we are but expressions of God Itself. Nothing can separate us from the love of God. Nothing!"

Tyler asked, "So then what keeps us from just being bad and mean to others in life if I know I will never be punished?" "Well," Gramps replied, "Nothing! But knowing that, does, that make you want to do bad things? "No," replied Tyler. "What about you Jared?" Jared said, shaking his head, "Based on the ideas in this book, and like you said, we don't know who wrote it, but it still seems even though we are not punished, we still enter a lower level somehow. What is that all about Gramps?"

Mr. Reed said, "I do not see it as something to be afraid of because the souls, you and me, all of us on this earth, are making decisions before we enter earth as to what we want to experience. People like Hitler and all that took part in the holocaust I believe made a decision to help shock humanity to its core and look closer to what it really wants in life. We have been killing each other for so many centuries, and governments and religions slowly taking more and more control over its people, that to save the world, the very planet, something drastic needed to take place. Hitler knew before he entered the earth in form, that he would be guided to do the things they did, and because of it would die and return home at a lower level and have to begin the cycle, if I can call it that, to work his way again over who knows how long back to where he may have been when he stepped forward to take on the assignment."

Tyler and Jared both just stared into the fire pondering on what their grandpa just said. Both were thinking about how that unique perspective caused them to feel compassion for Hitler where only hate existed before. God was for a moment shining light and love into these boys' hearts. Both had heard the story from their families and school and never had they considered the truly courageous man Hitler was in spirit when looking past what took place in form. Jared said, looking up at the stars, "I think I just felt a little of God's love for real as I realized how anger and hate could be turned into love just by considering things from a more spiritual perspective," looking over to his grandpa who was looking at him with a warm smile. Gramps said, "Shall we continue?" Tyler and Jared both nodded.

From Animal to Man

At the appropriate time, The Spiritual Families agreed to Speed up the Process of Evolution with the help of the Pleiadians Who were already Thousands of Years more Advanced than the Earths Civilizations. They had come from another Dimension to visit the Earth Dimension by Lowering Their Frequencies to that of Earth, Creating a Vortex in the Fabric of Space and Time. The Pleiadians took many of the upright walking Ape Kinds on Earth, that many of the Old Souls were experiencing Earth within their Forms, and re-engineered the Biology and DNA with that of Themselves which took numerous Generations of Manipulating the Biology of Form into Their Own Likeness.

"Well, that was a bit unexpected," said Mr. Reed. "the

church would not like to hear that we were created out of apes! But I guess when the Bible says that God created man, that too has no real evidence that he did it himself or the way it is mentioned in Genesis." Tyler said, "Well earlier the book said that creation creates creation!" "Yes, that is true Tyler, it did say that," said Mr. Reed nodding. Jared said, "In school, we have talked about the missing link from apes to man. I know the Bible says that God created man and breathed into the breath of life and he became a living soul. But like you said Gramps, maybe evolution was part of it, but that these aliens, the um, Pleiadians, got in there and created us to look like them."

Jared continued. "Also, speaking of Pleiadians, Gramps, didn't you say you knew something about them?" "I did?" Mr. Reed looking a little puzzled. "I don't remember sharing anything about that." Tyler kicked Jared's foot and glanced at him and whispered on the left side of his mouth, "Gramps just mumbled that when looking for the earth story." Jared remembering said, "oh, um, maybe I was just thinking of something you read. Gramps, never mind!" Now looking at Tyler with that shut-up look in his eyes.

"Speaking of the Pleiadians," Mr. Reed said, "you know when I was stationed in Nevada, there were elevators that went down several miles into the ground… Oh, and just for the record, don't share this with anyone ok, this is between us?" The boys both agreed in anticipation. "There is a tunnel down there that goes to California, under Mt. Shasta that the military is not allowed to travel on. They say that it goes to a large place called the inner earth where there are huge cities that exist in massive caverns hundreds of miles across. These are more rumors, but I do remember one day when this strange fellow came to Area 51 to work for a time because his adoptive father was also stationed there years before. I don't remember his name, but I remember he had six fingers on each hand and that his blood type was not of any known to humans." Tyler and Jared looked at each other for a moment and back to Gramps who continued. "Anyway, one day he left and rumor has it he went down to that tunnel and met with two very tall and thin, blond and blue-eyed beings, a male and a female that looked human. The train was like a tube and travels several thousand miles per hour, so it only took about five minutes to get to Mt. Shasta." Tyler asked, "So who were they?" "From my information, they are called the Pleiadians. But I have no idea if what this book is referring to is the same thing or not."

Jared said, "Well the universe is infinitely large, so it does not surprise me that there are others visiting earth." Mr. Reed nodding his head in agreement. Tyler said, "That sounds like they are different than the movies I have watched about aliens. I would not ever hope to meet some of them!" Mr. Reed said, "I have a feeling if they are all a part of God's creation, I would hope they would be friendly, but then again, humans can be incredibly scary and bad, so who knows if beings from other planets are the same as us." Then he said, "Let's keep reading, it's getting late, and I want to get through this section, looking down and turning the page. "Oh, this should be interesting! He said."

The Gods of Earth

As Earth became a newer Technological Realm, and other Forms entered Earth's Dimension from Lower Consciousness Realms and Dimensions. One of these outside Forces was called the Draconians who some say fell to the Earth because they were Kicked out of the realms of the Heavens. Free Choice existed with many Universes and on different Star Systems and Planets. Others would be called the Nephilim, Who were Created in proportion to the Planet they came from, but were Giants on the Earth. Their size alone made them Powerful and allowed them to Conquer Many Lands. They went into the Woman of the Earth and Bore them Great and Mighty Men of Renown who would become Kings and Rulers over the People of Earth.

Jared said, "The Bible talks about fallen angels, who we think of as demons. It kind of sounds like these Draconians were kicked out of the heavens, which that does not make sense to me because I thought the heavenly realms were spiritual and safe." Tyler, looking at his grandpa with the same eagerness as his brother. "Oh! That was a question," said Mr. Reed. "Well, I think you are on the right track, and your heart is in the right place because you know God is a God of love, and duality cannot exist in the heavens. However, I think this is related to what we call the heavens, looking up and pointing to the stars in the sky. Maybe they were banished from another planet within the 'heavens,' the 'cosmos' and found their way to earth which happened to match their frequency. Who knows the advancements that exist in other realities, or maybe I should say within other illusions we know as a form? But I am beginning to see how the people of the earth, especially those who write down history or metaphors and mysteries express themselves based on what they understand at that time in history."

Mr. Reed continued. "I know that even in recent history during world war two, that there was a village where we dropped supplies to the native people there, and years later when civilization came to visit them, that they learned that the natives of that village erected a crude statue that looked like an airplane as they believed it was a god and hoped it would return because of the gifts of food and clothes the god dropped to them years ago. We have something in us that wants to worship something greater than ourselves for the hope of being saved from the pain of life. We believe it will come from the outside when it has always been inside from the beginning."

Tyler said, "I want to talk about the giants. Doesn't the Bible talk about giants Gramps?" "It sure does, and it seems to be something most pastors keep their distance on because it contradicts the flood and that only Noah and his children were the only people to survive and repopulate the earth. Suddenly we have the Nephilim on the earth who made the human race feel like grasshoppers. We know David fought against a giant called Goliath who stood nine feet something tall, but I believe some of these giants were over thirty-five feet tall at one time. Don't ask me how they passed their seed onto human women, but we do believe they all died out over time. Archeologists have been uncovering some pretty amazing bones and remains of very large humans. Like femurs taller than a grown man and skulls with two rows of teeth. But all of these findings are quickly confiscated by the government which I don't fully understand why."

"Gramps, what about the flood, do you think there was a flood that covered the whole earth," asked Jared? Mr. Reed replied, "Well, again I go back to who these people were at the time, and to them, their world was not very big. When I look back on my childhood, there were globes and maps to look at, but I had no concept of how big the world was. Then I think back to most of these people most likely never traveled much outside of their own villages, especially back in Noah's days. Do I think there was a flood, absolutely! There are many flood stories from all over the world, some that predate the scriptures of the Biblical story. In fact, a few that you would be hard pressed to say that the person who wrote the story about the flood in the Bible got it from predated stories.

Like I said earlier, the solar system has its functions in the galaxy and push and pulls on one another causing tilting, earthquakes, volcano eruptions, tsunamis, and flooding. I have software on my computer that shows me all the earthquakes and volcanic eruptions around the world, and today as predicted in the Bible in the last days, all these things will increase. Over the past several decade's many things have been happening all over the world, but most of the mainstream media is not going to cover it, you need to dig for it. Anyway, the tilting of the earth most likely caused by this planet Nibiru coming in also caused the flooding back in Noah's days. The water rises, and it rained and flooded and killed many people. However, the indigenous people of Australia have been occupying their land for 30,000 or 60,000 years depending on the source. The Native Americans came from Siberia and Alaska about 12,000 years ago, both of these predating the Biblical record."

Tyler said, "I have wondered how God could destroy all the people of the world. Doesn't the Bible say that God was angry with them and wish he never made them?" "Yes, it does Tyler," Mr. Reed replied. "I have heard this same question from many people. Again, it goes back to how we have come to know God and love as both rewarder and punisher. These are human traits. What is happening on this earth is part of the experience we are all taking part in. Same as with Hitler, these people knew the earth was passing through some cosmic journey of its own and would tilt causing catastrophe to the land. And while we don't remember our agreements we made in the spirit world, we knew, or a part of us always knows within our spirit, that we were partaking in that adventure. It is possible that you, Jared and I were all there sitting around a campfire when the waters roared through our village sending us back into the presence of God in a moment."

Tyler said, "I don't want you ever to leave me, Gramps," tears welling up in his eyes and holding back a cry. Jared said, "oh Tyler, Gramps isn't going anywhere, he's built like an ox and healthy as a horse!" Tyler laughed which came out as a snort which made everyone laugh. Gramps said, "Let's keep moving, there are only a few more pages to go. Turning the page, he continued to read.

The Draconians were far more Advanced in Their Technology being able to bend Matter and Form and Shift Their Forms into whatever they wanted. They would soon become the leaders of the Earth, controlling the Great and the Small among the Earth. The people of the Earth understood them as Gods because their Technologies were so Advanced that it just looked like Miracles to them. Anti-Gravity Sound Systems were used to Build the Pyramids of the Earth which became Communication Systems to Their Home Planets and to others within the Galaxy. For many Thousands of Years there was War and Strife among the Nations of the World, fighting over Whose God was Greater, Bowing down and Worshiping Idols and Offering their Children as Sacrifices to Appease Them.

"Who wants to start on that?" asked Mr. Reed. Jared looked at his brother who was still wiping away tears on his sleeve, so looking to his grandpa he said, "Well, I know Tyler likes the idea of shapeshifting," looking at his brother who just looked back and nodded. "Tyler likes Transformers so we can both kind of understand what it means to change form. What do you think Gramps?" Mr. Reed said, "I am not real sure what I think about changing form, although there are those who claim that many leaders in today's world have Reptilian genes, DNA, another form of alien race some have speculated that live underground and have been among us that can change their form to look human. If they do exist, it would be my guess as to where the idea of demons comes from if I were to imagine what they might look like."

"Anyway, what caught my attention," Mr. Reed continued, "well, several things here did, but related to the science of sound and vibration, I happen to know a lot about it, but did not think about this until after reading, that they may have built pyramids using sound and levitation devices as some blocks are over 30,000 tons, something we cannot move with today's technology." Tyler spoke up and said, "Yeah, I heard that but thought maybe you read it wrong." "No," said Mr. Reed, "not that I know of this specifically, but there are several government secret programs that have developed anti-gravitational devices already back in the 1960's." Jared looked at his grandpa with disbelief in his eyes. "Yes, it's true Jared, I have seen these first hand." "Why do we not know about it Gramps?" asked Tyler. "Well, like many things the government knows and even the Vatican, there are higher powers at play than the presidents of their respective countries. The monetary system was put into place a long time ago for the purpose to control the population, and as I read this account here, I'm tempted to believe this goes back to what this book is talking about."

Jared said, "You know, maybe the God of the Bible is one of these beings!" Mr. Reed looked at Jared a bit shocked, "Jared, you took the words right out of my mouth! As I got older and began to question the stories in the Bible about God sending kings in here and there to destroy whole nations, men, women, and children, or ask parents to stone their sons who were rebellious, or even ask

Abraham to kill Isaac. These commands are not coming from The Source of All. The Great Spirit. A God of love. This is all about fear and torment. Then I thought they were just stories of people's imagination, or hold a meaning somehow symbolically, which may be the case. But now I am inclined to believe that all the gods of the Bible may have actually been real beings that actually ruled the earth and the people. When they left, man just mimicked them and became the Kings of the earth and carried on behaving the same way enslaving and controlling the lessor of the population…" Jared and Tyler could see their grandpa was acting a little strange and deep in thought. Then he just sat there for a long moment, a little awkward for the boys who turned to play with the fire.

Mr. Reed then looking at the boys with a bit of a smile said while holding up his pointing finger as if he was about to give a lecture, "So…" Recognizing what he just said. "…All the Egyptian myths, the Greek myths, the Mayan myths about all their gods…" Again, he stopped and thought again staring into the fire. "I think we have a mixed bag here! Yes! There were these gods, beings from outside earth who lived at one time among us... and it is where all this king and queen stuff comes from. I always wondered!"

Don't say anything he said quickly, making sure they did not interrupt his thoughts. "But God, the Creator, The Eternal One, was slowly revealing Itself… Yes, why on earth if we really knew of this Great Energy Source, This Divine Light of Love would we refer to It as he, as a male? That never made sense to me other than to create a masculine overtone to remain in charge which of course made women subject to the men which is evident throughout the Bible. Sorry boys, hang with me here…"

Mr. Reed stood up and began to pace a little and turning now rubbing his beard between his thumb and pointing finger, staring again into the fire. He shook his head as if disappointed he didn't see it earlier, amazement in his eyes. Then his eyes cleared and he returned to his seat and said, "so, are you ready to read some more? Tyler and Jared both nodded unsure of what just happened. "Great!" Mr. Reed said, turning the page to continue.

The Prophets of Old

One by One Prophets were sent into Earth from the Spiritual Realm, Born as Babies with more DNA available so that They upon growing up would remain closely Connected to Spirit and remember the Love that was Lost from the Earth, and to know Their Mission. The People were living in great Sin, Lost to Their True Nature, Unaware of Their True Reality as Sons and Daughters of The Eternal One.

Earth had become the greatest of all the Planets of Free Choice because more was allowed to enter Its Dimensions, both in Form and Spirit, Seen and Unseen. The Mightiest of Old Souls from the Greatest of Challenges over the Ages were coming into the Earth Realm to help Raise Its Collective Consciousness. But these Prophets were Killed over and over as the Centuries passed. Moses, Ezekiel, Jeremiah, Krishna, Siddhartha Gautama,

Jesus, Muhammad, Mirza Ghulam Ahmad and many Others all Sharing a message of Love and Unity to Save the People from the Control They allowed Themselves to be subject to, and to bring Peace and Harmony back to the Earth and all of Her Creation.

"You know, there is something more that I was think about on the last pages related to the gods," said Mr. Reed. "And that is the idea of worshiping God. Here we have gods who ask for worship and offer grace and mercy! Why? Love does not ask for these things." Mr. Reed took another sip of his beer and again got lost in thought, then looked at Tyler and said, "How much do you trust me?" Tyler smiled and looked at his brother a moment and back to his grandpa and said, "I trust you completely Grandpa!" Mr. Reed then said, "Well, if I would tell you that from now on, I want you to worship me, you know like bow down whenever I enter the room, what would you think?" Jared laughed and said, "I would think you have just lost your marbles!" Then he looked over at Tyler. Tyler said, "I would be a little freaked out and afraid Gramps!" Jared nodded in agreement with his brother looking back at his grandpa. "Exactly!" Mr. Reed said as he clapped his hands. "Exactly!"

"So, let me ask you, based on all that we have been talking about this evening, would 'The Eternal One' ask you to worship It?" Tyler thought for a moment and then shaking his head said, "No." "Jared?" Mr. Reed asked looking at him for an answer. Jared said, "No," and added, "since we have been talking tonight, God has become so much bigger to me than ever before." Mr. Reed nodded. Then he continued… "Love is the flow within life that allows without consequence. The truth may demand consequences, but love can only give Itself away. The word friend or companion hold with it the idea of equal in the relationship, like what we share between us, even if I am your grandpa and older and placed in authority over you. In reality, who we really are at the core, our essence, there is no one among us that is over the other. The love between friends is mutual, and if there was any indication whatsoever that one of the friends wanted to be worshiped by the other, the relationship would no longer be called equal, nor would we consider it held together by love."

Mr. Reed continued, "In fact, it would be kind of psychotic if you stop and think of such a thing. If it does exist within a relationship, it would be slavery because one has no choice. It could be codependence because one is incapable of leaving the relationship. It might be other dynamics as well, but in no case, will it ever be called love because in any case there would be fear on the part of the person worshiping." Tyler asked, "What about going to church, we call that going to worship, what does that mean then?" "That is very insightful of you, young man," said Mr. Reed. "I still believe in community and getting together to share in each other's lives as that is how love grows, and if we want to call that worship, that works for me!"

"What about grace and mercy?" Jared asked. "How do grace and mercy fit into a God that loves without condition?" Mr. Reed said, "As I think about this, it is not something that God bestows on Its children, but that we as humans bestow on each other. These are human concepts that come from a heart of compassion for our fellow man.

The idea that God offers grace and mercy is to imply that something or someone has fallen out of grace or does not deserve something. It also implies separation. Again, as I said with worship, If God is love, and you and I are a child of God as a part of this love, how can God offer grace to Itself, or mercy if perfect?"

Mr. Reed stopped as he knew he was again going on too much. "Anyway, I know that was not the subject of this page, do either of you have thoughts about what I just read about The Prophets of Old?"

Tyler said, "The thing that stood out to me was about how the prophets seem to have a greater connection to the spirit. I know Pastor Jenkins would say that God no longer speaks to us today like he did back in the Bible days, but that we have the Word of God today written down in the Bible to speak to us. But we have been talking a lot about knowing in our heart, and I was just wondering if God still speaks to us today and how?" Gramps looked at him with a soft smile that made Tyler relax. "When people believe that God can Be both loving and angry, there is nothing consistent about him that you could rely on, right?" Tyler nodded. Mr. Reed continued, "But we have been learning that God, is a loving God and that It allows us to do as we please. And because we are really expressions or extensions as one with God we can count on Love to guide us."

Tyler and Jared were listening intently as their grandpa continued. "If you think about it as we look back to where this whole book started tonight, there is only really The Eternal One. There is only Love. As we go about our day there are things we want to do, we can ask ourselves, is this the best thing for me? Is this my greatest joy at this moment? We choose and spirit guides the way and walks with us on every step. It's not as much as listening to an external voice to tell you what to do but to listen to your heart right now, right now and right now. You are the Creators because you are God's joy fulfilled within form called Tyler and Jared."

Tyler and Jared were absorbing what their grandpa just shared with them. It made them somehow feel more alive and more loved than they could ever remember. Both sitting there with the glow of the fire on their faces, perfectly at peace with themselves within the world. Mr. Reed could tell they were somewhere else at the moment so he waited to allow them time to enjoy whatever connection they may be experiencing. Then Jared said, "Gramps, I hope I learn to love my grandchildren the way you love us." Tyler smiled while looking out into the water where the moon was casting its light across the waves. Mr. Reed said, "Thank you." And then asked if they were ready to continue. The boys nodded their heads and breathed in deeply.

Mr. Reed continued on the topic of the prophets. "The prophets were people that were more closely connected to God because they learned to be aware of who they really were. They didn't need scripture to lead them, they became the scripture. Jesus knew who he was as an expression of his Father. He healed people because he could see the energy that made up the biology of the body. Jesus was also tempted by the adversary in the wilderness, that part of him that was human and flesh. Like him, we too can conquer our fears and weaknesses by trusting first in God alone to guide us by His love. In the wilderness, we cannot always hear the love speak, the joy is but a small light we can only hope for in the distance. But then that is the guide, that is what is speaking to you, and you need to pay especially close attention then and be strong. But then in time life will flow once again like a river, your steps will be sure, and your path made straight as you remain focused on love. Focus on love at every moment."

He could tell the boys were getting tired as they were quiet but also allowing love to have its way in their awareness. Mr. Reed looked down at the book and turned the page. "This is the last section, then we will go in have some ice cream! How does that sound?" They both nodded and smiled.

Prophecies and Probabilities

In addition to the Prophets, the Spiritual Realm worked harder to Communicate to Themselves in Form through the Christ Consciousness. The Communication System put in place when These Duality Systems were put in place to Experience Light and Dark. Different Prophets and Individuals all over the World were Writing things down. They Heard from a Voice, or in a Dream and even Visions. Warning Humanity and the Earth of Its Pending Doom if Love and Unity are not Brought Forth as the most Important Attribute to Live by.

"Gramps," Jared said, "I think that is just what you were saying, right?" Mr. Reed replied, "That's right, but there is also a growing number of phenomena happening in the world today that is allowing more and more people to communicate with their guilds, or angels or what we call God or expressions of God in some form of higher consciousness that is once again like the prophets of old trying to get humanity to see who they really are.

Love needs to be allowed to step out in front, and the truths even if right, need to step aside to allow love to have its way in our lives. No one will be left behind in the end, but while there is time, some will deny the love that is asking them to let go of their belief systems, let go of the truths you know are right, let go of the fear that we justify. Just let it go."

Tyler added, "Let go and let God!" "That's right," Mr. Reed said with a chuckle, "that's right." This is it, boys, we've come to the end.

The Revelations about the World Ending has Passed, for today the Desire for Love has surpassed the Desire for Control in the Collective Consciousness of Humanity. These were Probabilities from the Spirit Realm as Spirit can witness a larger Picture of Understanding. Man has Always been in Control of Its Own Creation and Destiny and must Decide what It wants for Themselves and Their Mother Earth. The Eternal One will get It's Way One Day through Love's Compassion. And when that happens, throughout All of the Cosmos, All will hear Laughter and Celebration over the Greatest Game Ever Played.

Tyler said, looking over to his brother, "Do you think dad is looking down on us right now?" Jared, moved by the moment and then the question let a tear slip out of his eye, but he didn't try to hide it and replied, "I know dad is watching over mom and us every day, Tyler." Jared thought about what he just said and realized it is what mom told him at times when Jared wondered about his father. Now he realized that those words meant more to him tonight.

Mr. Reed said, looking over to the empty fourth seat between him and Jared, "It wouldn't surprise me if he hasn't been with us all night boys." They all gathered in the moment and gazed into the embers left burning in the fire pit. With that their grandpa slowly closed the book and set it down. Then they all got up and walked toward the cottage with their grandpa embracing each one under each arm. Then Tyler said, "Gramps, I think that was the best treasure we could have ever found!"

At the center of the universe is love and laughter
~ Bernie Nyhof

ABOUT the AUTHOR

Steve Nyhof grew up in a large family with four boys and three girls. His mother Lillian was a multi-tasker, and gave her entire life to serving her husband and children with countless skills from home making to designing and selling kitchen and bath cabinets and much more. His father Bernard was a home builder and all the boys initially became building contractors except for Steve who took up machining while designing homes on the side. Later Steve built two companies, designing thousands of homes over the years and building custom homes.

From as young as he can remember, Steve loved to draw pictures as he has a very creative imagination. As he grew older his love for cars reflected in hundreds of drawings he would draw and even restoring and painting cars over the following decades.

Steve went to Africa with his mom and dad and several of his brothers and sisters when he was nineteen, as missionaries to help the people of Namalu Uganda settle back into their home village. The people were dispersed when Idi Amin was president and much civil war had ravaged their country and livelihood.

Today, Steve and his wife Mary live in Holland, MI. Their sons Jordan and Travis are married and also reside in Holland. Alicyn, their daughter, still lives at home with her mom and dad.

68617655R00232

Made in the USA
Lexington, KY
16 October 2017